Sophie Willock Bryant

Celtic Ireland

Sophie Willock Bryant
Celtic Ireland
ISBN/EAN: 9783337297213

Printed in Europe, USA, Canada, Australia, Japan

Cover: Foto ©ninafisch / pixelio.de

More available books at **www.hansebooks.com**

BY
SOPHIE BRYANT, D.Sc.
AUTHOR OF "EDUCATIONAL EN..."

> "The only better is a Past that lives
> On through an added Present—stretching still
> In hope unchecked"
> GEORGE ELI.

LONDON
KEGAN PAUL, TRENCH & CO., 1, PATERNOSTER SQUARE
1889

CONTENTS.

INTRODUCTION. SOURCES OF EVIDENCE ...

CHAPTER I. ETHNOLOGY OF IRELAND
,, II. ERIN AND ALBA ... ...
,, III. ERIN AND EUROPE ...
,, IV. PAGAN IRELAND AT HOME
,, V. CHRISTIANITY IN IRELAND ...
,, VI. SOCIAL AND POLITICAL INSTITUTIONS
,, VII. THE ARTS IN ERIN ... ...

MAPS.

PAGE

(1) CELTIC IRELAND, showing the Divisions of the Kingdom, the important Pagan Centres, the Chief Monastic Schools, and the Danish Settlements ... ... *Frontispiece*

(2) ETHNOLOGICAL MAP OF EUROPE AT THE DAWN OF HISTORY, showing the probable Lines of various Race-Migrations to Ireland 1

(3) EUROPE EARLY IN THE SEVENTH CENTURY, showing the Range of Irish Missionary Influence in the Dark Ages ... 60

BIBLIOGRAPHY.

ETHNOLOGY, Etc.

"Origins of English History." Charles Elton. (B. Quaritch.)
"The Races of Britain." John Beddoe. (Trübner and Co.)
"Rude Stone Monuments." J. Fergusson. (John Murray.)
"Celtic Scotland." W. F. Skene. (Edmonston and Douglas.)
"Early Britain." J. Rhys. (S.P.C.K.)
"Pre-historic Times." Sir John Lubbock. (Williams and Norgate.)

HISTORY, TRADITION, AND LITERATURE.

"History of Ireland, Critical and Philosophical." Standish O'Grady. (Sampson Low and Co.)
"History of Ireland." Jeffry Keating. (E. O'Mahoney, New York.)
"History of Ireland: Heroic Period." Standish O'Grady. (Sampson Low and Co.)
"Early Bardic Literature of Ireland." Standish O'Grady. (Sampson Low and Co.)
"Origin and Growth of Religion as illustrated by Celtic Heathendom." J. Rhys. Hibbert Lectures, 1887.
"Manuscript Materials of Irish History." Eugene O'Curry. (Williams and Norgate.)

"Ireland and the Celtic Church." G. T. Stokes. (Hodder and Stoughton.)

"St. Patrick, Apostle of Ireland." J. H. Todd, D.D. (Hodges and Figgis.)

"Writings of St. Patrick." G. T. Stokes and C. H. Wright. (Hodges and Figgis.)

"Tripartite Life of St. Patrick and other Documents." Whitley Stokes. (Eyre and Spottiswoode.)

"Celtic Romances." P. W. Joyce. (Kegan Paul, Trench and Co.)

LAWS AND INSTITUTIONS.

"Manners and Customs of the Ancient Irish." Eugene O'Curry, with Introduction by W. K. Sullivan. (Williams and Norgate.)

"The Brehon Laws." Translated by O'Donovan and O'Curry. (Longmans, Green and Co.)

"Early History of Institutions." Sir H. Maine. (John Murray.)

THE FINE ARTS.

"Early Christian Art in Ireland." Margaret Stokes. (Chapman and Hall.)

"Notes on Irish Architecture," with Photographs. Lord Dunraven. (Bell and Sons.)

"Ancient Music of Ireland." E. Bunting. (Hodges and Figgis.)

"Manners and Customs of the Ancient Irish," Introduction, pp. 484-636, and vol. iii. ch. xxx.-xxxviii.

INTRODUCTION.

SOURCES OF EVIDENCE.

THE study of history, at its best, implies inquiry into the means by which human character, in any of its national varieties, has developed itself. In the study of Irish history, more perhaps than in that of any other, writers and readers are alike apt to lose sight of this. Attention is concentrated, not unnaturally, on the melancholy story of the Anglo-Irish quarrel, and generally with a view to either excusing or accusing one or other of the parties concerned. While the quarrel lasts, it may, indeed, be unavoidable that its history should be studied in the spirit of the partisan. Nevertheless, it, as well as all else in Irish history, derives its highest interest from the light it can shed on the inquiry,— What manner of people were the ancient Irish, and how have they, with the infusion of other races now settled amongst them, developed into the modern Irish nation? And this, it may be said with truth, is the fitting prelude to the further question,—What are the characteristic qualities of the Irish nation now, and what are the circumstances necessary that it should accomplish its destiny—should fulfil that mission among the nations which is laid upon it by its gifts? Englishmen are called upon to-day to understand, in part, the answer to this question; and Irishmen, in all times, are called upon to feel the answer to it, for they it is who will have to work out that mission to its fulfilment.

In the spirit of such inquiry, I propose to deal with that portion of Irish history which preceded the Norman invasion—the Irish period of free development. Abundant ancient materials exist, out of which have been constructed, by careful scholarly minds, valid accounts of that history in all its most interesting and important aspects, although a single complete and critical history of early Ireland has never yet been written. Nor is the reason for delay in the production of such a history far to seek. It were an easy task to write the story of a people who had left a few annals and no great mass of poetical literature; but the ancient Irish were not such a people. The first glimpse we catch of them shows us a society literary to the heart's core, and so devoted to the memory of the national past that all literature revolves round the doings of the national heroes—who are represented sometimes as gods no less than heroes—and concerns itself solely with the real history of the "men of Erin." The bard is in the place of honour higher than the warrior, and he has a definite duty to the society that supports and honours him. His public duty it is to preserve in his memory the historical tales of the Irish race, to enshrine in verse new events as they occur, and to recite this bardic history, so composed and so preserved, for the pleasure and instruction of the people. In later times we find a division of labour among the bards, and the emergence of two bardic or academic classes—the class of historians, whose duty coincided with that of the more ancient bards, but was probably conducted in a more prosaic and critical spirit, and the class of poets (or Filidecht), *litterateurs* proper, to whom fell, perhaps, the larger share of the educational work which formed such a conspicuous feature of early Irish society. But, whether as poets or historians, it is quite clear that the definite duty of the Irish bards was to know compose and teach, in its various branches, the gradually accumulating literature of the Gael; and that literature had the one clear conscious purpose, to give an account of the past of Ireland and the Irish. In the Book of Leinster we are told that the qualification required of a poet, before he could obtain his bardic degree, was that he should know by heart seven times fifty stories, namely five times fifty prime stories and twice fifty secondary stories. It is evident that this requirement, or any such as this, was an effective guarantee against the invention of bardic tales out of relation to the general current of historical tradition; and in consequence we find, as we should expect, a remarkable positive, as well as negative, consistency throughout the bardic literature, so that each portion gives evidence to a consciousness of the whole in the narrator's mind.

Thus, by carefully trained memories, assisted by the use of the metrical form of literary composition, and checked by the presence in the country of a considerable literary class, all bent on remembering the same tales, and meeting periodically for the exchange of bardic ideas and refreshment of bardic memories—thus the history of the nation, steeped in the forms and colours of imagination that were native to the people the soil and the age, was handed down from generation to generation. When it began to *be* we do not know: when it began to be *told* we do not know: nor do we know even when it began to be written down, though there is good reason to think that written books were in Ireland before the coming of Patrick in the fifth century. The question of dates is of little consequence, however; for of one fact—the one that does matter—we are quite sure. The old bardic literature gives us the history of the ancient Irish, as told spontaneously and believingly by themselves in the pagan times before Europe had begun at all to influence their ideas. It is Irish of the Irish, more valuable for the imaginative element in which it moves than even for the historical truth which it certainly enshrines. It is the fount at which the pagan Irish drank in their moral and religious ideas—the source of their martial aspirations in the heroic age—the well whence they drew the inspiration of gentle and noble thoughts, of family affections, of loyalty to friends, of social justice, of faith in treaties, of fair play in war, of respect for the weak, of reverence for the heroes and the immortal gods of Erin. "Those heroes and heroines," says Mr. Standish Grady, "were the ideals of our ancestors; their conduct and character were to them a religion; the bardic literature was their Bible. . . . Under its nurture, the imagination and spiritual susceptibilities of our ancestors were made capable of that tremendous outburst of religious fervour and exaltation which characterized the centuries that succeeded the fifth, and whose effect was felt throughout a great portion of Europe. It was the Irish bards and that heroic age of theirs which nourished the imagination, intellect, and *idealism* of the country to such an issue. Patrick did not create these qualities. They may not be created. He found them and directed them into a new channel." And truly it is in the reason of things that the best sequence of events for the moral history of a nation should be that characteristic Irish sequence of an age of saints to an age of heroes. When the longing for great deeds, the contempt for ease, is at its height, no need is greater that that of an object, a worthy cause for self-devotion. A religion of self-devotion preached at such a time is like seed sown on well-tilled land. It strikes its roots deep and fast, and plants for all time the ideal of self-devotedness in the hearts of the people.

The ancient Irish emerge in history a mixed race, predominantly Gaelic, and, as such, tall, fair-haired, blue-eyed. They were gentle, as we shall see, in peace, fierce in war, loving enterprise and the joy of great deeds—the gathering together, doubtless, in that remote island on the shores of the Western world, of the most adventurous, the most high-spirited, the minds most curious to see new lands and find the limits of the world, the hearts most susceptible to the tender influences of Nature and apt to be fascinated by the quest of that land which is nearest the setting sun—the most imaginative and aspiring and poetic spirits in all those communities that moved slowly or rapidly westwards to find new worlds. So, out of the foremost waves of the great human drift that covered Europe, the Irish people was built up, to issue forth presently in the same spirit of enterprise that had brought them thither, speeding all over Europe and as far north as Iceland, first as warriors, and secondly as missionaries carrying scholarship in their train.

After the introduction of Christianity, the bardic literature began to be committed to writing with probable completeness. Then, too, the work of the

annalists commenced—a much more conscious work
of historical record, and somewhat less valuable, therefore, than that of the bards. Historical manuscripts
accumulated as time went on—stories and annals, as
well as law-books and other literature. These were
kept either in monasteries or in other houses of learned
communities; but, during the troubled times of the
Danish and Norman invasions, many of the manuscript collections were dispersed, and a large number
must certainly have been lost and destroyed. Allusions to books no longer forthcoming occur in the
books which we still have, and so enable us to form
an imperfect idea as to some part of our loss. A
considerable body of manuscript literature has, however, come down to us, dating from 1100 onwards, and
dealing with a great variety of subjects. Most of
these manuscripts are copies, or embody copies from
older books, and internal evidence based on the
structure of the language shows that some parts of
them have been handed down from early times.
Thus we have, as a survival to our own time of the
old Irish intellectual activity, a quantity of literature of well-ascertained antiquity, and certainly
known to reflect correctly, by means of verbal tradition, the ideas and tastes of an older antiquity still.
This Irish literature is now to be found not only in
Ireland, but scattered through the great libraries of
Europe. Collections exist in the library of Trinity
College, Dublin, in the Royal Irish Academy, the

British Museum, the Bodleian Library, the National Library at Paris, the Louvain College, Belgium, and the College of St. Isidor at Rome. The nature of all this literature is very various. Besides the bardic tales and the annals, Ireland produced many ecclesiastical books in Latin; but she produced a larger number in the native Gaelic, and Irish glosses on the Latin text are numerous. Classical stories translated into Irish are common; and, as one example of other subjects, I may mention a work on geography, extraordinary for its time, written by an Irish monk, Dicuil, about 825, which was discovered in the French National Library in the year 1812.

But I have already said enough, and more than enough, to show that the difficulty of the Irish historian is not the lack of valuable materials. His difficulty is the quantity of material, and the existence in it of that very literary character which makes it so valuable from a philosophic, as well as interesting from a literary, point of view. The bardic literature is there, and the historian cannot neglect it: it is too historical to be treated simply as romance, and too romantic to be treated simply as history. And so it is probable that early Irish history, as a chronicle of events, will always be more or less immersed in the atmosphere of speculation; and perhaps it will be, for that very reason, more true by far to the facts of the case than the history of other peoples who have had less to say about themselves.

Certainly, it is for that reason likely to exercise a much more powerful influence over the people whose past record it registers.

It is not the object of the following pages, however, to deal with details in the record of Irish events. The main facts of that record are attested by the unanimous voice of tradition, supported by collateral evidence from the history and tradition of other people, and finally confirmed by the testimony of later investigation into the traces left among the Irish people of a social and national life, the substance of which had been destroyed. It is not with the record of events, except in outline, that these pages will deal, but with the salient features of this social and national life—the laws, customs, and institutions of the old Irish people. These are revealed to us, with a completeness and evidence that leave little to be desired, in the bardic stories and annals and, above all, in the books that have descended to us containing the Irish or Brehon law.

In any intelligible account of these we may see the common characteristics of early institutions among all the Aryan peoples. But we see more, and it is not difficult to determine the line of distinction. In Ireland these institutions had a longer life, and therefore a more elaborate development, than elsewhere in the Western world; because Ireland, protected by her island isolation, and perhaps also by the reputed fierceness of her warriors, was never interfered with by the Roman power, nor ever came under the influence of the Roman Imperial idea. So far as it goes and generally, the Irish social organization represents what the free development of the North-western Aryan tended to be; though, no doubt, it contains certain characteristics of its own which do not appear elsewhere, and which, moreover, can be traced as determining elements in the history of the Irish nation throughout all times—elements which enable us to understand the forms taken by the Irish national movement in our own day, and to understand, too, the secret of that extraordinary assimilative force by which the idea of Irish nationality has absorbed into itself, despite all efforts to prevent it, the self-devotion of the motley groups of strangers settled from time to time, as enemies, within the borders of the land.

CELTIC IRELAND.

CHAPTER I.

ETHNOLOGY OF IRELAND.

WHO were the ancient Irish? To Irishmen, at least, this will always be an interesting question, and none the less interesting because it does not admit of a simply definite answer. Long before historic times the Irish were in Ireland; and early in history, if not at its dawn, they appear to have had well-marked traditions as to their origin. Later, the monastic chroniclers improved on the tradition and, connecting Irish story with the Biblical narrative, completed the history of the race backwards to the flood. This idea of the monks makes it not hard to distinguish the early from the late traditions. In estimating the value of the traditions as we have them, the first step, therefore, is to separate the mediæval monks' additions from the bardic story, by means of internal evidence; and, then, the historical value of the bardic story must be estimated according to the most reasonable tests. First, sift out the miraculous element which belongs to the atmosphere of the times, and does not detract from, any more than it adds to, the value of the residuum. Then, consider the probable motives *unconsciously* at work in the construction of a tale *intended* to be true, and select that part of the tale the most probable motive of which appears to be its truth. More—much more of it—may be true, but this much of it cannot at least be disregarded.

There are, however, other sources of evidence besides Irish tradition. The physical characteristics of the human remains found in ancient tombs give a clue to a theory of race-connections among the peoples who once inhabited the countries where these remains are found; and something can be made of this evidence for our present subject, though it is much obscured by the fact that cremation was practised by many tribes in both Ireland and Britain. In Ireland and in North Britain this practice prevailed most extensively, and it is in South Britain, or England, therefore, that the observation of the pre-Celtic types within these islands may best be made. We can reason, then, by analogy to Ireland and Scotland where the same types of tombs and monuments are to be found. Comparing the evidence of pre-historic ethnology and archæology collected in these islands with similar evidence in continental countries, it is possible for ethnologists to construct the most probable theory of the early race-history of either Ireland or Britain. But the subject is complex and difficult, and all the available evidence has by no means been yet collected, while some of it has been destroyed in the pursuit of archæological, apart from ethnological, studies.

The earliest class of tombs, in which stone implements only are found, fall into two sub-classes, distinguished by the presence or absence of a stone-built chamber inside. The huge "long barrows" of Salisbury Plain are unchambered mounds, and are probably the graves of the earliest immigrants; while the long chambered cairns of Caithness exemplify a more advanced order of ideas. In these tombs are found the remains of a long-headed, short-statured, lithe-limbed race, with brain capacity good, and features well formed. It has been thought that these people were of the same race as the stout-hearted Silures, who kept at bay for so long the Roman power in South Wales, and as the Atticotti, another hard-fighting foe beyond the southern wall. If so, this race has left its mark on the features of a considerable portion of the population in both islands, and to its admixture may be assigned, with probability, most of the dark hair and dark eyes that are found amongst us. As we proceed, however, it will appear that Silures and Atticotti, or at least the former, represent a probably different and more distinctive ethnological element, which can be traced through south-western Europe by the track of the stone monuments known as dolmens or cromlechs.

Later, came to Britain another and very different race — broad-headed, large-limbed, powerful — who built circular tombs for their dead, and buried bronze implements with them. As metal-workers they were comparatively skilled in the arts, and had thus advantages for conquest. But they appear to have settled down peaceably by the side of the older inhabitants, and with so much respect that the earlier and later ancestor-revering peoples are found to have buried their heroes in close proximity. The round tombs of the bronze age men are built in numbers on spots that were sacred to the elder race. Around Stonehenge, long barrows abound, and there are indications that Stonehenge was built by this tall, powerful, and probably fair people.* It is not improbable that the earlier settlers may have learnt to substitute the chambered tumulus for the mound of earth, from the example of their later-coming neighbours. If so, it may be that they, and not the so-called Iberians, were the original builders of those rude stone monuments throughout Europe, part of Asia, and the North of Africa, which seem to indicate the presence, or the passage, of one people in the countries where they are found. This theory would solve some difficulties, though it leaves others.

* Elton's "Origins of English History," ch. vi. p. 146. See also Greenwell's " British Barrows," for full account of both classes of tombs.

It appears, from the sepulchral remains, that this tall race had established itself along the opposite coasts from Sweden to Finisterre before they became acquainted with the use of bronze, and, therefore, before they came to Britain. From their physical characteristics, it is inferred that they were "of the fair Finnish type that still prevails so largely among the modern inhabitants of Denmark and in the Wendish and Slavonian countries." * A strong light is thrown on the subject by the comparison of this inference with the theory lately put forward by philologists, that the probable home of the Aryan language was in southern Scandinavia, and the speech of the Finns its nearest relative. † The early Finnish or Ugrian type, that wandered westwards from the north-east, was likely to be amalgamated easily with the more numerous Aryan tribes that followed, and may have acted too as a medium of solution between them and the ancient people that preceded both. Later immigrations into England, Scotland and Ireland may have included mixtures of a Ugrio-Iberian and afterwards of a Celto-Ugrio-Iberian stock, as well as mixtures of the Ugrian with the Celt. Such a mixture as the latter may have been the tall, red-haired Caledonians described by Tacitus,‡ and the Belgae of

* Elton's "Origins of English History," ch. vi. p. 144.

† British Association, 1887, Inaugural Address to Anthropological Section, by Professor Sayce; and paper on the "Primitive Seat of the Aryans," by Canon Isaac Taylor.

‡ These Caledonians were located in mid-Scotland, north and west of the Tay basin, while we must look to the south-west of Scotland or north-west of England for the Atticotti.

Gaul may have been distinguished from the Celts by some duplex or triplex mixture of blood.

In Ireland and Scotland the pre-Celtic evidence of the early tombs is much more obscure, though it is certain that the dark short race was there. It is, moreover, quite clear that, in semi-historic times, builders of one class of Irish stone monuments, the circles and the tumuli of circular form, spread over these countries; and their distribution points to the conclusion that they came from the North, down the west coast of Scotland to Ireland, where are found the most remarkable examples of circular tumuli in the historic cemetery of the Irish kings on the Boyne.* Numerous stone circles mark the spots where Irish tradition reports that two great battles were fought between the Firbolgs and the later-coming Tuatha Dé Danann, who are said to have replaced them in the domination of Ireland.† Tradition also assigns to the Tuatha the honour of having introduced a knowledge of metals and of the arts of life; and this fact suggests some association with the bronze age men of Britain.

The monuments known as cromlechs or dolmens are also found in Ireland, the finest examples, built with very large stones, being in the north, and the smallest in the west. These are also found in North and South Wales and in Cornwall, but scarcely at

---

* Fergusson's "Rude Stone Monuments," p. 199, *et seq.*
† *Ibid.*, p. 175, *et seq.*

all elsewhere in England. Hence it is clear that these parts must have been the homes of the people who built the dolmens, at the period when this type of architecture grew up. The North Europe dolmens are found in Sweden and Denmark, along the shores of the Baltic and North Sea, as far west as the eastern parts of Holland and no further. The second and greatest European group belongs to the west of France and the coasts of Spain. In the large tract of country between eastern Holland and the line of the Rhone, Loire, and Seine there are no dolmens; and these were the parts peopled by the Celts and Belgae in the time of the Romans. The Celtic peoples thus are marked out clearly as *not* the original dolmen-builders, though later they are found abundantly in the dolmen districts.*

Considering the distribution of the dolmens, it seems probable that their builders crossed over from Brittany to Cornwall, where they are very abundant, and were thence propagated to Wales and the south of Ireland; while the larger northern Irish dolmens may have come into Ireland by a different route, as an instalment of the tumuli and circles. There is, however, one piece of literary evidence connecting Spain with Britain which should be noticed. D. O'Campo, the compiler of an important Spanish chronicle in the sixteenth century, records that, " Certain natives of

---

* Fergusson's ",Rude Stone Monuments," ch. viii. p. 326, *et seq.* See also map showing distribution of the dolmens.

Spain called Silores (the Siluri)), a Biscayan tribe, joined with another, named Brigantes, migrated to Britain about two hundred and sixty-one years before our era, and obtained possession of a territory there on which they settled." * According to this, there were early migrations from Spain, as well as from France, to Britain, and possibly to Ireland also. If the dolmen builders did proceed direct from Spain to Ireland, it ought to be possible to find evidence of the fact in the nature and contents of these rude structures in both countries. At present, we are still very ignorant on the subject generally.

We are ignorant, too, as to the ethnology of these dolmen builders, who have left traces in Asia and along the African Mediterranean coast,† as well as by the Baltic and the Bay of Biscay. More investigation will solve some questions; for the dolmens were erected as tombs in honour of their heroes and kings by a people who must have highly reverenced and possibly worshipped their dead; and the tombs have not yet been asked consistently to yield up their secrets. Probably, they are not all due to the hands, or built in honour of the dead, of one race, but do all mark the dominance, or at least influence, of

---

* See a paper on the Migration from Spain to Ireland, by Dr. Madden, "Proceedings of Royal Irish Academy," vol. viii. p. 371, etc. Dr. Madden has brought together a quantity of evidence showing that the tradition of an emigration from Spain to Ireland is well marked in the Spanish annals.

† Fergusson's " Rude Stone Monuments," ch. x. and xii.

some one great family of mankind, which wandered forth to various parts and mixed its blood with, while it imparted its ideas to, the other races that either preceded and were controlled by it or followed and controlled it.

The indications, so far, are that a people from the south, through western Britain, and partly perhaps direct from Spain or France, came to Ireland in early times; while another came from the north, round Scotland and in part through it; and that neither of these people were Celtic, though both were possibly mixed in blood, and both may have contained a Celtic element. It is likely, indeed, that the northern race may have had a large, even a predominant, dash of Gaelic blood; but this suggestion depends rather on the direct literary evidence to which we shall come presently.

The Celt and the other Aryan peoples throughout Europe have not left in their path the same kind of monumental evidence as those who preceded them. Perhaps their tendencies to ancestor-worship were always less, though we cannot doubt that they went far in the direction of deifying their heroes. It may have been a natural consequence of a more vivid and poetic imagination that they deified Nature at least as much, and worshipped rivers and grottoes, no less than they performed religious ceremonies at tombs. Be that as it may, it appears to be quit certain that, though they often adopted, they never invented the practice of erecting stone monuments such as those which enable us to see dimly the track of their predecessors. For the movements of the Celtic and Teutonic nations in Europe we must look mainly to history and tradition. To the Irish records, and their evidence as to Irish ethnology, we shall come presently. But first let us consider another source of the same kind.

This source of evidence is one which Irish writers might naturally be apt to neglect—the evidence of old British history and tradition as preserved by Wales, and of old Alban history and tradition as found in the records of the ancient Pictland. Both Wales and Scotland can shed some light on Irish ethnology. In historic times, the Scots of Ireland and the Picts of Alba were close allies. Together, they harried the coasts of Roman Britain, and in the Welsh chronicles we find their races so closely identified that they are spoken of as the Gwyddel and the Gwyddel Ffichti. The Pictish chronicle, having been compiled in the tenth century, and therefore long after the Scottish dynasty was established in Scotland, may perhaps be regarded as a source tainted with the amiable desire to unite in social sentiment the branches of one nation; but it is impossible to regard as quite worthless for evidence the fact that it makes out Scots and Picts to be different branches of the same race. The names too that occur in the early part of the list of Pictish kings are Gaelic, and such British elements as are found in the names of the southern Picts are Cornish, not Welsh, thus pointing to an affinity with some Celtic race that preceded the settlement of the Britons, and may have been mixed with non-Aryan stock. Again, in the chronicle of the Picts and Scots, which was compiled in the fourteenth century, an important piece of traditional evidence is recorded. We are told that in very early times seven kings of the Cruithnigh, or Picts, of Alba, reigned over Erin in Tara; and we find that the seven are mentioned in the Irish annals as kings of the Firbolgs, the first of them being the celebrated traditional character, Ollamh Fodhla, to whom some legends refer the foundation of Tara as the capital of Ireland. Thus both traditions point to a time when the same race was settled over considerable portions of the two islands under different names, and so impressed themselves on the imagination of their successors as to appear to have been the dominant races for the time in each.

Coming now to definitely historic times, we find a colony of Picts settled in the north of Ireland under the name of Cruithnigh, and the Irish annals contain no hint that they spoke a different language from the Irish proper, whom the Romans called Scots. Either these Cruithnigh were a remnant of the old settlement from Alba to which the Pictish record points, and the Scots some new race, different though kindred, now dominating the island, or the colony was a new one, differentiated from the earlier settled people of the same race by its mere newness. We shall see reason presently for inclining to the former alternative, so far at least as the divergence between the two races is concerned. The identity of language is, however, important, and there is much evidence to show that historic Picts and Scots spoke the same language, or languages differing only as dialects of the same Gaelic speech. For example, in later times the Picts of Galloway, who were surrounded by Britons spoke, not Cymric, but the Gaelic tongue; and we know that St. Columba, in his mission to the Picts, did not need an interpreter for his intercourse with the king, but only when he or his comrades went to outlying districts, where probably the language, as well as the race, of the early non-Celtic settlers still held ground.

The whole evidence as to the racial character of the Pict is carefully collated by Mr. Skene,* and goes far to prove his conclusion that the Pict, as he stands out in history, is a variety of Gael, whatever other races may have been associated with him, or absorbed by him, in the formation of that unconquered little kingdom of Pictland. Professor Rhys's main conclusion does not differ so much from Mr. Skene's as appears at first sight. He finds the Picts to be a non-Aryan people—the original Iberians—whose his-

* "Celtic Scotland," vol. i.

tory is mixed up, however, with that of the Caledonians dwelling to the south of them, and whom he considers to be undoubtedly Gaelic.* Mr. Elton, again, finds the Ugrian element in the Pict,† and his conclusion must be to some extent admitted if there is anything in the conclusions to which we have already come. The exact limitations of the Gaelic element in the ethnology of Scotland does not, however, affect the question of Irish ethnology very greatly. If there was a large Gaelic and Gaelic-speaking element within the area of Pictland, which paved the way for its ultimate development into Scotland, this was probably the element that co-operated with the Scots, who were certainly Gaels, in their warlike expeditions, and was called Gwyddel Ffichti by the Welsh. This was undoubtedly the Pict to which the traditions of the Pictish chronicle refer.

This Pict is naturally identified with the Caledonian whom Tacitus describes as the most powerful foe which the enemies of Rome met in North Britain. The Gauls, he tells us, are somewhat like the Germans, tall and fair-haired, and the Britons are not reported to be different from the Gauls, while the Silures, remnants of the older race, are dark and curly-haired, like the Iberians of Spain. The Caledonians, on the other hand, are larger-limbed than any of these, and

---

* Rhys's "Early Britain," ch. v.
† Elton's "Origins of English History," ch. vi.

with redder hair, more similar to the Germans than are the Gauls. On account of their appearance, Tacitus imagines that the Caledonians had a German origin, but the evidence of language, and the fact that the Germans were still east of the Rhine discredit this idea. It seems, however, to be a probable inference that the Celtic stock whence the Caledonian sprang had a dash of some other race in it, which tended to the production of larger limbs and redder hair; and the men of the circular British tombs, who also resemble those found in the stone-age tombs of Denmark, rise inevitably to one's mind. And here we are reminded of a tradition recorded, not only by the Pictish chronicle, but by Bede, by the "Historia Britonum," and by the Welsh triads, to the effect that the Picts came from Scythia, and first acquired Orkney and Caithness, spreading thence over Scotland from the north. In the Irish legends we also find one of the Irish races—not the Scots—with physical characteristics not unlike those of the Caledonians, or Picts, as described by Tacitus, and with associations pointing to an origin in the north-east.

But, probable as it is that the Scots and Picts were ethnic brothers up to a certain point, with some relationship, whatever it was, to the Briton, it is still more certain that a great historical gulf must, at some time, have yawned between them. The difference between their social institutions sufficiently proves this, showing a marked divergence in their past, and in the influences of racial admixture which had acted on them, by different survivals in the institutions handed down from the past. It is pretty generally known that the Pictish law of inheritance was in the female line. A Pictish king based his right to the throne, for instance, on the fact that he was his mother's, rather than his father's, son. Not a man's sons, but his sister's sons, were his natural heirs. Such a law is a very clear reminiscence of a time when, for some reason or other, the tribal idea took a shape which prevented the formation of new families by marriage—a time when the woman and her children belonged always to her tribe, the husband attaching himself to her tribe rather than, as in the ordinary case, she attaching herself to his. Now, the Gaelic tradition of Ireland gives not a single trace of any such idea. Either the race never had it, or had had it so long ago that even the imaginative memory of the Gael had lost all hold of it. This single fact is, it would appear, enough to show that, if the Gwyddel and the Gwyddel Ffichti really were ethnic brothers, they were brothers that had parted long ago and made their way by different paths to the sister lands in which history finds them.

Professor Rhys considers that this institution of descent in the female line is one of the strongest proofs that the Picts were essentially non-Aryan ;* and it might, on the face of it, very well be that they

* Rhys's " Early Britain," pp. 166, 167.

derived the institution from their non-Aryan side, the primitive inhabitants with whom they amalgamated more or less—perhaps more in days after those when Tacitus described the tall, red-haired Caledonians. The difficulty still remains, however, that we have no particular reason to assign these institutions to the earlier settlers any more than to the Aryan folk, and it seems more reasonable on the whole to think that they represent the survival of a custom based on a long-vanished state of society, which custom survived in this particular case, and not in others, because circumstances did not arise to require or suggest its abolition. On that supposition its existence on one side of the channel and not on the other indicates a separation of history very considerable between two branches of the same race.

So much we might infer if the Irish ethnic traditions were non-existent; but they do exist, and are the most light-giving of all the traditions that bear on the history of the early peoples in both islands. Let us see now what they say. Do they tell us anything of that long-headed, lithe-limbed race, whose weapons were of flint and their graves oblong, who are thought by some anthropologists to be of Iberian stock, and to have contributed an element which can be perceived in the British and Irish populations of to-day? Do they tell us anything of the round-headed man? And is there any traditional evidence that a Gaelic or semi-Gaelic race from the north, similar to the Pict, preceded the Scot, or Gael proper, in the settlement of Ireland?

Throughout the whole of the early literature, deeply imbedded in the Irish idea of Irish origin, we find the tradition of three Celtic races who established themselves successively as lords in the land. The first of these is called the Firbolgs, the second the Tuatha Dé Danann, and the third are the Milesians from South Europe,* victors over all, traditional depositaries of the vigour, enterprise, and chivalry of the Irish race, and presumably of the literature, since they are its prime heroes. To their immediate predecessors, however, are more especially assigned powers of magical skill and nature-knowledge; but this may be connected with the fact, which constitutes the main difficulty in interpreting the legend, that these Tuatha Dé Danann appear in two distinct characters, first as a real people preceding the Milesians in the occupation of the country, and secondly as that race of immortal beings to which the *soil* of Ireland—not the *race* of Miledh—was sacred, the mighty "Sidhe" of Irish mythology, who degenerated later into the fairies of Irish folk-lore, dwelling

---

* The Spanish records agree with the Irish, as already noted, that there was emigration from Spain to Ireland. Colmenar, in the "Annals of Spain and Portugal" (1741), vol. ii. p. 55, sums up the matter thus: "History informs us that two hundred years before Jesus Christ the Biscayans plied on the sea in vessels made of the trunks of trees hollowed and covered with leather, and with a fleet thus constructed they went to Hibernia, now called Ireland, and took possession of it."

in the lakes and hills and at the bottom of the sea. This confusion may be partly due to a natural rationalizing tendency in the monks who wrote out so many of the stories—a tendency to minimize the mythical element and represent the race of gods as a race of men; but it is likely enough to be as largely due to the native genius for idealization, which alike transformed the Milesian hero into a heroic god and the Dé Danann magic-worker into the immortal who controls in Ireland the power of earth and air and sky.

Taking the Tuatha Dé Danann to be a real race of men, they may have been the builders of circles and circular tombs from the north, who came south by the Orkneys and Caithness, and were identical in part with the Picts of Scotland, though separated in their later history. If so, the bronze-age men of Britain cannot be wholly dissociated from them; though, since these came probably by a different route, from the Frisian coast to Yorkshire, quite different mixtures may be represented by the two. One contrast is remarkable. The Scotch and Irish tombs of the same kind as those in England show that cremation had been more generally adopted by the races which buried in them. This indicates some quite different dominant idea,* and points to the conclusion

---

* It is only a surmise of my own, but I suspect that this practice implies a more spiritual conception of immortality in the races to which it was indigenous, and indicates the presence of the Aryan intellect with its wide grasp of imaginative reason.

that the Scotch and Irish tomb-builders of this class were not in the main of the same race and period as those in England. If they were the Tuatha Dé Danann, they spoke Gaelic. Perhaps they came out from their Scandinavian home after the dominance of the Aryan had been long established there, the Finnish element having mainly migrated to other parts. But, however that may be, this wave of immigration to Ireland was, without doubt, chiefly Gaelic, if the evidence of tradition counts for anything at all.

The Irish legends, however, have something to say about earlier settlers than the three races already mentioned, and the Fomorian sea-rovers, who, according to the story, settled and fought in the north-west of Ireland before the coming of the Celts, may have been a tribe of pure Ugrian extraction coming round the north of Scotland from Denmark or Scandinavia. If this Ugrian race settled, however sparsely, in Scotland, and the Tuatha Dé Danann came to Ireland from that country, it is easy to imagine one way in which the modification of Gael by Ugrian might have come to pass in them. It is Mr. Skene's opinion,— and the description of physical characteristics in Irish legend tends to bear it out,—that the Tuatha Dé Danann correspond to Tacitus's large-limbed, red-haired Caledonians, and the brown-haired Scot to a purer Celtic type, or a type which, if mixed, was a different mixture.*

* "Celtic Scotland," p. 179.

It seems so natural to identify the Firbolg of Irish tradition with the so-called Iberian or dark-haired stock, that writers not familiar with the Irish literature often do so unhesitatingly. The evidence of the literature is, however, a stumbling-block to this identification. The Iberians were small; the Firbolgs, we are sometimes told, were of great stature—taller than the Milesians, though less beautiful. The Iberians were dark-haired, but the Firbolg Ferdiad in the greatest of the Irish heroic tales has golden hair and blue eyes, as well as noble stature. Cuculain, his Milesian foster-brother, who has been compelled to slay him in single fight, mourns over him with these words—

> "Dear to me was thy beautiful ruddiness,
> Dear to me thy comely perfect form,
> Dear to me thy clear gray-blue eye,
> Dear to me thy wisdom and eloquence."*

Of this kind of evidence there is abundance, and it is impossible to reconcile it with the idea that the Firbolgs were simply of Iberian race. If they were they must surely have left a different tradition behind them, even supposing that they were very early fused in the rest of the peoples. Hence Irish scholars see in the Firbolg, not the Iberian, but the first wave of the Aryan immigration—of Celtic extraction like the other two, though it may be mixed with non-Aryan

* Introduction to O'Curry's "Manners and Customs of the Ancient Irish," p. lxxii.

elements before it arrived in Ireland, and further adulterated in the same way afterwards.

The more the Irish tradition is studied, with the other evidence and the antecedent probabilities, the more probable it seems that it reflects an exact fact, a really threefold Celtic immigration. The Firbolg came, as some scholars think with good general reason, from the Belgic coasts, across South Britain and Wales—an impure Gaelic type absorbing still further the earlier British races before it reached the Irish shores. Next came the Tuatha Dé Danann from the North through Caledonia. Last came the warlike Milesian from Spain or South France.

Nevertheless, the Iberian is there even now in the land. Once he may have been the ruler there; and it may be that Irish legend has faintly reflected the memory of that time in its story of the Partholanians, who preceded, not only the Gaels, but the Fomorians also. However that may be, it is certain that in Ireland, as in Britain, the Iberian has left his stamp on the physique of the people. "There are," writes Dr. Sullivan,* "a few broad facts regarding the ethnology of ancient Ireland which may be considered as fairly established. In the first place, there were two distinct types of people—one a high-statured, golden-coloured or red-haired, fair-skinned, and blue or grey-blue eyed race; the other a dark-

* Introduction to O'Curry's "Manners and Customs of the Ancient Irish," p. lxxii.

haired, dark-eyed, pale-skinned, small or medium-statured, lithe-limbed race. The two types may still be traced in the country, and are curiously contrasted in their blushes ; the fair-haired type has a pinkish tinge, the other a full red, with scarcely a trace of pink, in their blush. The same, or an analogous type, form the basis of the Welsh population, and to a varying but often inconsiderable extent of that part of England west and north-west of a line from Dorsetshire to the Tees. . . . So far as the early ancient tales, such as the Tain Bo Chuailgne, the Tochmarc Eimire, and the Bruidin Daderga enable us to judge, the Firbolgs, Tuatha Dé Danaan, and Milesians belonged alike to the first type." As regards the second and earlier type, Dr. Sullivan argues that it probably now exists in a much smaller proportion in Ireland than in the west of Britain, since the people belonging to it, having been dispossessed of the land at a very early period, were the poorest, and must, therefore, have fallen victims, in a larger proportion than other races, to that plague of famine and war which has fallen upon Ireland so much more often and more bitterly than upon Britain. Against this fact must be set another important fact with an opposite tendency, namely the just and sympathetic government, under which all races in Ireland at an early date lived, which showed itself in the institution of customs and laws for the protection of the poor and weak against the rich and strong, and in the opening up to talent and industry of the path that leads to honour and wealth.* Dr. Sullivan's argument goes, however, to prove that only the descendants of the "fittest" among the Iberian race in Ireland are very likely to be there now—only the able and industrious families who had used the advantages of the Irish law to win a social vantage-ground for themselves, or those endowed with such a vitality of physical constitution as enabled them, poor as they were, to live through the horrible periods of privation and physical suffering so familiar to students of later Irish history.

The Irish legends, however, throw little or no light on this subject of the aboriginal Iberian settlement. Evidently there was early a bardic fiction that all the "men of Erin" were of the same race. Hence it is that, despite evidence to the contrary, it is so tempting to identify him, in part at least, with the Firbolg. Perhaps the most satisfactory hypothesis would be that the Firbolg represents the result of a Celtic wave of immigration, which had partly absorbed the aboriginal element on its way, and continued still further to absorb it after the Milesian conquest had brought the preceding colonists into subjection. The rent-paying tribes of the second century would, then, consist mainly of this mixed Firbolgic element, with a Milesian infusion of those who, by the action of natural causes, had fallen in the social scale till the servile ranks were reached.

* See Chapter VI.

The most definite account of the distinctions between the three Irish races that I have been able to find is given in Mac Firbis's book of the genealogies, *compiled* in the years 1650 to 1666, and said by him to be "taken from an old book" as "the distinction which the profound historians draw between the different races which are in Erin."

"Every one who is white (of skin), brown (of hair), bold, honourable, daring, prosperous, bountiful in the bestowal of property, wealth, and rings, and who is not afraid of battle or combat; they are the descendants of the sons of Milesius in Erin.

"Every one who is fair-haired, vengeful, large; and every plunderer; every musical person; the professors of musical and entertaining performances; who are adepts in all Druidical and magical arts; they are the descendents of the Tuatha Dé Danann in Erin.

"Every one who is black-haired, who is a tattler, guileful, tale-telling, noisy, contemptible; every wretched, mean, strolling, unsteady, harsh, and inhospitable person; every slave, every mean thief, every churl, every one who loves not to listen to music and entertainment, the disturbers of every council and every assembly, and the promoters of discord among people; these are the descendants of the Firbolgs, of the Gailiuns of Liogarné, and of the Fir Domhnaans in Erinn. But, however, the descendants of the Firbolgs are the most numerous of all these." *

* O'Curry's "Lectures on MS. Materials," p. 223.

The description is clearly Milesian in sentiment, and breathes somewhat strongly the spirit of ascendency; but, passing that, it brings out very clearly the idea of *two* dominant races well contrasted, and a subject-race containing miscellaneous materials. The black hair of this race is an unmistakable indication of Iberian affinities; and if all the rest of Irish tradition were consistent with this passage, from a writer whose date is unknown, there would be nothing to prevent our acceptance of the hypothesis that the Irish Firbolgs were mainly Iberian. As it is we cannot accept it.

It is certain, however, that at the dawn of Irish tradition all the peoples of Erin spoke one language, and were settling down together side by side under one set of social ideas and institutions, with an obvious tendency to obliterate race-distinctions, and to make such natural paths of communication between the aristocracy and the democracy that the social rise of families, on the one hand, and their fall, on the other, should be very possible. Doubtless, it was the pressure of this social tendency to national unity of thought and feeling that, acting on the bardic mind, produced the beautiful legend of Nemidh and his sons, in which the three peoples of Ireland are exhibited as having sprung from a common Irish ancestor in Ireland. Thence they parted in different directions, and, after many wanderings, returned one by one to the old home, meeting each other as foes, but soon to be reconciled and to rejoice in the recognition of the old common language which all had kept. The children of Nemidh, so runs the story,* were scattered over Europe in three bands. The band first to return, after wanderings in Northern Europe, was that of the Firbolgs. The second band went to Scythia, and, returning thence, met their brethren in Ireland and fought a mighty battle for the possession of the country. The story tells us how when the two ambassadors from the rival hosts met, each was surprised to hear the other speak in his own language, and delighted to discover the common lineage of their tribes. But when they examined each other's weapons, these were found to be different: the Firbolg was armed with two heavy, thick, pointless spears, rounded at the ends, while the Dé Danann carried two beautifully shaped, thin, slender, long, sharp-pointed spears. The third band went forth to Southern Europe, and, after many years had passed, set sail from Spain for Ireland, where they set up their royal dynasties, and played the principal part in moulding the fortunes and character of that nation in which distinctions of race were perhaps as easily lost in those times as they have always inevitably tended to lose themselves since—that people whose most familiar title was "the men of Erin," who never suffered a mere race-name to be given to their island.† I have told this legend

* O'Curry's "Lectures on MS. Materials," p. 245.
† For etymology of the name Ireland, from the Gaelic Eriu (old

not because I believe it to have any probable bearing on the actual history of events, but because it shadows forth an ideal truth which is much more important. In terms of ethnic legend it expresses the fact, so potent in its effects on later Irish history, that no race once planted on Irish shores can escape absorption into the substance of the Irish people.

Some may think it improbable that a band of immigrants should come to Ireland direct from the Continent without naturally landing in Britain first; but, as a matter of fact, the idea that the way from the world to Ireland lies across Britain is one of quite modern origin. In the historic period of the early Christian centuries, Ireland was in constant direct communication with France and continental Europe generally, and we have it on the authority of Tacitus that the ports of Ireland were well known to merchants in his time. Indeed, it is sufficient to look at the map of Europe, and realize the conditions of travelling before the growth of the Roman empire, to see that nothing could be more natural than the descent from the South of the Milesian Gael on the south-west coast of Ireland, which is the traditional place of his landing. Nor could anything be more improbable than that a southern tribe should reach Ireland through Britain, as northern and eastern tribes prob-

Irish Iveriu), see note by Mr. Whitley Stokes in Professor Max Müller's "Lectures on the Science of Language," vol. i. p. 284. He thinks it is probably connected with the Sanskrit *avara*, meaning "western" or "posterior."

ably would. Add to these considerations the fact that the early historic Irish were much given to travelling,—having explored the northern seas in Christian times as far as Iceland at least,—and the improbability of the Milesian story entirely vanishes. Indeed, we may go a step further, and see that the general, though vague, Irish tradition that the island was in more distant periods a home for various settlers from the south and east is probable enough, though it lacks sufficient positive evidence.

In the making of the Irish people, as we first find them, the last band of Gaelic-speaking immigrants played, as the rulers of the country, a leading part. What further evidence is there that they came direct from Spain, without contact with Britain, as the legend clearly tells us? We have already seen good reason to associate the Irish Gael with his Alban brother the Caledonian Pict, and yet to dissociate them also. The theory of an immigration direct from the continent of Europe does this, and the legend fills the gap unintentionally. Thus it has an independent antecedent probability. It accounts, too, for the difference between the fair-haired and the brown-haired Gael, though this is not important. Again, the discovery by Grimm of a Gaelic element in the language of Aquitaine, in the fourth century,* affords substantial support to the Irish tradition that the Milesians came

---

* Sullivan's Introduction to O'Curry's " Manners and Customs of the Ancient Irish," pp. lix., *et seq.*

from Spain (or at least thereabouts), since it shows us that a Gaelic-speaking people were at some time settled in the south of France, near to the place whence the sons of Miledh are said to have come, in search of new lands and with a spirit high for adventure, preferring the more distant Erin, we may infer, to the less distant Alban coasts. Aquitaine, it may be noticed, between the Garonne and the Pyrenees, is the one piece of south-west France which yields no dolmens;* and this, as we have seen, is a mark of the Celt.

Another link in the chain of evidence for the Milesian story is suggested by the presence on the west and south-west coast of pre-historic forts, very large and strong, which are not to be found, with one or two exceptions, in the rest of Ireland.† We shall have occasion to refer to these again later. Here it will suffice to remark that as defences they are incomparably superior to the earthen forts, so-called, of the ancient Briton and of the Irish in the eastern parts, and that it is difficult to imagine why they should be where they are, unless built by some race bent on settlement, making good their position in the country. That race could not have built them coming direct from Britain, for that would imply a sudden architectural inspiration of a fabulous sort. Moreover, such a race would have been more likely to build them on the side of the country where it first planted itself.

* Fergusson's "Rude Stone Monuments," p. 328.
† Dunraven's "Notes on Irish Architecture," with Photographs, pt. i. sect. i.

CHAPTER II.

ERIN AND ALBA.

THE first event in Irish history of which we can feel any certainty that it happened, is the one marked out as his point of departure by the great Irish historian Tighernach, seven centuries ago. As the testimony of scholars since goes on the whole to support his selection, we cannot do better than follow his lead. The chronicles compiled by the monks take us back into far distant regions of time, thousands of years before the birth of Christ. But the critical intellect of Tighernach pronounced the accepted chronology to be uncertain. So, while a protest should be entered against the neglect of all this mass of tradition and even the chronology inferred from it, the *historical* line will probably best be drawn where Tighernach draws it.

In 299 B.C., Kimbay Mac Fiontann, the chief of the children of Iar, founded the royal palace and entrenched seat of Emain Macha, and established in Ulster a powerful confederacy. His wife is represented to be Macha, who appears in Irish story as the war-goddess of the Ultonians, and he built the palace on the heights of Macha, called Ard-Macha, in Gaelic, —the place which is now known as Armagh. Thus the ancient capital of Ulster was that Armagh where St. Patrick afterwards established the primacy of the Irish Christian Church. The true capital of Ireland was not, however, Armagh, but Tara, so soon as there was a capital at all.

It is not the purpose of these pages to follow up the record of Irish internal history from this starting point. The fact with its date is rather set down here as a landmark showing the antiquity of that history apart from mere legend. Among the details associated with it and with much later events there is plenty of the mythical mingled with the history; but leaving aside such details, both of legend and event, let us pass on to notice certain broad facts. History has dawned; and we find four powerful tribes contending for the right to preside over the great national festival, the triennial Feis of Tara. The king who had that right was for the time the High King of Erin, with such honours, rights, and privileges as might pertain to his position. None but the four Milesian families had a right to celebrate the festival. These were known as the children of Heber, Heremon, Ith, and Iar, descendants of the four sons of Miledh according to the tradition; and in this distinction of families we may see the basis of the country's division into four provinces. The struggle made by one strong king or another, not only to hold Tara, but to gain an admission of his right to hold it, either for his own life or for his family, is at once the main source of internecine conflict and a striving to attain by force to national unity. Force of arms was not, however, the legitimate means by which a king was raised to the dignity of presiding at Tara. In theory, he was elected by the four families, and probably the presence in the country of many powerful non-Milesian septs contributed to the prevention of frequent combats that might otherwise have taken place. The main facts to be noticed are, however, these, that the Irish people had a custom of meeting triennially, for political, social, commercial, and probably religious purposes, at Tara on the plains of Meath, that it was usual to *elect* a king to convene the assembly and preside over it, and that the king who held this post was the High King of Erin. In later times, a fifth province was established side by side with the original four, and the king of this fifth province of Meath came to have for a time the right to Tara and the supreme monarchy.

About the middle of the first century after Christ, the Aithech Tuatha, or rent-paying tribes of Erin, rose up in rebellion against the great Milesian families, the aristocracy of the land. They succeeded in accomplishing a revolution which placed their own leader, Cairbre Cinn Cait, on the throne of Tara. But, after twenty-five years, Cairbre's successor was defeated and slain by Tuathal Teachtmar, the chosen leader of the royal tribes and son of the last legitimate monarch. Tuathal, we are told, immediately set about the task of reducing his enemies to obedience; and probably large numbers of them fled, or were driven out of the country. The remnant of the Aithech Tuatha were redistributed, so as to ensure better their continued quiescence and eventual absorption by the dominant races. And finally, Tuathal having reorganized the nation on a basis that is reputed to have been just as well as strong, received the allegiance of all his subjects, and established his dynasty on the throne of Tara.

It has been supposed that these Aithech Tuatha were identical with the Atticotti of contemporary history. The idea was founded on a fallacious resemblance between the two names, but there is essential truth in it nevertheless, for the word Atticotti is considered by authorities now to mean the ancient people,* and thus points clearly to the aboriginal inhabitants of Britain, the kindred of the Irish displaced tribes. It may very well therefore have been that the Atticotti in North Britain were strengthened by the forcible displacement from Ireland of the conquered tribes. Large bodies of them may also have acted as mercenaries to the Irish monarchs on their frequent warlike expeditions abroad. And in

* Rhys's "Early Britain," p. 275.

these ways they represent one element in the reflux of people eastwards that took place from Ireland during the first four centuries of the Christian era.

For at an early date the sons of Erin were known in the neighbouring countries as men of war and plunder. We hear of them in British history as the Scots who, with the Picts, contributed to the general discomfort of life on the British coasts. These expeditions began, or increased, about the beginning of the Christian era, and Irish tradition gives us some glimpses of plunder and sovereignty in the isle of Alba. Between 100 B.C. and A.D. 400, the Irish appear to have shared in the general movement of north-western peoples, by a reflux eastward, directed principally towards the neighbouring larger island; and during these times they left their mark on the ethnology and institutions of the British people in the west.

The comparatively settled state of the country which followed the completion of the Irish revolution and counter-revolution in the first century, bore its natural fruit in the result that the predatory excursions from Ireland to Britain assumed a more steady purpose of conquest.* The mineral wealth of South Britain had been largely developed under the Roman rule, and thus South Britain was a suitable object of prey to all the barbarian hosts from the north-west

* Introduction to O'Curry's "Manners and Customs of the Ancient Irish," p. xxxiv., *et seq.*

and east, Picts Scots and Saxons alike. In their common attack on Roman Briton, Gael and Saxon first met, and met as friends in that not quite holy alliance of plunder. It is curious to note that the first mention of the Saxons as enemies occurs in the seventh, and of the Danes in the eighth century, and that the first rise of hostility between the races had reference to the quarrel between the Irish and Roman Churches. But in these earlier centuries the Irish attack on Britain was simply a factor in the general descent of the young northern races—the barbarians —on the Roman empire. In one of Claudian's poems, Briton, personified, is made to speak of Stilicho the Roman general as protecting her from neighbouring nations, "when the Scots move all Ierne, and the sea foams with hostile oars." Cormac Mac Art in the third century, and Niall of the Nine Hostages at the end of the fourth, are conspicuous as leaders of the Irish forces in these incursions.

The relation of Ireland to West Britain was of a more interesting and permanent character. Welsh tradition and topography alike bear witness to the occupation of Wales by the Irish, after the British colonization, and before that determining event in Welsh history, the settlement of Wales by the north-western Britons, or Cumbrians, under Cunedda, who bound together in one nation, with a national literature that has never ceased to grow, all the tribes between the Clyde and the Severn, under the common name of Cymry or fellow-countrymen. The Gael retired, or was expelled from Wales, but he has left his vestiges behind him There appear in fact to have been two distinct settlements of Irish tribes in Britain, one of Munster tribes in South Wales, Devonshire and Cornwall, and the other of Erimonian Scots in Anglesey and North Wales, these being practically the same band as that which settled in the Isle of Man. The Rev. W. Basil Jones, in his work on the "Vestiges of the Gael in Gwynedd," (*i.e.* Wales), comes to the conclusion that the Irish at one time occupied the whole of Anglesey, Carnarvon, and Monmouthshire, with a portion at least of Denbigh and Radnorshire.

This inference is founded largely on the Gaelic topography of these parts, and on the presence of unmistakably Gaelic memorial inscriptions, showing that Gaelic was the language of the inhabitants in early Christian times. Three possible theories may be invented to account for these facts. The first is that Gaelic was the language of the main body of Britons once, and of these outlying branches so late as the time of the inscriptions, which belong to the fifth, sixth, and seventh centuries. The improbability of this theory is so evident, that no one seriously entertains it; the contrast between the districts of Gaelic ogam memorial stones, in North and South Wales, and the non-Gaelic district without ogams, or old memorial stones generally, in Mid Wales, is too remarkable to be accounted for, without the supposition of some national distinction. The second theory, favoured by Professor Rhys,* and other Welsh authorities, is that these traces of the Gael are due to an ancient Gaelic occupation, anterior to the true British settlement, which ultimately confined it within these corners of the land. First, it should be noted that there is no evidence of actual fact in favour of this theory. In Roman times, it does appear that the tribes of Mid Wales, the Ordovices, were pressing some earlier tribes into the corners, but there is no reason to think that these were Gaelic, or contained any dominant mixture of Gaelic with the aboriginal element. On the contrary, not only the fact that the Silures of South Wales were of the so-called Iberian type, but the evidence of the distribution of the rude stone structures, the cromlechs, throughout Europe, and the fact that Cornwall and the two extremes of Wales are conspicuously the cromlech districts of South Britain, point to the conclusion that these regions were *dominated* by the pre-Aryan race well into the cromlech-building period. From the facts collected by Mr. Ferguson, it is at least probable that this period extended into post-Roman times.† The evidence is slight, but it points in a direction opposite to the theory.

The inherent difficulties of this hypothesis are, however, more serious objections than its lack of

* Rhys's "Early Britain," ch. vi. and vii.
† Fergusson's "Stone Monuments."

evidence, which, indeed, would not be a positive objection taken in itself. The hypothesis implies that Gaelic inscriptions of the seventh and even later centuries belong to early settlers of a Celtic race who, during such long intervals of time, remained distinct, though contiguous, and were not even amalgamated with the British branch of the same race by the pressure of foreign invasion and oppression. An event more improbable in the history of Celtic races it would not be easy to imagine. It is supposed that the Gael, so far as language goes, had absorbed the tenacious and unimpressionable non-Aryan, but that two branches of the most quick-witted and impressionable of all the Aryan races lived side by side for centuries in the presence of foreign foes, and did not amalgamate to the extent of identifying two not very long divergent dialects of the same Celtic speech.

The third theory supplies the solution of these difficulties. North and South Wales were, in early Roman times, the strongholds of the warlike, tenacious, and probably unprogressive race, which preceded the Britons in the settlement of Britain, and have left their mark on Europe by the erection of cromlechs and similar monuments in all those parts that were not, at some undefined early period, dominated by the Celts or other Aryans. In the first century of the Christian era, the Celt had become permanently dominant in Ireland; and afterwards, more especially in the third and fourth centuries, he began to be aggressive towards the sister isle. We have it on the evidence of Cormac's "Glossary," written in the ninth century, that Irish kings collected tribute in the south-west of Britain.* This is a clear indication of dominion, established by aggression from Irish head-quarters. We know, too, that Niall of the Nine Hostages was slain in fight on the Muir n-Icht, the channel between Britain and France (A.D. 405), so that he must either have marched across Britain or sailed round it with an armed fleet. The Roman legions were withdrawn from Britain about the year 410, and near this time the last great Irish invasion was led by Niall's successor, Dathi, who was killed by lightning as far south as the foot of the Alps.

Here, then, we have the clear existence of a cause quite sufficient to account for the presence of the Gael in Gwynedd, as a distinct racial entity marked linguistically in later times. There was, in the fourth century and earlier, an aggressive Ireland seeking and establishing dominion in Britain. The Gaelic language for several succeeding centuries prevailed, and we may presume, therefore, that the Gael had dominated, in those parts of Wales where the pre-Aryan element was strong. It is improbable that this domination was pre-Roman, for reasons already assigned. It is highly probable that the aggressive Irish should,

* Introduction to O'Curry's "Manners and Customs," p. xxxix. See also reference to "Romance of Tristan and Iseult," for further evidence.

in the early centuries of the Christian era, settle in West Britain and dominate the old inhabitants—thus set between two fires—even if they did not, as is most likely, go, in a fitful way, much further when the power of the Romans declined. This then, it appears to me, is the true explanation of the Gaelic traces in Wales. These traces are the mark of a Gaelic migration eastwards to the southern parts of the larger island, under the influence of which the old inhabitants adopted the language and imbibed some of the ideas of the Gael, while the latter was not slow to absorb any element that might be useful in his civilization. It may be that the black-haired, grey-eyed Celt, in both islands, owes something better than the colour of his hair to that Silurian persistence of idea and tenacity of will which are so aptly complementary to the docile intellect and rapid impressionability of the Celt.

But this is the least interesting aspect of the early connection between the Welsh and Irish nations, for Ireland owes to that West Britain, which Wales represents, a debt of the kind that is sure to be a bond of national sympathy. About the middle of the fifth century, the Bishop Germanus, of Auxerre in Gaul, was summoned to their help by the bishops of the British Church, who were suffering much from the incursions of Scots Saxons and Picts, and the interference with study and religion these occasioned. Germanus organized the Britons, and defeated the combined forces in a battle near Mold in Flintshire, which is known in history as the Hallelujah Victory. These events drew the attention of Germanus to Ireland, still pagan, and therefore dangerous to the British Church. But about the same time it happened that a certain pious Briton, by name Patrick, was greatly moved to undertake the conversion of the Irish race. It is probable that Germanus fell in with this Patrick, and consecrated him for the mission. It is certain that Patrick went, and the story of his labours shall be presently told. What concerns us now is his origin only. Several places have disputed for the honour of being his birthplace; but the evidence of his own and other early writings makes it probable that he came from a place called Alcluith, which is identified with Dumbarton. This is now within the Scotch border, but was then in the region of the Strathclyde Britons, and bordered on the narrow part of the sea between the two islands. At the age of sixteen, Patrick was carried into slavery by the Scots from the opposite shore, and seven years of slavery were passed in an Antrim glen which can be identified to-day. At twenty-three he escaped and returned to his own people. But henceforth his heart was set on Ireland; to win the Scots to Christianity became the ambition of his life. The fulfilment of that hope is the first instalment of the debt which Ireland owes to the race now represented by Wales.

Most persons know that in the Dark Ages learning

of all kinds found its most natural and safest home in Ireland, the then famous School of the West. But before classical and theological learning had a home in Ireland, it had a less well-known home in Britain. St. Patrick brought the Christian religion from Britain to Ireland, but it would not be correct to say that he brought the scholarship of the British church also. St. Patrick was something much greater, but he was not a fine scholar, like the Irish saints of the succeeding century: the gulf between his Latin style and that of St. Columbanus is wide indeed. Nevertheless, in the wake of Christian knowledge, he brought with him the idea of new learning, and the keen-witted Irish people, prizing knowledge and literature with an ardour due to natural disposition and the national bardic education, needed no more than the suggestion of such an idea. So we find that, in the first half of the sixth century, the celebrated Irish St. Finnian, who founded the monastic school of Clonard—probably the first of the great schools in Ireland—went to Wales to complete his education, and was there the disciple of three eminent Welsh saints, David, Gildas, and Cadoc. Under St. Finnian, the school of Clonard became great and famous, and many were the scholars that issued from it; so that, as the Four Masters tell us this St. Finnian was called "foster-father of the saints of Ireland." Twelve of the most eminent saints—the twelve apostles of Ireland—were among his disciples.

Many were the torches of learning lit from the torch of Clonard: but the torch of Clonard was lit in Wales. And this is the second instalment of that spiritual debt which Ireland owes to the kindred genius of the gentle Cymric nation.

Not less important was the history that followed the settlement in Northern Alba of the Scots from Dalriada, or Antrim, who colonized the Airer Goidel (*i.e.* region of the Gael), now called Argyle. The close proximity of Scotland to Antrim is a fact which must strike every one who has spent even a day on the Antrim coasts. Looking out from the deck of the steamer, near the entrance to Belfast Lough, it is easy to mistake the Scotch coast for some part of the coast on the opposite side. The two islands lean towards one another at this point, and the geographical fact has probably influenced in several ways the history of each. On the seas between was made that alliance, already mentioned more than once, of Scot and Pict, in the Roman days; and the Roman generals showed their sense of the danger that threatened so constantly from the Dalriadic coasts, by the erection, in the second century, of a strong fort directly opposite, at Barhill near Kilpatrick on the Clyde. In the earliest times, as already stated, a settlement of Alban Picts was found established in a region called Dalaradia, which corresponds roughly to the present County Down, and are referred to in Irish history as Cruithnigh. On the other hand, the Irish Scots migrated indefinitely to the opposite shores. The definite settlement, however, of a Scottish kingdom in Argyle dates strictly from the year 502, when the Christian prince Fergus Mac Erc set up his kingdom there, an outpost of Scottish Christendom on the borders of the still pagan Picts. This settlement was a determining factor in the after course of Scotch national history; and, although it is an anticipation to do so, it will be convenient here to trace its effects. The little Scottish community was in no safe place, the old alliance between Scots and Picts being practically dissolved, and a new alliance of defence between Scottish and British Christianity having tacitly taken its place. The danger, be it noted, lay in the paganism of the Picts; and the Picts were old friends, with a special claim on their now more enlightened brother-race for instruction in the Christian faith. What worthier object could there be of the missionary zeal, then taking possession of Irish imagination and will, than the conversion to Christianity of these pagan neighbours? There was statesmanship, as well as self-devotion and charity, in the work which the great Irish saint Columba planned, when he set up his monastery in the Island of Iona off the Scotch Highland coast, in the year 563, and prepared for his mission in Pictland. Having wisely secured the assistance of two Irish Picts, Comgall and Canice, he commenced his spiritual campaign by an advance on the capital at Inverness ; and in 565, he preached to the Pictish king Brude himself, and converted him to Christianity. This success opened the whole country, as far north as the Orkneys, to his missionary efforts; for the king's favour secured a safe-conduct everywhere. Monastic establishments, which furnished to the people the example of a peaceful, industrious, and happy community, were established gradually throughout the land ; and, after nine years of missionary labour, the foundations of Pictish Christianity were laid on a basis which was broad and sure.

A year later (575) St. Columba was in Ireland again, pleading at a great national council, held at Drumceatt near Limavady, the cause of "Home Rule" for his brethren the Scots of Argyle, and, having succeeded in his object, he reorganized the little Scottish kingdom and placed Aidan, a descendant of the great Irish king Niall of the Nine Hostages, upon the throne. Nearly two centuries later, Pictland, or her kings, had a relapse into pagan ways; and, not only were the Scots driven temporarily from Argyle, but the Columban monasteries were expelled from the realm. This was not the end, however, but far from it. The Scots appear to have taken refuge in Galloway, where they formed a settlement; and a century later we find their king, Kenneth Mac Alpine, laying claim to the Pictish throne by descent on his mother's side—a claim which was sound under Pictish law. The rival claimant, however, resisted, and Kenneth entering Pictland with his followers, reinforced almost certainly by many of the Picts themselves, established his dynasty in the year 842. That dynasty was established permanently. It brought back with it to Pictland the blessings of the Columban monasteries, to the expulsion of which the Christian party in the nation referred the troubles that had come upon the Pictish dynasty. And, indeed, the probability seems to be very great that Kenneth owed his victory largely to the effects that had been wrought by Columba nearly three centuries before, and to the falling off of the Pictish kings from his teaching while its influence was still potent in the minds of the people. If so, the establishment of the Scots as the supreme race in Alba was not effected in any sense by force of arms, but was that much better thing, a conquest of heart and mind with the weapons of intellectual skill and moral self-devotion. Not Kenneth, but Columba, founded the modern kingdom of Scotland.

Under this name in time it came to be known. The kingdom of Scone, as it was called in Pictish times, became presently the kingdom of Alba, and not till two centuries after Kenneth's accession,—that is, in the tenth century,—was the name Scotia applied to it generally. By that time all the Celtic elements, Pict and Scot, and Strathclyde Britons, had become firmly welded with the non-Aryan remnant into one nation, having the common Saxon enemy on its southern borders; and this was Scotland.* In the course of centuries, as every one knows, the Scottish kings succeeded by inheritance to the throne of England, and thus the Queen of Great Britain and Ireland to-day is, through Kenneth Mac Alpine and Aidan of Columba's time, a lineal descendant of that Irish King Niall who flourished about 400 A.D.

Aidan was consecrated on a certain sacred stone, the Stone of Fate, which was presumably brought to Scone by Kenneth, and is now in Westminster Abbey. This stone is used very fitly as the coronation stone of the monarchs of Great Britain and Ireland. There it stands, a symbol of imperial unity, connecting by a "thread of poetry" not quite insignificant, the nationalities of three nations—the Irish Stone of Fate sacred to the memory of Columba and the Irish line of kings, brought, we may suppose, across the narrow sea where the islands lean over to meet each other.†

But the message of peace which Columba brought across the sea was not confined to the Celtic and earlier tribes which were still pagan in the larger island. Iona became the mother of many mission settlements, not only in Scotland and the distant islands of the north, but also in the as yet neglected Saxon south. At the time of Columba's death (A.D. 597), there were thirty-two mission stations

---

* See Skene's "Celtic Scotland," vol. i. for the history in full.
† The identity of the stone since the ninth century is quite certain, but its earlier history rests on an estimate of probabilities. See "The Stone of Scone," by W. F. Skene.

among the Scots of Alba, and eighteen among the Picts; and under his third successor the conversion of the Saxons began.

Oswald of Bernicia had in his youth taken refuge, during certain troubled times, with the monks of Iona, and from them he received a Christian education. When, in later years, having overthrown Penda of Mercia, he purposed to establish Christianity in Northumbria, he turned naturally to his early teachers and "sent to the seniors of the Scots" for assistance. Bishop Aidan came from Iona to Northumbria in the year 634, and a mission station of the usual Irish type was set up at Lindisfarne, an island close to the coast. "From that time," says Bede, "many from the region of the Scots came daily into Britain, and with great devotion preached the word of faith to those provinces of the Angles over which King Oswald reigned." Lindisfarne, like Iona, though in a minor degree, became the mother of many monasteries. Thus good and lasting work was done in England, although it happened that only thirty years after the coming of Aidan, the Northumbrian Church was separated from Iona by the king's acceptance, at a council held in Whitby, of the Roman rather than the Irish tradition.

Across the narrow sea came the Scots, with messages of war to their kindred the Britons on the other side; and back they carried, at one time, into slavery, Patrick, their future benefactor. Across that narrow sea came, for the second time, the British Patrick, longing to heap Christian coals of fire on his former master's head. Across the sea came Finnian, to learn of St. David in Wales, that he might sow in Erin those seeds of learning which yielded later such a plentiful crop. And presently the figure of St. Columba, mightiest of all, is seen, standing as it were on the Antrim cliffs, looking towards that Pictish land whither none had dared to take the message yet. So he took it and prevailed, planting the land with Christian communities, and organizing on its outskirts a kingdom confirmed in the faith, gentle as well as brave, and free to work out its own destinies. Across the narrow sea came one strand in the ancestry of the royal dynasty which reigns without rule over the four nations now, the fitting symbol of an imperial unity which should be founded on national sympathies and the convergence of national ideas after the Celtic and Christian style, not upheld by that weapon of blind and tactless force, on which the Norman conquerors mainly relied, though always in the end it breaks feebly in their hands.

The Normans, who conquered England and Wales, settled in Ireland, and fought long for supremacy in Scotland. Their faith was in force. Of Norse descent, and having imbibed the Roman imperial idea, they studied how to use force well. They had a military organization which was possible to them, because they worshipped force, and could, therefore, find it in their hearts to subject all higher human interests to the demand for national strength, as nations with a heart set on other ideas could not. The Englishman respected force, but the tenderest spot in his heart was after all for freedom. So, though he was patient when crushed by the Norman yoke, his instincts were unchanged and, circumstances favouring him, he, slowly and in his own doggedly instinctive rather than consciously idealizing way, wrought out the democratic England which is in these days coming for the first time to full consciousness of herself. The Briton of Wales believed not in force, and cherished high above all else the right to his own ideas. Violence done to the national ideas he resented more than restraints on his personal liberty. He knew the might of the strong arm, in the experiences of his hard history; he was patient, therefore, but had an indomitable nationality. He might have forgiven the force, but he could not forgive the Norman's blindness to this, his want of sympathy for sentiment other than his own. And so Wales marks herself off even now from that England where Norman manners still control the national style, as a nationality distinct and contrasted.

The Gael of Ireland believed so little in the Norman god of conquest that he did not realize, perhaps ever, what a terrible thing the rod of iron is. He had had experience in his wars with the Danes, and, though after much loss and suffering, had in his own manner broken the Danish rod. So the Gael let the Norman settle in his midst, as the Danes had settled before, as well as after, their submission; and it probably did not seem unreasonable to him that the king of England, being the greatest king in those parts, should claim the over-lordship, especially as his claim was recommended by the Pope. The Normans settled in Ireland, and kept up their connection with the English king. But the Gael kept up his own ways of thought and feeling, his love for the land, his instinct for liberty, and his faith in reason rather than force. By means of these he has accomplished a twofold result: he has effaced the idea of his own *race*, and has imprinted that of Irish *nationality* on the stranger races settled in his borders. He has by his ideas conquered the Norman force-instinct which in the sixteenth and seventeenth centuries overcame his race; and now he is in the van of the great democratic movement which agitates the four nations of the United Kingdom.

To the Scots of Scotland belongs the honour of having successfully resisted the Norman military power from first to last. Their kingdom was not founded merely on force, but they understood the organization of force for purposes of resistance better than the people of Erin or of Wales; and Scotland was in the military sense a national unity before the Norman landed on English shores. But the Norman instinct of force—blind force, deaf and tactless

—which descended to the kings and oligarchy of England after the genuine Norman period had passed—that force-instinct kept up, through long periods, a struggle with Scotland to destroy her independence which bears fruit now, not in the consolidation, but in the marked distinction of the two nations. After such a war of independence as Edward the First forced on the Scottish nation it was impossible that Scotland should be absorbed into England. A union of crowns and even a union of parliaments—these were possible, brought about as they were in later times, by the accident of circumstance and the consent of both nations; but Scotch sentiment is as Scottish to-day—as averse to the absorption of Scotland into England—as when Scots won the battle of Bannockburn. And so it will be always; the history made by Edward the First can never be unwritten to the end of time. Forcible consolidations have been effected among other races than those which peopled Alba and Erin, and by leading races more gifted with ideas and sympathy than the Normans were; but the attempt which the Norman made to weld the four nations of these islands into one has been defeated all along the line. To his instinct for dominance the English opposed their instinct for political freedom, the Welsh their racial, and the Scotch their composite national idea; while in Ireland the Norman instinct has through centuries been worsted in the spiritual struggle with that most subtle of all national ideas, a people's devotion to its mother-land. So the English arms triumphed, but the Irish idea conquered; the successful invaders, generation after generation, coming out fresh from England when each war was done, became presently "more Irish than the Irish themselves."

So the four nations are intact in the islands still; and the political heirs of the Norman rule are still there too, laying the heavy hand of force, though feebly, on the nations' soul. Feebly—for political power has gone over to the peoples, and faith in self-government is an ancient tradition common to them all. Through faith in such a tradition, is made possible a union of diverse elements stronger than any force-made union can ever be—a union of self-governing, self-developing, self-respecting nations, bound to support each other by every tie of interest, honour, and the new-made tradition of a confederate democracy—each nation bound to assist the other three against any infringement of popular rights on the part of the classes deputed freely by each to rule. Even now the four nations are drawing together as they never drew before, and the time, it would seem, is not far off when that Irish Stone of Fate in Westminster Abbey will symbolize at last a real union, based on those principles of justice and love in which the great Columba, statesman and missionary, laid the foundations of the Scottish kingdom.

CHAPTER III.

ERIN AND EUROPE.

THE history of early Ireland, in its relation to the sister isle, shows us external symptoms of a certain national development which it will presently be our business to study within the island itself. We have seen pagan Ireland aggressive and even conquering along the British coasts. Then comes the British mission of Patrick, and presently all is changed. Ireland abandons the rôle of the hero for that of the saint, though invested still with the heroic temper and its thirst for deeds. Her war-policy has ceased, and the peace-policy of missionary labour takes its place. Long after Columba's time, his followers carry on their spiritual warfare, and extend their conquests over Northern England and the Midlands. Monasteries tracing their origin to Iona are planted throughout Saxon Britain, and at one time it seems likely that Irish rather than Roman Christianity is likely to reign in the English land. Columbanus, who was twenty-two years younger than Columba, goes with a mission band to Burgundy, Switzerland and Northern Italy, to combat paganism and immorality in places which then were very dark, by establishing, after the Irish fashion, industrious and saintly communities, as examples and for instruction, in the people's midst. The old passion for adventure and enterprise which we may imagine to have possessed the Milesians on their journey west, "moved by an ancestral spirit urging them to great deeds"—that spirit is found anew in the Irish missionaries. They visit all the islands on the north-west British coast, they go north and discover the Shetlands, they go further north and make a settlement in Iceland. "In A.D. 870, when the Norwegians came to Iceland, there were Christians there who departed and left behind them Irish books, bells, and other things, from whence it may be inferred that these Christians were Irish.' So says an old text which Zeuss quotes in his "Grammatica Celtica." In all directions they go forth, some in search of missionary labours, some moved by a desire for world-knowledge and new fields of learning. So the Irish monk travels to Egypt and measures the pyramids. He goes east studying the customs and scholarship of the Syrian Church. There is the clearest evidence that, after Christianity was established in Ireland, there began to be a communication of the liveliest sort between the Eastern and the extreme Western Churches. The iconoclastic policy of the Greek emperors in the eighth century drove Eastern ecclesiastics west, bearing their peculiar heritage of art and learning with them. This they brought to Western Europe, and no other country was so ready at that time as Ireland to benefit by it. Celtic art was a reality long before then, but it may well be that it found use for the artistic ideas of the East, with which Irish travel had already made it more or less acquainted.

Greek was certainly studied in the Irish monasteries, or some of them, a century earlier. We find that a certain monk, Aileran, displays a knowledge both of this language and of Hebrew as early as about the middle of the seventh century, for he died no later than 665. But it is probable that the flight of Greek scholars from Constantinople created fresh opportunities for the development of Irish Hellenistic studies. The fact that there were Greek ecclesiastics in Ireland left its mark on the tenacious Celtic memory till as late as the troubles of the seventeenth century. Probably Greek became, in the eighth century, a general subject of study in all the Irish ecclesiastical schools, whereas it was exceptional before that time. The conspicuous evidences which have come down to us of its existence belong to this and the succeeding centuries. The Irish scholar, Sedulius, lived in the eighth century, and wrote a Greek Psalter, which survives now. Cormac Mac Cullinan (831–903), king and bishop of Cashel, compiled a glossary, which is clearly marked by a knowledge of Greek, since he occasionally derives, absurdly enough, the names of places from Greek roots, as Tara from the Greek θεωρεῖν, "to behold." The Book of Armagh, too, bears witness to the same fact of Greek study, as, for instance, by the writing of the Lord's Prayer in Greek characters.*

But the man who most of all makes Irish scholarship stand out conspicuous in the European world was Joannes Scotus, also called by his contemporaries Erigena, or Eriu-gena, "Irish-born." John of Ireland was summoned to France, to the court of Charles the Bald, where he alone was able to translate the Greek works of the Pseudo-Dionysius. This John, who appears to have been educated at the School of Bangor in County Down, was the one great philosopher of the Dark Ages, preceding by two hundred years, and indeed in the width and depth of his philosophy far surpassing, the scholastic philosophers of the eleventh century. And, truly, there is a strong flavour of his Gaelic origin in Erigena's thought, an unmistakable dash of that Gaelic love of enterprise, fearlessness of consequences, and joy in conflict which can find a field in philosophy and literature as well as in deeds of war and difficult feats of self-devotion. As a thinker he follows without hesitation the lead of reason, not fearing that the end of philosophy could be other than *truth*, though

* See Stokes's "Celtic Church in Ireland" for a more complete account.

charges of heresy and the thunders of the Church abound.* The qualities of the race which have made many of its difficulties are yet the qualities which make individual Irishmen, and which will yet make the Irish nation great.

In the eighth century, European scholarship was at low ebb, but it was about this time that Irish scholarship reached its high-water mark, just before the Danes embarked on their pagan crusade dealing out destruction specially on churches and monasteries; for the Danish attack on Christian Europe was at the outset a genuine crusade, a retaliation for Charlemagne's "Christian" mission to the Germans, whom he attempted to convert by fire and sword. The Danes first appeared off the Irish coast in 795, and, though Irish scholarship produced its finest personal result in Erigena (810–877) about half a century later, it is manifest that the great struggle of the three next centuries must have prevented much further development at the outset, while it ended by bringing very low the school of the West. The consequent destruction of books was certainly great, since the famous monasteries were burned down time after time. But enough remains to give us some measure of the hold which the idea of learning had taken on the popular mind. There are books in Irish giving accounts of various foreign events, and translations of

* In Erigena's case, the Church thunders abounded freely (see Stokes's "Celtic Church in Ireland").

classical stories into Irish. These and the Latin texts with elaborate Irish glosses and the Irish, as well as Latin, theological literature, show us that classical and theological learning had taken a place beside the genuine Irish literature in the curriculum of an educated Irishman's studies. They never, however, ousted that literature from its place. Every bishop and priest in Ireland was a Gaelic scholar down to the seventeenth century.*

On the Continent and in Great Britain this condition of scholarship made Ireland famous. Not only were scholars found in foreign lands, but students from abroad flocked to the Irish schools. In the great school of Armagh alone, one third of the city was, it is said, devoted to the use of foreign students, and the schools of Lismore, Bangor, Clonmacnoise, and Kildare rivalled it in importance. Twenty-six of these schools, all on an ecclesiastical foundation, are known to us by name.† These do not represent, however, the whole of the provision made for education in Ireland ; for a regular system of national schools was established in connection with the bardic classes in the year 590. But it was no doubt to the ecclesiastical schools that the foreign students came. On this subject we have the testimony of the Anglo-Saxon Bede, writing in the

* O'Curry's "Manners and Customs of the Ancient Irish." vol. ii. p. 84.
† *Ibid.*, vol. ii. p. 76.

seventh century, who tells us how certain of the nobles of Britain resorted to the Irish schools and were provided with food and clothes, as well as learning, without expense to themselves.

To understand rightly the significance of the work which Irish missionary and scholarly enterprise did for Western Europe in mediæval times, we must briefly consider the condition of the West, more especially after the decline of the Roman empire.

By the middle of the second century, Christianity had become an element in the Roman civilization, and began to be carried, with the Græco-Roman culture generally, in the wake of the legions throughout the empire. Before the close of this century it had reached the Rhine and the British coasts, and by the beginning of the fourth it was flourishing in Gaul and Britain and along the rivers of the Rhine and Danube. In the fifth century it reached Ireland, and at the same time began to be destroyed in the German and Romance countries, where the power of the Romans, and their influence founded on power, was fast going to ruin.

In the year 406 the Vandals from the Upper Rhine overwhelmed Gaul, the Alemanni and Burgundians settled on the Rhine. The Franks from the Lower Rhine presently established themselves in Northern Gaul, and the remains of the Roman power vanished there (481–500). The Germanic tribes of Angles and Saxons were conquering Britain, Attila and his Huns spread further desolation in Gaul and Italy, and the last touch was put to the work of destruction when the Lombards broke into the valley of the Po (568) and established their seat of government at Pavia. Thus by the end of the sixth century Germanic barbarism had overwhelmed Roman civilization like a flood, and Europe awaited a new and more deep-based enlightenment.

About the year 594, when the historian Gregory of Tours died, the Franks had become nominally, and in part, Christians; but the moral and intellectual condition of the Frankish Merovingian kingdom is described by this historian as truly deplorable. The Merovingian records are indeed drawn up in such barbarous Latin that one written more correctly is suspected as belonging to a later date. And the Christianity, we are told, was on a par with the Latin. That culture had declined in the centre of the Roman world itself we may gather from the fact that Gregory the Great knew no Greek.

In Spain and Ireland only, had learning still a home at the beginning of the seventh century. Of these two, Ireland, being enthusiastically Christian, was seized with the desire for missionary enterprise in foreign lands. The wandering instincts of the race were not without influence in prompting to this work, nor was the eagerness of intellect which urges to new fields of activity. Enterprise, as well as religious enthusiasm, characterized the Irish preacher, though he was by no means a wandering missionary only, but the settled founder of many famous monastic establishments.

In 590 Columbanus and his twelve comrades proceeded to the land of the Franks. They founded first the monastery of Château Annegray, and later, as the number of converts increased, the second establishment of Luxeuil. These became centres of influence and the parents of other similar establishments. After about ten years' work, Columbanus, having ventured to reprove the regent-queen Brunhilda, and refusing to conform to the Roman custom of keeping Easter, was forced to leave the country. Hostile winds prevented his return to Ireland, so, with a band of companions, he betook himself to the Rhine and, having rowed up the river, they settled at Lake Constance. Here they lived mainly by fishing, and preached to the people for some time. But in 613 Columbanus went to the Lombard princess Theodelinda, and founded at the foot of the Apennines the famous monastery of Bobbio.

Another Irishman, Gallus, had shared the fortunes of Columbanus up to this last stage, but was prevented by illness from accompanying him into Lombardy. So he remained on the north of the Alps, and presently founded, in the wild Steinach valley, that monastery of St. Gall, the Iona of Germany, which became the most celebrated, as it was the most frequented by Irishmen later, of all the Irish monasteries.

Numbers of Irishmen, like Columbanus and his comrades, came into the Frankish kingdom in the seventh century, and established mission stations. Thence issued Franks and Germans as disciples, to continue the work of their teachers. Of the details we are ignorant, but of this much we are certain that at the beginning of the eighth century a broad belt of mission stations, founded either by Irishmen or by their disciples, and after the Irish type, stretched from the mouths of the Maas and Rhine to the Rhone and the Alps. In monastic records, Irishmen, recognizable by their names, appear everywhere, as abbots or distinguished brothers; nor did their distinctive influence decrease in many centres, and especially in St. Gall, for a couple of centuries. In the ninth century St. Gall became specially conspicuous for art and learning under the abbotship of the Irish Moengal.

The Irish mission work advanced beyond the Rhine into the eastern settlements of the Franks and into Bavaria. According to the testimony of Jonas of Bobbio, missionaries from Luxeuil went out to Bavaria about 620, and towards the end of that century the Irish Kilian, with two companions, suffered martyrdom at Würzberg, on the frontier territory of Thüringen and the East Franks.

Nor is Ireland altogether unconcerned in the efforts made late in the seventh century to convert the Frisians and Saxons. The missionaries Victberct,

Wilibrord, and the two Hewalds were Englishmen, but we have it on the authority of Bede that they had received their theological education in Ireland. Alcuin says of Wilibrord, the apostle of the Frisians, that he had passed twelve years under celebrated teachers in Ireland. Britain gave him birth, but Ireland education. These missions, we may therefore infer, were conducted on Irish principles, and after the Irish manner.

That manner has been already described, and was as different as possible from that of the emissaries who about this time began to be sent out as organizers, no less than missionaries, from the Roman see. Apparently, neither the Irish missionaries nor their Germanic disciples made any attempt to receive the heathen masses into the Church by the mere external rite of baptism. Their methods were slower, though infinitely surer. But in 723 the Englishman Winifred, under the ecclesiastical name of Boniface, came as Roman legate to the land of the Franks; and the Christian fruits of more than a century's Irish and German work he organized and established under Rome, not scrupling, moreover, to use the secular arm for the more speedy addition of converts to the Christian Church.

Not only in France, but elsewhere, the Celtic and Roman ideas met, and the opposition between them gradually developed itself. So early as the sixth century, Columbanus, at Luxeuil, could see no sufficient reason why an Irishman should conform to the customs of Rome, with respect to the time of keeping Easter, rather than follow the traditions and customs of his own country; and, though it does not appear that this Paschal controversy greatly disturbed, at a later date, the relations between Rome and the Irish abbots on the Continent, it certainly, as well as the dispute on general questions of church government, waxed very hot between the papal see and the Irish British and Columban Churches. In England the most definite trial of strength for the Celtic idea abroad was made, and the Columban monks were worsted in the famous conference at Whitby, by the decision of the English king to follow the counsels of the papal legate. The Irish and Scottish Churches still held out at home, and the Roman system of government was not accepted in Ireland till the twelfth century. Probably this long adherence to the native forms, and the national habits which it created of relation between Church and people and non-relation between Church and State, may account for peculiarities in the Roman Catholicism of Ireland now which puzzle English Protestants who happen to observe them.

During the eighth and ninth centuries the scholarship of the Irish schools continued to rise in repute; but from the middle of the seventh century the Irish quarrel with Rome produced much confusion of motives in the minds of those who esteemed at once

F

learning and orthodoxy, the latter being measured, out of Ireland, by the Roman standard. There was no confusion in the minds of some, and we get a quaint piece of testimony to Irish scholarship from the lips of Aldhelm, an earnest Roman adherent who viewed with orthodox horror the practice of sending young Anglo-Saxons for education to Ireland. In a letter to Ealfrid, who has returned from that country, he exclaims, "Why should Ireland pride herself so highly that thither students from England should stream in crowds, just as if Greek and Latin teachers were not to be found upon England's fruitful soil, able to solve the most serious religious problems and to train scholars eager for knowledge?"

As the innovations of Rome and her claim for ecclesiastical supremacy made Ireland seem heterodox to mechanical souls, so Irish influence in the Christian mission to Europe declined. That work was taken up by other hands, and carried out by other methods, of which the religious wars of Charlemagne were one characteristic sign. But another field for Gaelic enterprise was opened up, as the taste for scholarship developed in foreign countries, and a demand for Irish teachers as such sprang up. Charles the Great and his successors, in the eighth and ninth centuries, strove to make a home for learning in France, and the learned "Scots" were received with open arms. So, just as we find Irish missionaries everywhere in the Merovingian land of the Franks during the seventh century, so Irishmen during the ninth century under the Carlovingian empire are found in abundance, as teachers of all the branches of knowledge then cultivated in the schools of the court and the scholastic monasteries.

With the general spread of culture the pre-eminence of Ireland disappeared; but this brief review of the evidence, condensed and imperfect though it is, will be sufficient to prove her claim as not only the home, but the mission-home, of learning in the dark interval that followed the collapse of the Roman empire. Nor should it be forgotten that she produced the most profound, as well as the earliest, of all the mediæval philosophers, and that he was a layman, as none of the others were.*

* For readers of German, an excellent account of the Irish Christian mission to Europe is given in an article "On the Significance of the Irish Element in the Culture of the Middle Ages," in the Prussian Yearbook, 1887.

CHAPTER IV.

PAGAN IRELAND AT HOME.

The age of Irish military enterprise abroad ended about the middle of the fifth century, when Irish paganism had received its deathblow at the hand of Patrick; and within a single century a new Ireland was revealing itself to Europe. Let us now inquire into the history of Ireland within her own borders corresponding to these different glimpses we have had of her from an external point of view; and, first, let us try to understand the main social and historical features of pagan Ireland.

For a definite historical starting-point our purpose will best be served by taking the time of Cormac Mac Art, who reigned at Tara from A.D. 218 to 260. The events of Irish history reach much further back than this period, but in the time of Cormac we may feel sure that the main features of Irish pagan society had developed themselves into the characteristic form which shall be presently described. Cormac was an active warrior, and followed the war-policy then customary to his nation. In the year 222, as the Annals tell us, "the large fleet of Cormac Mac Art went over the sea for the space of three years." It went to ravage the British shores. But the domestic labours of Cormac have a higher interest. He found the nation with certain settled political and social habits. He organized the customs of the tribes into a social and political system. Thus he had the Brehon law revised and, in a manner, codified, and he secured his labours in this direction by settling the national convention at Tara on a regular basis, appointing a meeting every third year, for the popular proclamation and acceptance of the law, and the administration generally of public affairs.

Cormac did not invent the national parliament of Tara, nor did he invent the Brehon law, but, like a wise ruler, he did that work of reorganization and confirmation which he deemed necessary at his time. To him also, Dr. Petrie attributes all the monuments now remaining at Tara,* the vestiges of which exactly correspond to ancient descriptions. *Tara is, however, older than Irish history.* The bards tell us that the assembly was instituted and the buildings erected by the Firbolg king, Ollamh Fodhla, "who was first a learned bard and then king of Ireland," and to whom also they attribute the general organization of the country. But this is a bardic tale: its hero may fitly

* Petrie's "History and Antiquities of Tara Hill."

be taken to symbolize the Irish people, who unconsciously created their own habits and then invented a definite maker of them.

The political purpose of the assembly is very clearly summed up in the following lines written by a poet of the year 984 :—

> "The Feis of Temur each third year,
> *To preserve laws and rules,*
> Was then convened firmly
> By the illustrious kings of Erin."

Tara was not the only place where such assemblies were held. Two different lines of Ulster kings had their royal hills of assembly at Aileach* near Derry and at Emain Macha, now Armagh; and the assembly at which St. Columba pleaded successfully the cause of Scottish Home Rule in A.D. 590, was held at Drumceatt, near Newtown Limavady. The fair of Carman too, in Wexford, is almost as famous as the fair of Tara itself. In fact, it would seem that such assemblies were for every king, provincial or even tribal only, the regular way in which the laws and customs of the tribe were preserved and developed. The kings, nobles, judges, poets and scholars met in the national assembly to discuss national affairs; and new decisions were proclaimed afterwards to all the "men of Erin" that might be assembled, at the same

---

* There still stands on the hill of Aileach a remarkable specimen of the Irish stone fort, and the marks of the ramparts surrounding the royal seat are evident to this day. Every visitor to Derry should see Aileach.

time, around the royal hill of Tara, pursuing their national amusements of feasting, racing, athletic, musical and literary contests, to say nothing of the social intercourse which Irishmen have always prized. So, likewise, the minor kings took council with the corresponding fit persons within their realms, and summoned the assembly of all the people from time to time. Of the constitution of the tribal assemblies, more will be said in a later chapter.

Probably this habit of tribal assembly was the earliest political habit the Irish tribes had, for their whole social system shows that they could have had no idea of a source of *power* other than the popular will, though they were peculiarly susceptible to the notion that the reason of the wise man should be the determining motive to that popular will. Certainly it was a habit that died hard, if it ever really died at all. Edmund Spenser, in his " View of Ireland," written in Elizabeth's time, tells of the meetings of the Irish on their ancient accustomed hills, where they debated and settled matters between families and townships, going in large numbers and armed. What did die, and died early, was the habit of meeting as one nation at Tara; and so thoroughly republican was the whole elemental structure of Irish society, that all the reality of national unity began to fade with the decadence that fell upon Tara in the sixth century. This decadence seems to have been closely connected with that decline of the bards which slowly followed the rise of monastic scholarship.*

Cormac was zealous for discipline as well as orderly legislation ; so he organized a national army, and established a school of military training. This was the most important step that any king of Ireland, as king, had hitherto taken. In early stages of social development the army of the tribe, or nation, is identical with its whole adult manhood, and indeed, in the Irish case, womanhood too ; for the Irishwomen, like those of Britain and Germany, were not slow to take the battle-field. Armies of regular warriors come into existence as differentiation of function in general between the members of the society proceeds—as the bulk of the people engaged in other pursuits find military service an irksome interruption. The Irish were pre-eminently a fighting race, and, for that very reason, they were slow to form for themselves a strong military organization, or to permit such a formation by their kings. Hence it was that the Irish kings seldom had any army other than their people ; and hence two results. First, there never was an Irish king who could establish his dynasty, or himself, as a real ruler over the minor Irish kings ; and, secondly, no Irish king, small or great, got a right of absolute power over his people.

Still, there were professional warriors in Ireland

* See Sir Samuel Ferguson's poem, "Congall," for an interesting view of the relation between these events.

from very early times; they appear as the heroes of Irish bardic history. There was a system of military education, too, by which the student was brought up as the foster-son of some eminent warrior. The teachers of great champions are frequently named; and from these references we learn that the principal champions, whether kings or inferior chiefs, were prone to preside over the physical education of the more promising youth. We hear, too, of champions who were foster-brothers in arms—fellow-students of war—learning champion-feats together; and, though regular military colleges probably did not exist before the time of Cormac, schools for the joint military and literary education of the upper classes almost certainly did.

The nearest approach to a regular army which we find in earlier times, was the band of valiant Ulster knights, the Red Branch of Emania, which flourished in the time of Conor Mac Nessa, king of Ulster at the beginning of the Christian era. The history of Ireland was so far affected by the institution of the Red Branch, that Ulster became at this time a great power in Ireland, and a terror consequently to the other provinces.

More than three centuries later, the High King, Cormac, carried out a similar conception more completely. The following note is quoted in the Book of Ballymote from the Book of Navan, which is now lost, and refers to Cormac. "The monarch of Erin appointed an army over the men of Erin; and over it he appointed three times fifty royal Fenian officers, for the purpose of enforcing his laws and maintaining his sovereign rule and preserving his game; and he gave the command of the whole and the high-stewardship of Erin to Finn Ūa Baiscné (that is, Finn Mac Cumhal)." This was the famous Feni of Erin, the Irish militia of the third century; and its commander was the still more famous Finn, son of Cumhal,* the father of Oisin and other celebrated persons, the central figure of a most interesting cycle of Irish bardic literature, in part of which the Feni are projected back into distant ages and appear as demi-gods and mythical heroes, rather than as the really practical warriors and hunters that they were. It is from them that the modern Fenians, the "physical force" party of Irish nationality have taken their name.

The Feni were quartered on the people from November to May; and from May to November they lived by hunting. They acted as a force against internal disorder as well as against foreign invasion, and thus fulfilled at once the duties of police and army. According to the accounts that have come down to us, the rules of the force, when viewed in the most prosaic light, partook in marked measure of that

---

* "Cumhal" is pronounced "Cool." Finn was the grandson or descendant (*i.e.* "Ūa," modern O') of Baiscné and the son (*i.e.* Mac) of Cumhal.

moral strictness which should pertain to the idea of it as guardian of the realm's internal peace. In a poetic light, however, they read as rules of chivalry; and as pagan knights of chivalry we must indeed regard Finn and his Feni in this early, but by no means uncultivated, age. Finn, the typical Fenian, was a poet as well as a warrior, learned in all the bardic wisdom of the Gael, and gifted with the bards' keen enjoyment of nature. Thus at least the bards describe him.

"The music that Finn loved was that which filled the heart with joy and gave light to the countenance, the song of the black bird of Letter Lee, and the melody of the Dord Fian, the sound of the wind in Droum-derg, the thunders of Assaroe, the cry of the hounds let loose through Glen Rah, with their faces outward from the Suir, the Tonn Rury lashing the shore, the wash of water against the sides of ships, the cry of Braan at Knock-an-awr, the murmur of streams at Slieve-Mish and oh, the blackbird of Derry-Carn. I never heard, by my soul, sound sweeter than that. Were I only beneath his nest!" *

Cormac, we are told, made another advance on previous practice by founding three great colleges at Tara for the instruction of the men of Erin; and one was a School of the Art of War. In it, we must suppose, he intended to have carried out, under the

---

* See Standish O'Grady's "History of Ireland," vol. i. chap. xii., for this modern version of Oisin's description of Fenian delights.

control of the High King himself, a system of splendid physical training, similar to the best that had been adopted hitherto by scattered teachers up and down the country. And it is well, perhaps, to remember here that the spirit of mediæval Christianity, elsewhere certainly and probably in Ireland too, was not very favourable to anything like that splendid physical education in which our pagan forefathers delighted, and which Cormac sought at this time to centralize at Tara. That old joy in physical ability has now revived in full force, and finds its fit expression in the Gaelic Athletic Association, the democratic modern equivalent of Cormac's school of championship.

But Cormac's attempt to organize the "strong arm" of Ireland in relation to the high king's throne went the way of all later attempts to solve the Irish national problem by "physical force." There was plenty of it in the country—perhaps too much; every corner had the spirit of fight so strong in it that it could not be repressed for more than one generation. *The fighting force could not be organized unless every fraction of the popular will was organized too.* And it was a will difficult to organize in some respects, because each considerable unit was affected with a marked individuality of its own—a strong self-will, not uncommonly accompanied by a keen egoistic sensitiveness, apt to resent a supposed insult more than a substantial injury. Irish history bristles with self-will, and is also marked at every stage with the individual Irishman's fearlessness of the arm stronger than his own. Force has consolidated many nations, compromise has consolidated some; but the only way in which Ireland could ever be consolidated was by the way of reason and sympathy. Nor has Nature been slow to compensate this nation for the qualities which have been her trouble. She prizes them rightly, nevertheless, for they are a power. The Bard and the Brehon understood Irish nature—or rather they were it. The bards held up before the people the ideas of Ireland, heroism, gentleness, and justice; and, travelling as they did constantly from one end of the country to the other, they familiarized the inhabitants of every part with the heroes and associations of every other, telling of the Red Branch champions of Ulster in the South, and of Finn and his heroes and the great King Cormac in the North. The bards were a national brotherhood, with their hands on the strings of the popular heart, their minds in close touch with the popular imagination. Through their unity of mind and heart Ireland was united while their order prevailed. Tara was their great festival, and Tara was the political link of the provinces. And as for the Brehon, he set up his court of arbitration in all quarrels that might occur among this self-willed and fight-loving people, trusting in the might of reason alone. And the disputants came to him, keen of wit no less than rapid of imagination as they were; and in the might of reason he made the law prevail. No fact strikes more forcibly a student of the Irish social system than this, that, side by side with careful provisions for the administration of an elaborately developed law, there exists no visible means for carrying it out, except, indeed, so far as the physical force of the whole community might be called upon to do so. A passage from Sir John Davies, who wrote in the time of James I., throws, however, a light which is quite sufficient on this point. The Irish people at his time had been going through terrible struggles, which must have roused to the full all their fighting and non-rational instincts. Yet this is what he, an observer of the opposite camp, tells us, soon after the Ulster plantation—

"I dare affirm that for the space of five years past there has not been found so many malefactors worthy of death in all the six circuits of this realm (thirty-two shires) as in one circuit of six shires, namely, the western circuit, in England. For the truth is, that in time of peace the *Irish are more fearful to offend the law* than the English or any other nation whatsoever. . . . There is no nation under the sun that doth love equal or indifferent justice better than the Irish; or will rest better satisfied with the execution thereof, although it be against themselves."

Hence it is evident that in Sir John Davies's time, either the fact of the Brehon's constant reliance on popular reason had developed popular reason, or the fact that Irish popular reason was peculiarly accessible, had enabled the Brehon to rely upon it. And, indeed, it is a truth open to easy observation by any one to-day, that the Irish peasant is peculiarly ready to see any matter from the universal or rational point of view. Now, as in olden times, he despises force and loves his personal will, but reverences law, respects other wills, and is capable of much self-devotion.

Cormac's attempt to organize the army of the high king failed. Finn and the Feni quarrelled with the king; and the people, weary perhaps of having the Feni quartered on them, put themselves behind the king and defeated the army, enfeebled too, as it was, by internal dissensions.* So one part of Cormac's ideal failed.

Of the other parts we are left to suppose that they succeeded; the element of success was in them. The king, who was a scholar and judge as well as a warrior, reorganized the learned classes, and established, besides the School of War, a School of Law and another of Literature. A manuscript, now lost, the Saltair of Tara, is ascribed to his authorship, as well as a portion of the Book of Aicill, which is part of one of the Brehon law tracts. With his nobles, ollamhs, and kings around him at Tara, Cormac is said to have ordered a new code of laws and regulations to be drawn up, to have revived obsolete tests

* One of the most beautiful of the Irish romances, *i.e.* the story of Diarmait (Dermat) and Grania, is connected with the Fenian dissensions. See Joyce's "Celtic Romances."

and ordeals, and instituted new ones, thus making the law of evidence as perfect as it could be in those times. "The world," says an old manuscript, "was full of all goodness in his time; there were fruit and fatness of the land, and abundant produce of the sea, with peace and ease and happiness in his time. There were no killings nor plunderings in his time, but every one occupied his lands in happiness."

It is clear that Cormac's reign made a deep impression on the national mind as the time in which all the wise laws and customs of the nation flourished, standing out specially from the reign of his predecessor. For this reason, I have taken it as a fixed central point in Irish pagan history, to which we may refer the flourishing existence of that social condition to be presently described, or the elements in it that are not clearly due to Christian influence and which form the main portion. It is believed, indeed, that Cormac was not himself a pagan, but had imbibed some Christian ideas during his wars with Britain, which found expression in a request, made at his death, not to be buried with his fathers in the pagan cemetery of the kings of Tara on the Boyne. But, though Cormac may have been Christian, it is quite certain that the institutions which he reorganized were not.

Before proceeding to consider the nature of Irish paganism as a religion, let us glance more particularly at the organization of the learned classes. Of these

Again, the most conspicuous fact about Irish moral character is the warmth of its affections for kindred and the Irish foster-kindred of friends and neighbours. We might expect, therefore, beforehand, that pagan religion, as developed by the Irish, would be marked somewhat emphatically by the presence of the two great ideas in an Irish form—for Nature, the spirits of Ireland; for Humanity, the Irish race.

And so it turns out. All the available evidence points to the conclusion here expressed in somewhat abstract form. Perhaps there is no object of worship so natural as the memory of ancestral heroes, and no belief more real than that the great and good live after death. We have no evidence to show that the ancient Irish had any form of worship for their dead kindred, but we know that funeral games were held in their honour, that the cemeteries were deemed to be sacred places, and that they believed it possible for their dead heroes to help in battle or distress. One example will suffice. Mac Erc is in tradition the king of the Firbolgs, a hero; but he appears as a deity in the following lines, discovered by Professor Sullivan:—

> "Twice during the Treena of Taillten
> Each day at sunrise *I invoked Mac Erc*
> To remove from me the pestilence."

This is a case of prayer to a hero. The same hero's wife affords us a good example of games and ceremonies held in her honour. A manuscript quoted by

Professor O'Curry,* gives an account of the sports, games, ceremonies and lighting of fires at Tailltcn (now Telltown, to the north of Tara), for which that ancient place was celebrated, and which took place in the beginning of August. These were said to have been instituted more than a thousand years earlier than the time of which the writer wrote (A.D. 405), by Lug, the king of the Tuatha Dé Danann, in honour of Tailltè, the wife of Mac Erc. At her court he had been fostered; so he raised over her a mighty mound, and instituted games in her honour. In this example, it should be noticed as very characteristic that the person honoured is reputed to be not of the same race as those who honour her. The idea of a common country has prevailed over the idea of common kindred, but is related to it in some measure by the fact, or presumed fact, of fosterage. The tomb of a Firbolg queen is, according to the story, made a sacred place by the Tuatha Dé Danann, and accepted as such by the Milesians later. It does not greatly matter whether the story be true. The important point is that it should be believed to be true by the Milesians. It illustrates a tendency, which may very well have taken effect throughout the whole island, to accept the sacred places of the earlier races as sacred, and pay honour to their heroes as *national* heroes.

It would appear, indeed, that the Tuatha Dé Danann made a deep impression on the imagination

* "Manuscript Materials of Ancient Irish History," p. 287.

of their successors. Of the historical people themselves we hear that they were noted for their skill in magic and druidical arts. More important is it that the heroes and heroines of the Tuatha Dé Danann, Lir, Mananan, the Dagda Mor, Angus his beautiful son, and the three fair sisters Eire and Fohla and Banba, "from each of whom the island has a name"—these and others appear in the literature as, if not the gods, at least the immortal spirits who love, and sometimes foster the children of Erin. Nor is this all; in one aspect of it, tradition assigns to the Tuatha generally an immortal life in the midst of the hills and beneath the seas. Thence they issue to mingle freely with the mortal sons of men, practising those druidical arts in which they were great of yore, when they won Erin from the Firbolgs by "science," and when the Milesians won Erin from them by valour. That there really was a people whom the legend of the Tuatha shadows forth is probable, but it is almost certain that all the tales about them are poetical myth. The idea of them, however, as a wise and mighty race which preceded the Milesians in the possession of the island, and who dwell there still, in that invisible land, within the visible land, of everlasting youth, strong in the possession of a druidism that could bend all nature to their will, the immortal spirits to whom the soil of Erin is sacred, foster-kindred oft to the sons of Miledh and intermarrying with them—this idea is rooted firmly in the bardic imagination, and we must take it as a fair expression of the ideas towards which the popular religious sentiment tended in their time.

In the hymn written by St. Fiech in honour of St. Patrick, we are plainly told that before the coming of Patrick the Irish *worshipped* the Sidhe,* and the bards identify the Sidhe with the Tuatha Dé Danann, or rather with the palaces in which these mighty beings dwelt. For instance, there is an ancient poem in the Book of Ballymote on the wonders of that Brugh-na-Boinne, which is familiar in the literature as the hall of the great king of the Tuatha Dé Danann, the Dagda Mor, and is associated also with Angus, who carried thither after death one of the famous Fenian champions, Diarmid, his foster-son.† This is the second stanza of the poem.

> "Behold the *Sidhe* before your eyes;
> It is manifest to you that it is a king's mansion,
> Which was built by the firm *Dagda*.
> It was a wonder, a court, an admirable hill."

The same place is spoken of as the fairy mansion of Brugh on the Boyne, in a tale relating how a certain poetic lover, finding that the only condition on which the lady of his affections would accept his suit was the composition of a poem describing her possessions, then unknown to him, goes to the fairy mansion on the Boyne to see his *nurse*—evi-

---

* Pronounced "Shee."   † Joyce's "Celtic Romances."

dently a fairy foster-mother—and with her aid makes the required poem.

The identity of the Tuatha Dé Danann with the degenerate fairy of Christian times appears plainly in the fact that while the Sidhe are the halls of the Tuatha, the fairies are the people of the Sidhe, and sometimes called the Sidhe simply, just as St. Fiech calls the Tuatha. In bardic times, however, the people of the fairy mansions are frequently called by a name indicating, as a primary characteristic, their connection with the places reverenced as Sidhe. We hear of the ben-sidhe and the fer-sidhe, literally the woman and the man of the fairy mansions. The ben-sidhe, pronounced *banshee*, has descended to our times, as the guardian spirit of certain Irish families, which manifests itself in some way when a death is at hand. Here, again, is a curious fact : the ban-shee is an immortal being mysteriously connected with the destiny of a particular group of kindred, and associated in modern times solely with the idea of death. The inference seems probable, to say the least, that the Sidhe, whence these racial spirits were supposed to come, were within those great sepulchral mounds, which the ancient Irish raised above their honoured dead. What more natural than that the ancestral dead should be laid in those spots where the spirits of the race's destiny dwelt immortal, and would care for the heroes in the ghostly life after death ! What more natural than that reverent hands should build the mound broad and high and round, for the comfort of the spirits that dwelt therein! What more natural, too, than that the spirit of the race as in the modern superstition—the foster-parent of divine race as in some of the bardic tales—should draw nigh at the time of death, and bear the immortal soul to its fairy home!

The similar ideas that the fairies carry off the young men and women who die, and that the dead come forth on November Eve to dance with the fairies on the hill—these linger in the minds of the Irish peasantry now, and represent the common people's share in that idea of a relationship after death to the invisible Irish nation whose home is in the centre of the hills, which yields, for the aristocratic folk, a family ban-shee, dwelling once—but this is now forgotten—in the sacred family mounds. Whether fairyland was first in the hills and reflected itself in the sidhe and ben-sidhe of the tombs, or was first ancestral in the tombs, where the Milesians found and honoured it, and then reflected itself into the nature-spirits that populate the hidden districts of the land, it would not be easy to say. Probably, however, the latter supposition is nearer the truth, for the fairy myth would have required a certain development of imagination such as no race, and certainly not a race with strong family affections, would be likely to attain, without having previously imagined the continued existence of its heroes after death. It may be that the choice of the ancestral sacred places of their predecessors as their cemeteries by the Milesians, and the double tribute of respect henceforward paid to them, occasioned the peculiar form of the Irish fairy myth. The Milesian tombs were the abode of the aristocratic Tuatha, but their common people were gradually connected with the underground world of the island generally. So all Nature came to have a sacred meaning, instinct with the feeling of kindred through the idea of fairy fosterage on Irish soil,—fosterage by the elder race to which the soil of Eire, sweet daughter of the Dagda,* is sacred. And thus it is easy to see how, as developed and refined by bardic influence, Irish religious sentiment contributed to that effect of merging the feeling of kindred in the feeling of Ireland, without in the least detracting from its force, which so characterized the early Irish people that they have infected all other races since settled among them with the same tendency. To every settler in Ireland, sooner or later, the sacred places of Ireland become sacred; and every place in Ireland has a poetic sacredness.

Respect for the dead, and reverence for the Tuatha of Erin, observance of the great feasts, the periodical celebration of games in the sacred places (of which Tara must certainly have been one), and such superstitions as we still find dying out among the peasantry—these are the chief positive elements

* This is the bardic derivation of the country's name.

that can be discovered of Irish paganism. Of sacrificial rites or any elaborate ceremonial not a trace in bardic times is to be found. Whatever they may have been elsewhere, or in times of which even Irish memory holds no hinted record, Ireland of the bards knew its druids simply as men skilled in all magical arts, having no marked relation either to a system of mythology or to a scheme of ceremonial practice. The head of the kindred would have more to do with the sidhe than he, and the king it was who presided over the periodical festivals. Hence, perhaps, their natural association with politics.

It was not, therefore, to a land of obstinate *idolatrous* paganism that Patrick came, nor to a land where superstition was organized definitely in relation to a priestly caste. Celtic imagination could well dispense with idols,* and Celtic freedom was averse both to hard and fast ceremonial and to precise definition of doctrines to be believed. Moreover, the land was full of active intellects, in want of more thought-material on which to spend themselves, of eager souls touched by a tender sympathy for the poetic beauty of a noble life, and of vivid imaginations

---

* The "Tripartite Life of St. Patrick" makes mention of a group of idols which stood in the plain of Magh Slecht, and were there destroyed by the saint. The "Tripartite Life," however, is very mediæval, and, as there is no hint anywhere of a systematic worship connected with these, the suspicion arises that they may have been, if they existed at all, mere memorial stones, raised to the dignity of idols by the iconoclastic imagination of the mediæval Christians. The earlier lives of St. Patrick do not mention them.

ready to be stirred. Before Patrick, the sacred bard had been in the land; superstition had paled before poetry; the noble deeds of self-devoted heroes had been sung and heard; the gentle, ever-open nature of the Gael was ready to take a higher flight. The Isle of Song was soon to become the Isle of Saints.

CHAPTER V.

CHRISTIANITY IN IRELAND.

ST. PATRICK'S Christian mission to Ireland was not the first, but it was the first to produce any important results. For the facts connected with it we have a vast mass of later information that cannot be relied on, and a few sources of knowledge that cannot reasonably be doubted. The most important of these are two acknowledged works of St. Patrick himself, his "Confession," and his epistle to a British prince Coroticus. There are also two early histories of his life in the Book of Armagh, both of them belonging to the latter half of the seventh century, about two hundred years after St. Patrick's time. From these sources the account given in Dr. Stokes's "History of the Celtic Church in Ireland" is derived, and they are also the staple material relied on by Dr. Todd in his older and more elaborate history of the great Irish saint. They are quite sufficient to enable us to form a clear idea of St. Patrick's character, the nature of his missionary method and its effects.

St. Patrick was probably a native of Strathclyde, in Britain, born at Alcluith which is now Dumbarton, but it would seem that his family was derived originally from Armoric Brittany. The interesting point to notice about his origin is that it was connected with British Christianity, and that, therefore, Armoric Brittany being Celtic also, it was a Celtic form of Christian thought and organization that he brought to Ireland. At the early age of sixteen he was taken prisoner, and became slave to an Irish chief Milchu in North Dalaradia, in County Antrim. The scene of his slavery has been carefully identified. It is in the valley of Braid, near Broughshane, five miles from Ballymena. There, near the hill of Slemish, Patrick spent six years tending his master's cattle, and there, as he tells us himself, his mind awakened to a genuine realization of the Christian doctrine he had learned as a child. At the end of that time, he made his escape, the means having been, as he believed, revealed to him in a dream. Thus he returned to his family, then probably in Brittany, having gained the threefold requirement needed for his after-work. He had developed the missionary temperament, its spiritual aspirations and its human tenderness; he had learned to love the Irish people, and be at one with them; and he knew their language, their customs and their character. And so, ere long, he felt himself greatly moved towards this people lying in spiritual darkness; his sleep was troubled with visions, and he heard voices calling to him from Ireland for help.

The question has been much discussed as to who it was that sent Patrick on his mission to the Irish, and especially whether he was sent by the Pope or not. All that he himself tells us is that he was moved to go by the visions he had and the constraint which he felt to be laid upon him ; and these he took to be a direct call to his work from God. As neither he nor the ancient lives mention a mission from Rome, such a mission is extremely improbable ; but since it would be necessary that Patrick should be consecrated by some bishop for the work, and since we know that the events connected with the mission of Germanus of Auxerre to Britain had drawn his attention to Ireland about this time, it is antecedently probable that this Germanus was the person technically responsible for that Irish mission of which Patrick himself was the real originator.

About the year 432, or, according to Dr. Todd,* a little later, Patrick landed for the second time in Ireland at the spot where the town of Wicklow now stands. He did not remain here, however, but sailed north towards Dalaradia, on which his heart was set, landing as he passed at Inis Patrick off the Skerries, and at the mouth of the Boyne. Finally he halted at Strangford Lough, and proceeded into the country from that point, speedily to make a convert of a

* "Life of St. Patrick," p. 391, *et seq.*

certain chieftain, Dichu, who was "the first of the Scots to confess the faith under Patrick's ministry." Dichu made a grant of land, on which Patrick established the first Irish church, at a place called Saul, where he afterwards died. Thence, he continued his way towards the scene of his servitude, bent on the conversion of his old master Milchu; but legend relates that Milchu, hearing of the approach of Patrick and the triumphs that attended his progress, feared lest the magical powers of his fugitive slave should reduce him in his turn to servitude, so he set fire to his house and perished in the flames, to avert the possibility of such a result. And Patrick, grieved, returned to his new friend and convert Dichu.

Soon, however, he determined to take the decisive step of making a Christian attack on the centre of Irish paganism and Irish nationality—Tara itself. Like a good general, he saw that success to his mission at Tara would mean, in the first place, a great moral victory which must powerfully affect the popular imagination, and, in the second place, a political achievement, which would open up the whole country to his missionary efforts.

Accompanied by a party of followers, he landed at the mouth of the Boyne, and, following the course of the river, encamped at Slane, close by the great pagan cemetery, "the grave of the sons of Feni," where the kings of Tara were buried. He pitched his tent, we are told, on the hill of Slane, which is plainly visible from Tara, where at that very time the festival of Beltine was being celebrated. It was Easter Eve, and Patrick lit the Easter fires on the hill, thus, wittingly or unwittingly, contravening the immemorial custom, which forbade that any fire should be lit that night on all the plain till the royal beacon shone out from Tara. Hence it came to pass that attention was especially attracted to the hill of Slane, and the king Laoghaire, with his principal druids and various attendants, went in anger to see and punish the man bold enough to offend against the sacred customs of the land. After various conflicts with the druids, into the account of which the miraculous element enters largely, the king yields, though rather through fear of Patrick's power than for any higher motive. Tolerance for Christianity is thus obtained, and a safe-conduct through Ireland granted by the king. Laoghaire, himself, however, remained to the end a pagan at heart, and was buried after the manner of his ancestors—upright, with his arms by his side and his face towards Leinster, with the king of which the kings of Tara had a constant feud.

But Patrick made converts at Laoghaire's court—notably one Erc, a Brehon lawyer. Thence he made a tour through Meath, founded churches at Trim, and elsewhere, and made an important real convert at Donagh Patrick, in Conall, the brother of Laoghaire, and the ancestor of St. Columba.

From Meath St. Patrick made his way to Connaught, with which place he had specially connected the visions that first drew his mind towards Ireland. Pursuing his missionary labours as he went, and appointing bishops where he established churches, he passed along the great western road that led to Connaught, and crossed the Shannon near Clonmacnoise in the King's County. Thence he proceeded into Connemara, and remained in Connaught for the space altogether of seven years. The policy he had pursued at Tara is typical of the policy he pursued elsewhere: the first step was to win the king or chief—to make him a real convert if possible, and, if not, to gain at least his tolerance and approval so far as obtaining a grant of land to build a church upon and make the formation of a religious community possible. The establishment of religious communities, scattered in all sorts of places throughout the land, was in fact Patrick's way—as it was afterwards that followed by the Irish missionaries abroad—of converting the whole country to the Christian faith. Sometimes, a converted chief would be enthusiastic enough to hand over all his possessions and tribal rights to the religious community established among his people; and in such case it would often happen that he himself became abbot of the monastery thus endowed, with bishops under him though ecclesiastically superior to him. Patrick's object was to plant centres of Christian influence throughout the land, and he used the tribal system as he found it, to carry out this purpose by every available means. As a stranger having no status in the tribe, Patrick's only way of getting immediately a material footing on the tribe lands was through the chief or other powerful person who held demesne lands of his own. These he could either plant with stranger tenants or grant for purposes which he thought desirable. A converted chief would deem such a grant from him to the church as a pressing duty; and the religious centre once established, with a staff of Irish Christians, generally new converts, to manage it, the essential work of organization was, according to Patrick's Celtic ideal, done. The centre was expected to grow by its own vitality and to make the Christian idea dominant in its vicinity.

From Connaught Patrick went to Ulster, where he specially visited Donegal, Antrim, and Armagh. And there in the old city of Ard-Macha, he established (445) the primatial see of Armagh, having, as the story goes, induced the king, Daire, to grant him the high ground on which the cathedral now stands, by miraculous deeds which at last overcame his reluctance to give so strong a position to a stranger.

The king of Leinster's palace was at Naas, and thither Patrick next proceeded, to pursue his labours in the eastern province. That he visited Munster we are also told, but have no authentic account of his doings there. Last of all, as old age overtook him, he returned once more to the favoured province of Ulster, and to the scene of his earliest labours at Saul. There, among the brothers of his first church, he died.

After his death a contest arose between the churches of Saul and Armagh for the honour of interring his body. To settle the matter, it was determined to yoke two untamed oxen to the cart that bore his remains, and to leave them free to go which way they would. So runs the story. The oxen stopped at the spot where now stands the church of Downpatrick, and there, accordingly, the great saint was buried. This much, at least, is certain, that since the year 700, it has been positively believed that the bones of St. Patrick lie under the site of the Downpatrick cathedral.

But before Patrick died, the church which he had planted in Ireland had taken root. The soil was good soil, well prepared for the seed, and the seed was sown by a skilful hand. The bardic age had developed to a high point the heroic spirit of enterprise and self-devotion, and had developed also that still characteristic feature in Irish character—its accessibility to ideas and readiness to submit action to the sway of thought. To a people of enthusiastic temperament, vivid imagination and idealizing tendencies, Patrick preached a practical doctrine of self-devotion. To a people affectionate towards kindred, and, notwithstanding their warlike fierceness, sympathetic towards all men, he preached a practical doctrine of love. To a people of awakened intellect and quickened sense of the beautiful in things and thought, he brought a theory of nature and life fuller and more thought-satisfying, as well as more sublime, than any they had been able to forge for themselves. Irishmen had their faults, and faults that were troublesome, especially to themselves, but they were peculiarly susceptible then, as they are now, to the influence of a noble ideal that asks for self-devotion. And this is why Ireland was then a land of song, and the spirit of song has never died out in the hearts of her people.

The soil was well prepared; and Patrick sowed the seed with skilful hand. He sowed it in compact plots throughout the length and breadth of the land. When the chief of a sept was converted, he would sometimes confer his house and lands on the church, transferring also his right as chief; and thus a religious sept would be formed, consisting of the religious persons to whom the grant was made, and of the vassals connected with the land besides. The head was called the "comarba" or co-heir, inheritor of both the spiritual and temporal rights of the founder, and thus having the right of chieftaincy in relation to the freemen of the tribe, as well as other larger rights over the vassals settled on the monastic demesne which had been the private demesne of the chief.

In other cases, the chief would simply grant a piece of land for the establishment of a church and religious community. Into that community would come, as volunteers, the surrounding tribesmen and others from a distance, and thus, on the type of the corresponding secular institutions, a voluntary family would be founded, with an abbot as head, and a bishop usually attached for ecclesiastical convenience. Similar voluntary families were frequently formed, not only by the professional classes for the sake of learning, but also by the people in general for agricultural and other industrial purposes; and the bruighfer of the agricultural community held much the same relation to his community, and in the whole tribe, as the abbot of the monastery held in the case we are considering.

From the first, Patrick seems to have made his ideal of church organization in keeping with the Irish method of political organization. The nation began by being tribal, and developed slowly towards a national unity which, as a uniform, centralized, executive administration, it never realized. The tribal forms were prevalent in Patrick's time, so the Church in Ireland naturally began by being tribal too, and developed slowly, though not nearly so slowly as the State, towards such a centralized unity as under the Roman empire it assumed at the first start. Medieval Rome was often shocked at this tribal character of Irish Christianity, with its indefinite number of bishops and its somewhat fiery spirit of local independence. Yet it is evident enough that the extraordinary vitality of Irish Christianity, and the vivid reality of its influence on the national life, was largely bound up with the peculiarity of its form. Christianity established itself in Ireland after the manner of a natural growth in a way which is quite exceptional ; and the fact suggests that missionary societies might perhaps do well to study a little in detail the method of Patrick and of the great Irish missionaries who, after him, laboured in Great Britain and in Europe. A religious family settled in the midst of a pagan people, pursuing the ordinary labours of agriculture and handicraft for its support, exhorting its neighbours on all useful occasions, but without bitterness, to lead better lives, teaching its doctrine to those who would listen, and constant in prayer for the welfare of all—this is what Patrick aimed at establishing on all sides ; and it is easy to imagine the effectiveness of his method.

It is evident, too, that the tribal church organization, though it must surely have given occasion for argument and even fighting, was highly favourable to the growth of a tolerant spirit. With a felt sense of unity underlying it all, Irish Christianity left room for much diversity, and this implied necessarily an education in tolerance. Moreover, the Church was national just in proportion as it was not established, and it never at any time approximated to the position of a State institution. Thus, not only was the sword of the State never actually invoked to defend the

Church against pagan or heretic, but the machinery for that sort of thing did not exist. When the Church was centralized and brought at last to acknowledge definitely the authority of Rome, no earlier than the year 1152, Armagh was made the seat of the primacy, the seat of political supremacy being not there but in the south. This was done in accordance with Irish tradition, which had always assigned the place of honour to that see, as being sacred to St. Patrick himself. Armagh had long been regarded as the chief see and final court of appeal for the Irish churches. Indeed, we have positive evidence from the Book of Armagh that this view was held in the eighth century.

It was not till this year 1152 that, at the synod of Kells, held in the month of March, the diocesan system was established which has existed ever since, the pope having despatched a supreme legate to Ireland for the purpose, at the request of a synod held four years earlier at Holmpatrick. Cashel, Tuam, and Dublin were made archbishoprics, as well as Armagh; and the wise concession of the primatial dignity to Armagh transformed that powerful see, which had been hitherto the centre of opposition to Rome, into a faithful subject. Not even thus, however, was the spirit of Irish Church Home Rule destroyed. The monastic schools still held on their own way. So the primate Gelasius held a synod in 1162, at the abbey of Clane, on the banks of the Liffey, when it was decreed that no one should be admitted a reader or professor of divinity who had not studied at Armagh, or taken an *ad eundem* degree in that college. And thus it was intended to bring into subjection to Armagh, all the colleges, as well as all the bishops—now no longer to be indefinite in number—while Armagh itself held authority direct from Rome.

Thus after seven centuries the Irish Church, with its fiery spirit of independence, consented on the whole to fall into line with all other churches in Europe; though it is certain that the old spirit which died so hard was not quite dead even after the success of Gelasius, and probably there is a little of it left even now. It is interesting, however, to note that the process of centralization after the Roman manner was brought about by the action of forces within the Irish Church itself, and not, as some persons imagine, by Henry II. and his Papal Bull. The process had been a long struggle between two sets of ideas, the one set national and tribal, the other set cosmopolitan, and national too in a sense, since the loss of idiosyncrasies was accompanied by the gain of unity in organization. The struggle began with the controversy about the proper time of keeping Easter, as to which the Irish Church held out for its old customs with characteristic persistency, long after the rest of the Christian world had been reduced to uniformity. The cosmopolitan element in the general struggle is well expressed by one of the Irish controversialists in the eighth century, St. Cummian, of Durrow, who sums up a long argument in favour of the Roman custom, addressed to the Abbot of Iona, in these words: "What can be thought worse concerning the Church, our mother, than that we should say, Rome errs, Jerusalem errs, Alexandria errs, Antioch errs, the whole world errs; the Scots and Britons alone know what is right."

But we must return to the fifth century, and the system of missionary centres which Patrick set on foot, and which soon became centres of learning as well as of spiritual influence. It has already been shown that we have reason to associate the monastic learning of Ireland in its inception with the corresponding learning of Wales. The first name to stand out as that of a learned monk, founder of a monastic school, is the name of St. Finnian, who is said to have studied first at Trim and afterwards at Dair-inis in the Bay of Wexford, but to have specially associated himself as pupil with the eminent Welsh saints, David, Cathmael, and Gildas. After that he returned to Ireland and became Abbot of Clonard, the earliest of the monastic communities known to develop into a college or school. St. Finnian is called by the Four Masters the "foster-father of the saints of Ireland," and we may infer therefore that many other of the schools took their rise from the inspiration of saints who had been pupils at Clonard. The monastic communities were there already, and so was the old Irish zeal for knowledge: a learned abbot was quite enough to turn a community into a college. Clonmacmoise, Clonfert, Glasnevin, besides Devenish, Cluain-inis and Inis-mac-saint on Lough Erne, owed such a learned abbot to Clonard. The great Columba of Iona was also a pupil of the college there. Another of the earliest schools was established by a different St. Finnian, at Moville on the banks of Lough Foyle.

Since the first St. Finnian died in 549, at which time Columba was a young man of twenty-eight, we see that the scholarly movement was well under way in the first half of the sixth century. This, as we have already seen, was the age when Irish enterprise took on the missionary form, and it is specially associated with the name of St. Columba the apostle of the Picts and Northern England, and of St. Columbanus famous for labour in France, Switzerland, and North Italy. These are the two conspicuous men, but each of them was surrounded and succeeded by a number of less well-known workers, and their missions were the parents of many others. But it is Ireland at home that occupies us now, and the facilities which she then afforded for the training of men like these.

St. Columba, a descendant of the great King Niall, was born in 521, at Gartan in Donegal, and was baptized at Temple Douglas, which is not far off. After his education at Clonard, he made the round of he leading Irish colleges, according to the later fashion of the schoolmen. Then commenced his evangelistic work in Ireland, no less than the foundation of three hundred churches being attributed to him, among which are Derry, Kells, Tory Island off the Donegal coast, Drumcliffe in Sligo, Swords, Raphoe, Lambay near Malahide, and Durrow.

St. Columba was a poet, as well as an artistic scribe, a teacher, and a missionary. He had also something left in him of the warlike nature of his aristocratic ancestry, and so it fell out that he had a quarrel with St. Finnian of Moville, who claimed a copy which Columba had made, without his consent, of his Latin Psalter. When the quarrel was referred to the king of Meath, he decided that, on the principles of the Brehon law, the copy properly belonged to St. Finnian. Thereupon the Scot in Columba took fire; he summoned his tribesmen, and a great conflict ensued, in which at last Columba and his Ulstermen were triumphant and no less than three thousand, it is said, of the Meathmen were slain. Then Columba, repentant, retired to the monastery of Inismurray off the coast of Sligo, to consult his friend Molassius who was abbot there. Molassius advised submission, and prescribed, as a penance and compensation for the great evil he had done, that Columba should undertake that mission to Pictland with which his name is so honourably associated.

After that, the story of Columba's life belongs mainly to the history of Scotland and indirectly to that of England. It has been already told in these pages. Nevertheless, he does appear again on the Irish scene, as an honoured guest and ambassador at the national assembly of Drumceatt, in 590, which settled other affairs besides those pertaining to the Scottish colony in Alba. The poets of Ireland were in danger. They had roused popular indignation against them by their exactions, and now they were threatened with expulsion. But Columba, though a saint, was still a bard, and he came to Drumceatt to plead their cause as well as that of the little colony across the seas.

The memory of the great meeting at Drumceatt lasted till the seventeenth century; for Colgan, the great writer of that age, tells us that the site of the assembly was even then frequented by numerous pilgrims. The Irish lords and clergy encamped under arms during the entire session. This lasted fourteen months, so we may infer that much arrears of legislation were satisfactorily disposed of in that time. One piece of legislation is strikingly curious, and we are told that Columba was its principle promoter. It was decreed that women should henceforth be exempted from military service, whence it may be inferred that they still retained their military habits to some extent. And, indeed, it was found desirable by Adamnan, Columba's successor, to secure the exactment of a similar law a century later, at the synod of Birr, in the year 697.

The most important domestic business of the occasion, however, concerned the poets and the profession of teaching. It was solemnly resolved that the general system of education should be revised, and the following scheme was adopted.

1. Each king, chief, and lord was to have a special ollamh, or doctor, in literature attached to his court, to whom free lands were to be assigned by his chief, and a grant of inviolability to his person and sanctuary to his lands by the monarch and men of Erin at large.

2. Free common lands, or endowments, were ordered to be given to the ollamh for the purposes of education after the manner of a university, in which free education should be given to such of the men of Erin as desired knowledge.

Thus was established a system of free national secular colleges quite distinct from the ecclesiastical schools, and naturally founded on the older Irish institution of a State-supported academic class, living freely on the people and in general giving freely of their mental store to the people. Abuses in the working of the older institution, which had in its time achieved much for popular education, led to reform; and the reform amounted to the establishment of the same academic class as heads of schools with definite endowment as well as definite privileges. After that the days of the wandering poet, with his pupils around him, began probably to be over.

That the material which used to breed poets was gradually used up for breeding scholars in their stead is likely; although we know that Irish literature never was neglected in any of the Irish schools, and it is to those schools that we owe the preservation of the bardic traditions. The next great Irishman, however, was not, so far as we know, an Irish poet, while he was a remarkably elegant classical scholar, whose writings are still extant to testify to his scholarship. This was Columbanus, a native of Leinster, born twenty-two years later than Columba, in the year 543. He was educated at one of the schools in the islands of Lough Erne and afterwards at Bangor, then becoming famous as a place where the greatest attainments in learning as well as sanctity were possible. After forty-two years of a quiet life, the missionary zeal came upon Columbanus, and, in 585, he, with a band of companions, including St. Gall, turned their steps to France, then in a state of more than pagan immorality. His labours there and elsewhere have been already mentioned, and space forbids that we should dwell on them further. But in general we may connect with the missionary band of which he is the central figure, those remains of Irish art and Irish literature which are still to be found scattered here and there on the continent of Europe.

During the sixth, seventh and eighth centuries the School of the West grew and flourished, and, as we have already seen, it produced its highest result in the philosopher Erigena so late as the ninth century. But the eighth century was marked by an event fraught with much evil for the Church and the schools. This was the pagan crusade of the Danes. In 795, the Danes were first seen cruising off the coasts of Ireland, and when they descended it was on churches and monasteries that their heavy hand fell heaviest. The destruction to art-treasures and manuscripts must have been great; but, fortunately, the *spirit* of learning is hard to destroy, and, once acquired, not hard to revive. The struggle lasted, however, for more than two centuries on and off, and so it is probable that the energies of learning were to some extent paralyzed by the generally disordered state of society.

At first the Danes came as plunderers, but about the middle of the ninth century their movement assumed the purpose of settlement; for they were then seeking to escape the tyranny of their princes by finding homes in other lands. Later still, in other parts of Europe, they commenced the work of political conquest from which Ireland was saved, by the great effort made under Brian Boru to bring the Danes into subjection to the Irish crown. That effort, 1014, was successful, and henceforth the Danes were settlers in the land, living by their own customs in their own towns, but destined soon to be absorbed, like later-coming strangers, into the Irish nation.

The struggle with the Norsemen must have interfered seriously with the work of Irish literary and artistic production; but it would be far from the truth to suppose that anything like a collapse was the result. Political society was probably much more seriously shaken than the societies of learned and artistic monks. As a matter of fact, the blossoming period of Irish Christian art, to which most of the monuments now in our possession belong, was between the tenth and twelfth centuries, after the Dane had settled in the land. It seems likely that he did destroy earlier treasures; but by this time, having become a settler, he had ceased to be a destroyer, and, baffled in his purposes of conquest, was tending towards his ultimate fate of absorption into the individuality of the Irish nation. Cormac's chapel on the Rock of Cashel belongs to the end of the tenth century, during the interval between the first and second attack of the Danes.

The ninth century was the period of Danish plunder, and of settlement along the coasts and in convenient places for purposes of plunder. Towards the latter end of this century the Irish in Ireland, like the English in England, succeeded in driving out the enemy, and there was peace for forty years. Then came the Danes again, but bent more definitely than before on permanent settlement; and their most notable work was the establishment of the Danish kingdom of Dublin, with its centre at one of their old haunts, Ath Cliath on the Liffey, where the city of Dublin was built by them. The establishment of this kingdom dates from the year 919, and its extent may be traced to-day as conterminous with the diocese of Dublin, extending from Holmpatrick and Skerries on the north, to Arklow and Wicklow on the south, and inland no farther than seven or eight miles to Leixlip. Until quite recently this was also the district over which extended the jurisdiction of the Lord Mayor of Dublin as Admiral of the Port of Dublin. On College Green used to be held the assembly of the freemen of the kingdom of Dublin, while the chiefs took their seats on the steep hill that once stood where St. Andrew's Church now stands, opposite to "the old house on College Green" which is so dear to the national aspirations of the modern Irishmen. There the Danes held their parliaments, agreeing on laws, consenting to judgments and contracts, feasting and making merry, just as the old Irish held their parliaments at Tara, Carman, Armagh, and elsewhere.

Nor was Dublin the only Danish city. Limerick, Cork, Waterford, Wexford, all became the centres of petty Danish kingdoms, active in commerce, skilful, for those times, in domestic architecture, and with political and legislative ideas identical in their essence with those of the people among whom they settled.

In the course of the tenth century the Danes nominally became, for the most part, converts to

Christianity. But it appears that they derived their Christianity mainly from English sources; and when they began to organize their Church, they did so after the Roman manner, and in connection with the see of Canterbury. It was not, however, till after the wars of Brian Boru that Danish Christianity became either very real or at all organized. The forces arrayed against Brian at Clontarf represented mainly a pagan confederacy, although the king of Dublin was nominally a Christian.

The importance of Brian's work can hardly be overrated. In his youth the Danes of the South were a sore trouble to Munster, the province of which Brian became king, after the murder, by their joint enemies, of his brother Mahon; and he was the chief agent in achieving conquest over them. In his middle life, he established himself as supreme king over all Ireland. And in his old age he smote the Danes of Dublin, destroyed the pagan confederacy, and reduced that kingdom to a position of subordination to the Irish High King.

This was in 1014, and the memory of the old feuds lingered for a century or so. In 1038, for the first time, Dublin had a bishop. Sitric, king of Dublin, returned from a pilgrimage to Rome, much impressed with the power, magnificence, and organization, of the Roman Church; and we find that the earliest Peter's pence paid in Ireland, were those of Sitric, the Danish king. Sitric determined to establish a see in strict communion with Rome, unlike the ordinary Celtic ones; and the first bishop was called Donatus, probably a Latinized form of the Irish name Doonan. Sitric and Donatus have left their mark on the city, by erecting the cathedral now known as Christ Church, after the model of those they had seen on the Continent.

Donatus died in 1074, and then Dublin attached itself to Canterbury as the nearest ecclesiastical centre of the Roman type. This was an important step, but a perfectly natural one. Dublin was separated from Armagh by the fact that Dublin had started its ecclesiastical life after a different type from that of which Armagh was the centre. The other Danish communities followed the example of Dublin. Waterford did not get a bishop till 1096, when the king wrote to Anselm at Canterbury asking that he would consecrate to that office Malchus of Winchester. Thus an ecclesiastical union of the Irish Danes with England seemed to be setting in.

But the Irish tendency to local independence seems to overtake, like a fate, Irishmen of all races. So we find the fourth bishop of Dublin beginning to assert himself against Canterbury, and to assume the style and manners of an archbishop. And forces were about this time also at work to remove the difficulties that lay in the way of Irish Church unity on the side of the Celtic Church.

In 1117, the Archbishop of Armagh was legally

recognized at the synod of Usnagh as primate of all Ireland except Dublin, and in 1121, the then bishop of Dublin died. The primate, thinking the opportunity favourable to strike a blow at English intrusion, attempted to seize on the cathedral and see of Dublin. But the burgesses rose to a man, drove him out, and elected a layman, Gregory, one of themselves, to be consecrated at Canterbury as their bishop. In their wrath, they desired that even his lower orders should be Norman, not Irish. Gregory's predecessors seem, from their names, to have been Irishmen, but Gregory was a Dane, and all round Ireland, in the Danish cities, were bishops of the Roman and Canterbury party.

Yet, during Gregory's episcopate, the yoke of Canterbury was shaken off and the primacy of Armagh acknowledged, Dublin being raised to the dignity of an archbishopric, and the supremacy of the pope acknowledged by all. Armagh had been the centre of resistance to Rome; Armagh became the head of all the Irish churches.

This result was mainly brought about by the labours of an Irishman, Malachy O'Morgair, whose character recalls those of the missionary Irish saints in earlier days. It was due to him that the synod at Holmpatrick was held in 1148, when a petition was sent to the pope asking for the archiepiscopal palls for Cashel, Tuam, and Armagh. The synod of Kells in 1152 was a direct consequence of this, and at it the diocesan system was established, in which all the Danish sees were included, while Dublin was made an archbishopric. Thus Celt and Dane were reconciled, each making an approximation to the ideal of the other; and the second archbishop of Dublin was that very genuine and faithful Irishman, Laurence O'Toole, who has left behind him a name honoured for good service to the country in Norman times. The danger of the Danish settlement was completely passed, and the country seemed ready for a fresh outburst, with renewed vigour, in political, literary, and artistic development. Not many years later the Norman was in the land.

CHAPTER VI.

SOCIAL AND POLITICAL INSTITUTIONS.

EVEN this brief account of early Ireland would be incomplete without more careful examination of the social and political institutions under which the Irish people lived a life the external manifestations of which in history are so full of interest. In their early stages of development there can be little doubt that the Irish institutions were practically identical with those of the other European peoples; but the isolated position of the country enabled the Irish people to develop those institutions, apart from external influences, in a way that was exceptional, setting aside all question of the peculiar individual genius of the nation itself regarded racially. Hence it is that the record of Irish laws and social customs has a special instructive significance, for all the Northern European nations, while it sheds light on many a sociological inquiry.

The Irish nation, like all nations in early days, came to their country, not as individuals, but in tribes; and the tribal organization continued after they had settled down upon the land. Each tribe had its chief or king, its wise men or druids, and its custom of determining all doubtful matters by reference to the common sense and will of the tribe as expressed in the tribal assembly. In this tribal assembly we see the common origin of parliaments and courts of justice. The druid foreshadows the judge and the legislator—persons with power to give advice only, in the first instance, to the tribal assembly, and depending for their power on the popular wisdom they display. The king is the chief of kindred, the political head, the leader in battle, the convener of the assembly, but he derives his authority from the will of the tribe expressed in the assembly. The peculiarity of the Celtic tribal system was probably in the large proportion of influence ascribed to the druid or wise man as compared with the king, and the very early *intellectualization*, at the same time, of the general idea attached to druids. This is shown in the development of *several* learned classes dealing with different kinds of wisdom, and in the consequent check given to the growth of anything like a priestly caste-influence. These learned classes were—besides the druids—the brehons and the bards, with their several varieties.

Each tribe, as a whole, owned the land on which it lived. At first, no question would arise as to the quantity that each tribesman had a right to use, because land was unlimited in proportion to the uses for which it was required. But, as population increased, the theory developed that each tribesman was, in general, entitled to *use* as much of the common pasture land as he required for his stock, and to *use* tillage land in proportion to his status in the tribe. Originally, no individual tribesman *owned* any portion of the land, but each head of a family was entitled to claim the family's share. To the chief, as chief, a certain portion was allotted, which he appears to have held in addition to the share that fell to him as head of his family.

The Irish law of succession in landed property known as that of Irish gavelkind, was a logical consequence of the theory of tribal ownership. If a member of the tribe died, his piece of land did not descend by right to his eldest son, or even to all his children equally. Originally, it reverted to its sole absolute owner, the tribe, every member of which had a right to its use proportionate to his tribal status. This was undoubtedly the essential principle of inheritance by gavelkind, and the logically complete application of it would clearly require that at the death of each tribesman the lands of the tribe should be redivided among all the tribesmen. It is manifest, however, that such a procedure would be highly inconvenient, and never in fact likely to be carried out. Various customs would be developed for applying the principle to the various cases that might arise ;

and these customs, considered as laws of inheritance—which strictly they were not—would present the idea that a man's distant relations were equally with his own children his natural heirs to property in land. And as the custom of private ownership in land crept in, the law of succession would still reflect the principle that the land which a man held he owned in usufruct only, and the reversion of this usufruct at his death would therefore be to his family as a whole, not to his merely personal heirs. It is easy to see that such a law of succession would be sure to seem very perplexing and anomalous, as indeed it did, to the historical ignorance of the Elizabethan observers.*

In two ways, it was possible that private ownership should creep in. It would be convenient and natural that families should continue to use the same holding for generations; and, thus, approach to the custom of family, rather than tribal, ownership would be made. And, again, powerful and crafty persons, especially the chiefs, would be likely, unchecked and gradually, to appropriate to their sole use portions of the common waste land, as, being rich in flocks and herds, they had uses to which these lands could conveniently be put. Estates in severalty did gradually become established, and in later centuries the chief is found to have a private estate as well as the lands pertaining to his chieftainry. Nevertheless, it is a fact that at no time in old Irish history did the tribes-

* Sir Henry Maine's "Early History of Institutions," Lecture vii.

man lose his inherent right of free access to the tribal land, or the chief acquire general rights of ownership in it. He acquired a private demesne and no more, till a decision of the English King's Bench, early in the seventeenth century, made him the owner of his people's land in the eye of the English law. Rents had come into existence before that time, but not as payment by the tribesman for the use of the land.

The customs regulating inheritance cannot, however, be properly understood without considering the structure of the Irish family.* The primitive social unit was undoubtedly the tribe. In very early periods—beyond the reach of Irish, though not of all European traditions—the simple group of kindred was probably not divided into families at all. The establishment of definite marriage relations, and the rise of the family institution as we understand it, with the father at its head exercising acknowledged authority—these two events must have been contemporaneous. The tribal group of kindred became a group of families, and the families ramified, the individuals within them standing in various degrees of relationship to the head. In modern society, the individual, after he is of age, stands in a direct relation to the whole community, is responsible solely

---

* Sir Henry Maine's "Early History of Institutions," Lecture vii., p. 208, *et seq.*; Skene's "Celtic Scotland," vol. iii. chap. v. p. 176, *et seq*; Sullivan's Introduction to O'Curry, pp. clxii.–clxviii.

for his own deeds, and is the owner solely of his own property, all partnerships being matters of contract and definition. In such a society as that of the early Irish tribe, its constituents were families, not individuals: the family was responsible to the State for crime, the family owned property and especially held land in use; and, in the case of the Irish kings, it was to the royal *family*, not to the royal *person*, that the sentiment of reverence attached. Evidently, therefore, it was very necessary to define quite clearly the limits which separated the family proper from its ramifications outside those limits. This was necessary, and was done in Ireland, because the idea of family ownership and responsibility was preserved and developed as the general characters of social life became more complex, not allowed simply to decay as it did in other countries.

The Irish family, as we find it represented in the Brehon tracts, consisted, when complete, of seventeen men, and was distributed into four sub-families, the names of which may be translated as the hand family (geilfine), the true, the after, and the end families. The hand-family included the head or geilfine chief, and four other members; and each of the other divisions contained four also. The geilfine was at once the primitive family from which the others sprang, and consisted of the members latest born. When any person was born into the geilfine after its number of five was complete, its eldest member was promoted into the true family, the eldest member of the true family passed into the after family, the eldest of the after family passed into the end family, and the eldest of the end family went out of the organization altogether. Henceforth it appears that he belonged to the kindred of that family only —the sept which became afterwards the Highland clan—and probably he became the geilfine chief of a new and less dignified family.

It is exceedingly difficult to see how this system of promotion out of the range of family duties and rights worked in detail, but there appears to be no doubt as to its general principle. Every change depended, not on the death of seniors, but on the birth of juniors, who thus acquired the benefit of their birthright at their birth. Again, it is the younger children who are left with the father, to enjoy the geilfine share of the family holding, and to be subservient to his authority. The elder members lose their claim on that share by the birth of juniors, but they also gain the advantages of independence. These may have been very substantial at some early time, while the abundance of tribal land would secure to them an ample allowance in their new position. Sir Henry Maine suggests that the organization is founded originally on the idea of gradually emancipating the seniors of the family from paternal control; and that after this idea had ceased to be very apparent in it, the system continued to affect inheritance in a way that seems to turn upside down our modern ideas founded on primogeniture.*

At the time to which the Book of Aicill refers, each division of the family appears to have held separately a share of the land allotted to the family as a whole of seventeen men. Inheritance to this share proceeded within each division so long as there were any members to represent it. If, however, any of the divisions became extinct, its holding was divided among the other groups, not equally, but according to an elaborate system of distribution carefully laid down. As for the persons who had been promoted out of the complex group of seventeen, they must have had recognized claims on the unused lands of the tribe; and so long as land was plentiful, it seems clear that for purposes of land-tenure this artificially limited family arrangement probably worked very well, keeping up fairly, as it would, at once fixity of tenure in the families and a fair distribution of land according to members. It is easy to see how the principle of Irish gavelkind would have worked generally by its means without the constant redistribution of land which gavelkind seems at first to imply.†

* Sir Henry Maine points out that in the practice of Borough English by which the younger son inherits, we have probably a survival of the same idea.

† While the holding remained fixed in the possession of the group of seventeen, the outgoing members might be provided for by the opening up of new lands, or in some way, for the finding of which the tribe was responsible.

Joint ownership or tenure implies joint responsibility; and we find accordingly that each division of the family, and not the whole family in the first instance, is held responsible for the misdeeds of its members. The social convenience of this arrangement was probably very great, but there will be more to say on this subject presently.

The geilfine chief was the head of the family, and the rank of its members was higher or lower according as they stood more or less near to him in the group. As a body of kindred grew up outside, descended from those who had passed through the whole process of emancipation, these probably formed the outer and less dignified portion of the sept. And thus we see how the very barbarous and primitive tribe, having divided itself into families, became in course of time a group of septs or real kindred, each of which was a group of families, the tie of kinship in the tribe having become by that time imaginary, though still highly effective on the imagination as a social influence.

The law of succession to the chieftainship was that known as tanistry; the member of the royal family chosen as most fit by the tribe succeeded to the dignity. Originally, and in theory always, the tribe consisted of kinsfolk only, and the tanist was selected from the leading family, or family of traditionally the purest blood,* to lead all his kin. When

---

* Probably this was originally the family supposed to be descended direct through geilfines from the original geilfine.

a chief died, an assembly of the tribe was convened, apparently by the bruighfer, or borough magistrate, since it was held in his house.* The new chief was accepted by this assembly, and thus formally installed in office, while, at the same time, the heir was elected and known henceforth as the tanist. This mode of succession and election was manifestly intended to secure the political safety of the tribe by efficient leadership, and to maintain the popular control of the chieftainry, with the minimum risk of war between rival claimants, by the choice of an heir-apparent at the earliest possible moment. And it would appear from the annals of Ireland, full of war-tales though they be, that tanistry was at least as successful as primogeniture in preventing wars of this kind.

Within the tribe there was developed at some period an elaborate system of classes, founded partly on distinctions of birth and partly on those of wealth. This is described in the Book of Aicill, ascribed to the time of Cormac Mac Art, in the third century, and in part to the hand of that monarch himself. It is possible that the writer may have been over-subtle in his description; but the general tenor of his evidence it is impossible to set aside, the more so as it throws a singular light on the natural process by which an aristocracy is differentiated from a democracy in the primitive society.†

---

* Sullivan's Introduction, ccxxxiii.

† A good account of the system is to be found in Sullivan's Introduction, p. c., *et seq.*

Highest in rank are the noblemen or aires, the heads of families that have a certain dignity of birth, and that have possessed wealth appropriate to their position for many generations. Of these the writer mentions seven grades; but the higher grades are mainly distinguished by their official position in the State, of which more hereafter. Next in social grade we find the aire in actual process of manufacture, as the bo-aire, or cow-nobleman, who is simply a common tribesman rich in flocks and herds, the usual form of wealth in those times. When the bo-aire's family has acquired twice the wealth of an aire desa, the common kind of nobleman, and has held it for three generations, he becomes an aire desa. Thus wealth is a cause of rank, and, as industry is presumably the cause of wealth, this is very satisfactory. At any rate, it helps us to understand the absolute obliteration in Irish society of those racial distinctions in which aristocracies so often take their rise. Each grade of aires is distinguished from the others by the amount of wealth held on an average by one of its members, his consequent claim on the use of the tribal lands for his stock, his power of making contracts with his tribe, which was limited by law, the weight attached to his evidence in the courts, and his honour-price and eric, the special damages to be paid for insulting or injuring him. The king had the highest honour-price and eric. His testimony carried most weight, his power of making contracts with his tribe was greatest. Thus he was measurably, but not at all immeasurably, the most privileged person of his tribe. Short of the kingship, each aire family of lower rank could win for itself a higher and more privileged status by the acquisition of wealth and its retention through generations.

Next to the aires in dignity was the common tribesman, the peasant head of a family enjoying freely the use of the tribal land. The tribesman might, if he could, acquire wealth to any extent, and thus raise himself to the position of a bo-aire; or, by lack of wealth, he might fall into debt, make a contract with an aire or bo-aire, or the chief of his tribe, by which he borrowed cattle for his use in agriculture and undertook to pay interest in service and homage and material goods. This is the origin of rent in Ireland, and doubtless was the origin in all other parts of Europe as well. To this origin we can trace the inception of feudalism in the tribal organization. The peculiarity of Ireland lies simply in the fact that the Brehon land law was developed, parallel to the development of the feudal tendency, to check and regulate it at every turn.

The chief of the tribe, from his position as leader in war, as well as for other reasons, became possessed of large wealth in cattle or "stock." The peasant required more stock than he had, and the chief wanted to dispose of his stock for convenience and with advantage. So the needy peasant had to "take stock" from his chief, or some other rich man, and thus became a tenant to a lord or flath. The tenant or ceilé paid rent, rendered homage, and lost social status in proportion to the amount of stock taken. Thus there arose the class of ceilés and its subdivision into daer, or free, and saer, or unfree.

At this point the law-loving intellect of the Celt steps in, and makes the distinction which obtains to this day between the Irish *idea* of land tenure and the idea in all other European countries where landlordism still exists. The Brehon law regulated with the utmost exactness the rents which tenants were to pay their lords. The idea of a judicial rent is as old in Ireland as the institution of rent.

The saer stock tenant received a certain small portion of stock from his lord, and retained his tribal rights in their integrity. The normal period of his tenancy was seven years, and at the end of that time he became entitled to the cattle which had been in his possession. Meanwhile, he employed them in tillage, and paid rent to his lord by handing over to him the "increase," *i.e.* the calves and the milk, rendering to him also homage and service, such as aid in reaping his harvest and building his castle or dun. The daer stock tenant, on the other hand, having received a large portion of stock from his lord, parted with some of his tribal rights, and accepted a heavy duty in consequence. The stock was to be considered as divided into two portions, one proportional to the rent incurred and the other to the tenant's loss of tribal rank, the technical measure of which was his "honour-price" and his value as witness or bail. After rent and homage had been rendered for seven years, the tenant became entitled to the stock if the chief died, and, if the tenant died, his heirs were partially, though not wholly, relieved from their obligation. Thus the Brehon law aimed, not only at regulating the relations between landlord and tenant, but at the prevention of permanency in the servile relation. This tendency to conserve the ancient tribal idea of a community of freemen by limiting the power of the strong to make contracts with the weak is very characteristic; and it is evident that herein lies the explanation of the fact that Ireland never developed feudalism, as the rest of Europe, starting from a similar basis, did. Nevertheless, the shadow of feudalism came very close to the Irish tribesman in this respect, that, while he could refuse to "take stock" from any other man, it was not lawful to refuse to "take stock" from his king. The law, however, regulated the king's rents as well as all others.

Free or unfree, the ceilé was still a tribesman in the full sense of having a claim on the lands of the tribe. Although a tenant, he was still a co-owner in the tribe, and, as such, had absolute rights in the land he cultivated. Outside the tribe proper, there existed several other classes of inferior order, with definite relations to the lord rather than to the tribe, and having definite rights, relative to him and his estate, already recognized by the laws and customs of the land. We are told of the bothachs, both saer and daer, who served the lord, either freely for reward, or servilely as his permanent farm-labourers, and who possessed tenements on his estate. And we hear, too, of the sencleiths, or poor adherents of the lord, a lower class, who had no tribal status except that of a right—no mean one, many Irish tenants would think now—to shelter and to irremovability from the estate. These persons were not tribesmen, but they had rights: the duties which the lord owed them were recognized by the law. They were not outcasts and strangers in the land; and it was possible for a sencleith family, after a fixed term spent in service, to become bothach, and for a bothach family likewise to attain full tribal rights.

It would seem, indeed, that these classes represent the transition stage of stranger families becoming slowly adopted into the tribe by a process dependent on their good behaviour and industry. Side by side with them, and much more prominently, we find the true stranger and outcast class, the waifs and strays from distant lands, runaways from other tribes, prisoners of war, and broken men of all sorts who, having lost hold on the tribal life, had to begin afresh as individuals to build themselves once more into the social structure somewhere and somehow. Out of such materials, of which there would probably be no lack, the class known in Ireland as that of fuidirs was made up, with the two divisions into which it naturally falls, of free fuidirs and base fuidirs or slaves.

The origin of the base or daer fuidir class was probably very old, and its members, in the first instance at least, were prisoners taken in war. This class, the lowest in the society, had neither the liabilities nor rights of the ordinary tribesman. Nevertheless, in the times to which the law-tracts refer, the lord to whom a base fuidir was attached was bound to protect his life and to avenge insult on the women of his family; and for the ill deeds of his fuidir, the lord was responsible, just as the family was in general for the ill deeds of its members.

The origin of the saer fuidir is no less evident, and in him we find the type of the genuine feudal tenant, the type into which the European tribesmen generally were absorbed, as the tribal idea stagnated and decayed. The chief had no doubt, in very early times, access to the waste or spare lands of the tribe; and in course of time these lands were largely absorbed into private estates by him and other wealthy nobles, lords probably, though not landlords, so far as their own tribesmen were concerned. Here was one factor of genuine landlordism, control over land, vague but unquestioned. The other factor was the stranger, tribeless and homeless, needing not only land to settle upon and, perhaps, a little help to start, but also needing the protection of a claim on some society. The tribe was not open to him, unless he were a person of such skill, learning or other advantages that the tribe would be disposed to adopt him by public proclamation, as the tribes sometimes did. For a common man, the only refuge open was the manor of the lord. He might enter into a free contract with a lord, by which he obtained leave to settle on the land, and was secured in the protection of the lord, who thenceforth stood to him in the relation of family, *i.e.* was bail and witness for him in the tribal courts. On the other hand, he would agree to pay the lord a rent, and the law left him and the lord perfectly free to agree on that rent as best they might. The lord might accept the fuidir tenant's offer or let him go; the tenant was free to pay or go. It is noticeable that the rent of a fuidir is definitely distinguished in the Senchus Mor from the fair rent paid by one of the tribe, as a " rack-rent from a person of stranger tribe." So, from this point of view, it is clear that to be a tribesman was to have the protection of the land-law, and to be a fuidir was to be left to the lord's goodwill, the natural laws of demand and supply, and public opinion. Thus, looking on to later times, we see that the effect of English law in Ireland was exactly the same as that of turning the Irish people under the Brehon law into strangers in their own land. It only fell short of turning them into prisoners of war as daer fuidirs; and, by destroying at one blow the whole class of peasants with rights in the soil, it took away the wholesome check of their public opinion on the Irish landlords of olden times, and the ideal of peasantry towards which the whole system of the old Irish land-law tended.

For the fuidir was markedly better off than the modern Irish tenant in this respect, that his position was probationary under the law. In time, every fuidir family might be adopted into the tribe; and here we see one source of the Irish tenant's fixed idea that continuance in a holding for several generations constitutes rights. After two generations, the unfree fuidir family became free, after one more, a bothach, and after another, a sencleith. In the ninth generation, the stranger family was admitted to full tribal rights. Thus it was provided that every stranger family, however alien in race or even discreditable in origin, should be gradually adopted into the tribe, and this although the idea of the tribe centred with such intensity in the sentiment of kinship. The way in which this sentiment of kinship was supplemented by the related sentiment of foster-kinship is a subject on which there will be more to say hereafter. Both must be realized together before one can understand the extraordinary fusion of races in Ireland into one nation with a common racial sentiment, a deep and abiding sense of a common racial character between persons who are not of the same race.

It is not to be supposed that this elaborate provision for the slow absorption of alien elements existed just as it has been detailed from very early times; but no supposition could be more improbable than that it either came into existence suddenly or was a pure invention of the law-tract writers. It must have tended to exist from the very first occasion for its existence, and been gradually developed as the occasion for its use developed; and the law-writer cannot be reasonably suspected of more than a tendency to make explicit, and perhaps idealize, the notions of the customary law. It might, for instance, have been only his judgment that allotted the exact number of nine generations as the most reasonable and usual time for the process of absorption to last. But the matter of real importance is the nature of the absorption, not the time required; and, above all, the notable fact is that the Brehon law, by the provisions considered, aimed at making feudal tenure a mere temporary stage in the history of each family and therefore of the nation. The fuidir tenants of the chief and other lords represented the tribal means of growth from the outside, and their absorption into the tribe implied the resumption by the tribe of those lands which had been alienated as the manorial estate.

As a matter of fact, the poverty of the poor tribesmen and the wealth of the nobles must always have been operative to convert the former into tenants of the latter in the limited tribal sense. So, although the law provided for the termination of every tenancy, fuidir or ceilé, it is probable that the poorer tenants, by reason of their poverty, were forced to renew their tenancies again and again, and thus they may have become practically permanent in many cases. The Danish wars, and the consequent displacement of tribes in some parts of the country, probably increased the class of fuidirs, and thus perpetuated feudal tenure. After the Norman invasion, the causes tending to produce homeless wandering men, in need of shelter and protection, greatly increased. The Irish internal wars did not break up tribes and scatter them, but with the coming of the Normans the process of pulverization began; and every broken tribe meant a batch of feudal tenants for the Irish lords, to whom came those displaced from their ancient lands. So, despite the Brehon law and the tribal idea of rights in land for all, the relations between landlord and tenant, and those between chief and tribesmen, had inevitably degenerated when they came under the observation of the Elizabethan statesmen, even before the last blow had been dealt to the Brehon ideal in the reign of James I. by converting the chief into the lord of the tribesmen's lands (1605).

The whole structure of this tribal society, with its careful provision for promotion from rank to rank, cannot but strike us as likely to be very stable in its hold on the minds of the people. Intensely aristocratic as it is, in its unqualified recognition of the claims of birth and rank, it is peculiarly democratic too, in so zealously guarding the interests and liberties of each rank. Directed as it is against the unlimited concentration of wealth and power in the hands of any class, it is clearly conducive in a high degree to the production of national wealth by all. In fact, as natural causes tended to evolve the great social inequalities of feudalism and capitalism, the ideas of humanity as expressed in Irish law continually stepped in to give other developments to these natural causes. The lord and the fuidir in contact bring feudal tenure into existence. The law makes it a means by which the stranger can slowly and safely be incorporated in the tribe, and the manorial lands appropriated by the tribe.

By this counteraction of the feudal tendency, the Irish nation lost, no doubt, the political advantage which, in conflict with other nations, comes from concentration of strength in the hands of the few strong men. The cause of her early weakness in this respect may be, however, the sign of her high final destiny. She did not part with her social ideas for the sake of political strength. It remains for her to show how a power greater than the strength of armies can be attained by a nation that will labour faithfully for the perfect development of her social ideas. This, however, it is for the future to bring forth.

So far we have considered the order of ranks in

the tribal society as it developed directly on the lines of the great agrarian industry. The next point to interest us is the method by which the special enterprise, skill, learning and energy of individuals asserted itself within this apparently almost cast-iron order, and created the varied display of industry and talent which was so marked a feature of the national life. The tribe was originally a sum of natural families, each with common rights and responsibilities represented by its head. Arts, industries and literature were, no doubt, first created by individuals within the family; and these, being appreciated by the tribe, were honoured by treatment as separate units with personal duties and rights pertaining to their personality. The treatment awarded to the poet as such is the familiar case in point. He seems to have been treated always as a privileged servant of the State; and there is abundant evidence to show that the skilled metal-workers were dealt with in a similar spirit. Humbler workers, however, while probably able to drive a good enough trade in their personal capacity, would come to feel that their individual insignificance in the tribe was a source of inconvenience. And the humbler tribesmen, too, measuring their strength against that of the aires, would naturally be struck with the idea that numerical strength in their ranks ought to have its equivalent in social advantage. A family of high rank had definite social and political privileges. Might not half a dozen families of low rank *associate* and acquire tribal privileges for the joint body equal to the sum of those pertaining to its constituents?

And we find that this is just what the craftsmen and the peasants did, the latter more particularly, so far as Ireland is concerned.* The voluntary association was regarded, in the eye of the law, as an artificial group of kindred, with rights and responsibilities equal to the sum of its constituents and centred in an elected head. An artisan sept was exactly the same thing as a mediæval crafts-guild, and the agricultural sept, or Bruigh, is identical with the Saxon village, the germ of city guilds, and every other form of town communities. The Irish Bruigh plays no small part in Irish story. It had its own by-laws, the Bruigh-rechta; and its head, the Bruighfer, acted as magistrate, administering the law. The head of a guild, having rights in the tribe corresponding to the joint rank and wealth of the whole guild, was practically an elected aire. The weight of his bail and witness, and the amount of his honour-price, became by cumulation equal to those pertaining to noble rank. These rights he exercised on behalf of his fellows, whose rights were literally the constituents of his. He was their pledge and witness in the tribal courts, and their representative in the tribal councils, just as the noble heads of septs were for the septs, and the flath, or

* Introduction to O'Curry's "Manners and Customs of the Ancient Irish," p. clviii., *et seq.*

lord, for his vassals and dependents. Thus, while on the one side of the tribal organization there grew up the feudal manor, with the Flath, as distinguished from the tribal Aire, at its head, on the other hand there grew up, in Ireland as elsewhere—a rival to the Aire as well as to the Flath—the Bruigh, or voluntary association of freemen, some of whom probably saved themselves from the fate of ceilé tenants by this means. The Bruigh, with its Bruighfer and Bruighrechta, presents us with the elements of a local magistracy and borough government; and in the law's recognition of the Bruighfer's cumulative tribal rights we see unmistakably the germs of a directly elective parliamentary system, in addition to the indirectly representative system by which the noble heads of septs met in the tribal assemblies to settle the affairs of the tribe.* As time went on, the Bruighfer seems to have become an important official person, since we find that the election of the tanist and installation of the chief appear to have taken place in the house of the Bruighfer of the royal Bruigh, which makes it seem probable, though we have no certain information, that the Bruighfer may have been the proper convener of the assembly on this occasion.

The whole body of nobles, including probably the bo-aires, and more probably the elective aires, chose the chief or king of the tribe, who, as already stated,

* Introduction to O'Curry's "Manners and Customs of the Ancient Irish," p. cxcvii., *et seq.*, for development of this idea.

was a strictly limited monarch, with rights, privileges, and duties accurately defined by law, and differing from those of other nobles only in degree. The tribal king held in the confederacy of tribes a somewhat similar position to that which the aires held within the tribe. We hear of the Rig Mor Tuatha, the king of the great tribe or confederacy of tribes; and all such kings were partially subject to the Rig Ruradh, or king of the province to which the tribes belonged. Of these there were five, including the central province of Meath, which was founded about A.D. 400 by the great Niall, who sought to connect permanently with the provincial kingdom of Meath the Ard-Rigship of Ireland. The decline of Tara, however, in the sixth century, was a sign, and partly a cause, of the failure of this attempt. The Ard-Rigship remained, on the whole, what it was originally—a royal office nominally elective, to which the high kings not infrequently made good their claim by the sword. During the eleventh century, the O'Briens of Munster prevailed. They were successful in welding the Danes into the national unity, and that not only by the great Brian's victories over them in the field. In the twelfth century, the O'Conors of Connaught came to the head; but they did not succeed in driving the Normans out.

Particulars respecting the executive government of the country must be sought in the constitution of the tribes thus federated together, and may be understood to repeat themselves in the constitution of the federation. It has already been stated that the Irish law tracts distinguish seven grades of Aires, but the three highest appear to be simply distinguished as officials of State. The Aire Forgaill was the king's chancellor, who held the king's court, had jurisdiction over the common lands of the tribe, and determined the rights of each family therein. The Aire Tuisi seems to have been the official commander of the levy of the tribe. And, lastly, there is the Aire Ard, or high noble, of whom Dr. Sullivan conjectures that the Lord High Steward of Scotland is the logical descendant. It was his business to levy the tolls and dues of the king, and to hold the high court in which cases coming under statute law had to be tried, while the lower courts tried cases coming under customary law only.

These officials were the king's ministers. The Aire Cosraing, on the other hand, was elected by the families of the tribe, and probably corresponds to the modern Sheriff, who is descended from the similar popular official of the Teutonic tribes. It was his business to carry out the decisions of the king's courts about tolls, dues, tributes, etc., with which the Aire Forgaill and the Aire Ard had to do, and thus to act practically as their executive officer. He also had to distribute honour-prices and injury-prices to the families to which these were due.

Each family was of course responsible for the

maintenance of its own poor, and appear to have had a special officer charged with this duty. Each family was also responsible for the good behaviour of its members. If an offender failed to atone for his offence before the law, by restitution in some equivalent to the injured person, then the family must atone. It was for the family, therefore, to see to it that its criminals were forthcoming and submissive to their punishment. Hence, it is not surprising to find that the coercive power of the law was mainly represented by the presence in each family of an officer called the Dae, whose business it was to carry out judicial decisions against resisting members. Each family had, in fact, its own policeman.

If the family resisted, the physical force of the whole tribe appears to have been the remedy; and probably this is the reason why the Irish tribes, as Edmund Spenser describes them in a time when their organization must have fallen much into decay, assembled on their accustomed hills to give and receive judgment, always *with arms in their hands*. It may be that the duty of leading the military force of the tribe to carry out the decrees of the courts was the special duty of the official called the Aire Echtai, as distinguished from the Aire Tuisi, who was military commander in war.

The next subject to concern us is the means that existed for the administration of the law. Mention has more than once been made of the tribal assembly, and originally there can be no doubt that, in Ireland as elsewhere, this body was at once the parliament and the court of justice. With time comes the development of distinct bodies having the separate functions of legislation and administration, the organization of the latter being naturally the more complex of the two. In the Irish system of courts the idea expressed is very similar to that which at a later date was elaborated in England. The comparison is fully discussed by Dr. Sullivan, keeping the corresponding institutions of the Germanic tribes in view.*

The high persons of the tribe would naturally be regarded as those whose duty and privilege it was to preside over a court of justice, and this idea is aptly embodied in the Irish name Airecht for a court. The lowest kind of court was the Airecht Fóleith (similar to the Court Leet), presided over by an aire, in which minor cases under common law could be tried. Next to this was the Airecht Urnaidi, or Court of Pleas, in which cases concerning property and others involving technical law were tried. These were presided over by a special magistrate, the Neimid, and cases were heard in them by the lowest order of brehons, or Irish judges. The Court of King's Bench was represented by the Airecht Fodeisin or chief court of the king, in which justice was administered by his ollamh brehon or chief judge. The Rig Mor Tuatha held the

* Introduction to O'Curry, p. cclxiii., *et seq.*

Taeb Airecht, a court for dealing with cases arising between different territories; and, since this court, dealt with matters of fact as to traditional boundaries and tribal contracts, the king was supported in it by scanchies or historians, whose business it was to know facts, rather than by judges whose business it was to know law. Above all inferior courts, was the Cul Airecht (rear-court) or High Court of Appeal, one for each province, including the Cul Airecht of the High King of Erin, that used to be held in Tara while Tara was the centre of the nation's life. In these courts the judgments of the king and ollamh brehons were supported by the bishops and the state officials, and cases were stated by professional pleaders, called in Irish generally "arguers" and sometimes, more quaintly, "polishers," in reference to their duty of polishing up and brightening their clients' cases.

For the Irishman who had a cause against another there was, then, no lack of courts to award him his rights; and by Irish law every wrong done was a wrong done to some person who ought, in right and reason, to be compensated for the injury, by the offender. The business of the court was to decree, according to law, what the compensation should be; and it was the business of the state officers of the tribe to enforce the decree against the offender's family if he were in default. If the family defied the law, then the tribe was called to arms by the executive to enforce the decree against the family.

The following passage from Chief Baron Gilbert on the state of Britain before murder became punishable by death under the later law of Canute, is quoted by the writer of the article on Brehon Law in the "Encyclopædia Britannica" as illustrative of the Irish as well as the English system of family responsibility.

"If any offence was committed in any of the Decennaries (tythings), if the party was brought to answer, he was obliged to pay his fine for his offence, or he was imprisoned for ever; and if he fled, the Decenna was answerable for his offence to the king. So that by this discipline men were put under a necessity of being innocent, or paying a grievous fine, or being totally deprived of the conversation of mankind. And the laying of this fine on the tything, in case the offender fled, made it the interest of every man to bring the offender to light, and made it exceedingly difficult to conceal a theft or a murder."

The general character of the Irish criminal law cannot be better described than in the following passage from the same article.

"The law of torts regarded all offences, with the nominal exception of murder, as condonable by fines until the offender and those liable for him could pay no more, when the defaulter lost his status and fell into the servile class. For some of the offences of the individual the family were responsible, for others particular sureties. . . . The scale of mulcts for the several sorts of homicides, wounds, and personal hurts is in outline the same with those of the other Western European nations; but in addition to their definite fine of so much for such a lesion or bruise, *it provides by rateable deductions for excusatory circumstances* of intention, knowledge, contributory negligence, accident, and necessity, *all of which are considerable refinements on the contemporaneous systems of the continent."*

In its essence the principle of trial by jury was present in the Irish method of administering justice. If *twelve* good men and true could be found to come forward and declare their belief in the innocence of the accused, they were admitted as his *compurgators* in the eye of the law and his innocence allowed, while they were held responsible if it should turn out that their *witness* for him had been contrary to the truth. In form, compurgation was a witness to innocence and a surety for good behaviour; but its effects were so precisely those of the modern trial by jury that we must regard it as a primitive form of the institution. The fact that its practice was common to Britain and Ireland illustrates in an interesting way the truth of the remark made by the writer above quoted that "whencesoever derived, the common law may to so great an extent be recognized as substantially a common inheritance of all the populations now organized into the United Kingdom."

Passing from the law of criminal to that of civil offences, the most striking point in the Irish system is the very elaborate development of the law of distress. The court is ready to judge between debtor and creditor; the problem for the debtor is how to get the creditor into court. The general means are first by summons, and, if this fails, eventually by distraint on his goods. The peculiarity of Ireland lay in the greater complexity of the whole process.* We find, too, curious evidence of the link between the extreme Eastern and the extreme Western Aryan in the practice, common to India and to ancient Ireland, of fasting for a certain time at the door of a creditor belonging to the privileged classes, before proceeding against him by way of distress. Fines, awarded by the courts, were also exacted by process of distraint.

Coming now to consider the question, Who made new laws in ancient Ireland? it strikes us as at once evident that some kind of popular legislature is implied in the whole structure of the society so far as we have already considered it. We are not, however, left to theorize, by lack of evidence. The assembly of the people † is a frequent event, occurring in various ways: whatever has to be done is done by calling a meeting of those concerned. The habit of jointly taking action in assembly is of the very essence of self-government. Add to it, what indeed it already in part implies, the vigorous self-will of a freedom-loving people, the intellectual capacity for complex

---

* Sir Henry Maine's " Early History of Institutions," p. 279, *et seq.*
† " Introduction to O'Curry," p. cclii., *et seq.*

organization, and the moral capacity for self-control, and the self-governing nation begins to develop from the mass of self-governing tribes.

If the lord wanted anything done by his tenants— some special work or provision for an extraordinary levy, he called a Mithal Flatha, or meeting of his tenants, and they agreed to do it. This was convenient, but it was also wholesome for him and for them; tyranny never begins while the people are dealt with in masses, unless, indeed, there is an armed force behind the tyrant. Similarly, if the head of the tribe had any purpose to serve, he naturally called a meeting of the free householders of the tribe, the Mithal Tuatha, to set his requirements before them or to take counsel with them.

These assemblies, however, had no special significance as germs of a definite political constitution in course of development. Much more important was the Mathluagh, the assembly of all the householders of a sept, which was summoned by the chief of kindred, the Aire-Fine, to consider matters in which the kindred were interested. These might be acts of the king, decisions of the courts, measures of defence, and so on. Here we have an assembly of a very significant kind, capable of becoming, in proportion to the size and strength of the group, an organ of resistance to arbitrary power or to the popular will outside the sept. The Mathluagh was convened by its own natural head, the representative of the kindred in the tribal or national councils, and was in fact the meeting of his constituents, summoned for information, for counsel, and for support. If the institution of the Mathluagh were used to any considerable extent, it must have made contravention of popular rights by the kings and tribal chiefs very difficult; and, by its decentralizing tendencies, it may have added to the difficulties of such concentration of power in kingly hands as was required for the ultimate safety of the national life.

The Mathluagh corresponds most nearly to the modern public meeting of the constituents of a parliamentary division. It had no definite functions, no recognized powers to act, even as a local authority, in affairs of state. The germs of local government are to be found, not in the tribal Mathluagh, but in the analogous institution of the Bruigh, with its Bruighfer and Bruigh-rechta. This was analogous because instituted as a group of voluntary kindred—an artificial sept; but its outcome was very different, just because of that voluntary principle, and the consequent institution of elected officials and deliberately adopted laws instead of the customary tribal rules. We must look, however, beyond the Bruigh, as well as beyond the Mathluagh for the parliament of the nation in its original form.

Such a parliament was the Dal, the assembly of all the Aires—heads of kindred, including probably the elected heads—of the tribe, who met in the Dal to assess fines, levy taxes, and carry on the fiscal business of the tribe generally. The meeting of the heads of kindred was no doubt an institution as old as the existence of the tribe, and its functions as multifarious as the needs of the tribe, including certainly the administration of laws as well as legislative decisions. But it seems probable that when the division of functions came about, one of the first kinds of business to fall definitely into the hands of the full assembly of tribal Aires was that of the Dal, the transaction of all that is concerned with the *power of the purse*. Indeed, the practical necessity of having full tribal assent in matters of taxation is sufficiently evident; and the passing of money-bills in all primitive parliaments was probably an earlier event than the passing of bills to enlarge or control or amend the common customary law, which naturally has as much tendency to develop from precedent to precedent by the decisions of wise men or judges as by definite legislative enactment.

We find, however, that necessities for definite legislation did arise in ancient Ireland, and that, as we should expect, the same persons who in a Dal controlled the purse, formed also a true legislative assembly by which all new laws must be solemnly adopted. This assembly was called the Tocomrach, the distinction of the two parliamentary functions being thus emphasized by the use of different names for the same body as discharging them. No law was valid till it had received the assent of the Tocomrach, which body also elected the king; and, since it met in the house of the Bruighfer for that election, it is not improbable that the Bruighfer of the royal Bruigh, rather than the king himself, was its convener.*

Before a law could be adopted, it had to be drafted and proposed. This was the work of the Sabaid Cuirimtigi—council of the alehouse—which consisted of the chief men in the tribe, province, or nation, as the case might be, and was in fact the king's privy council. At this council measures were discussed and decisions on them taken, skilled lawyers being employed in the actual drafting; and thus they were prepared for the Tocomrach, much as measures are prepared for Parliament by the Cabinet in our own time.

It has been already said that the Mathluagh had no actual power, but it is clear that it had means of influence, however much or little used. The Aire-Fine, or head of the sept, was a true representative of his sept traditionally, and might well report the result of discussions in his Mathluagh to the Dal or Tocomrach, and, on the other hand, might report the decisions of the latter to the former, with the result probably of gaining for them a voluntary adhesion. It is indeed true that, being an hereditary, not elected, representative, he might very easily neglect this duty; but the

* Introduction to O'Curry's "Manners and Customs of the Ancient Irish," p. cclvii.

solidarity of his kindred or constituents being, it is clear, a matter of practical as well as sentimental concern to him, motives for promoting it by use of the customary means were not lacking ; and the extraordinary vitality of the sentiment binding kith and kin of all classes into solid local political entities is itself a sign that heads of kindred generally were prone to observe, in the spirit if not in the letter, such national institutions as tended to promote, by the maintenance of mutual confidence between head and trunk, the solidarity of the kindred.

There were, however, other means by which it was secured that popular consent to the decisions of the privileged classes should not be lacking. The Aenach, or Fair, which was the general assembly of all the people, is a much more conspicuous fact in the Irish annals and stories than any of these later developments of the primitive folk-meeting which we have been considering, though without them its functions in later times would not be very intelligible. The Aenach took place periodically, and was summoned by the king himself, generally, so far as we know, at certain places such as Tara and Teltown in Meath, Carman in Wexford, Aileach and Ard-macha in Ulster, which were probably sacred at some time to the memory of ancient heroic and religiously venerated persons. All new laws were promulgated at the fair in the hearing of the people, while also old laws were rehearsed, proclamations made, and genealogies recited, the people being thus kept acquainted with the institutions and traditions under which they lived. This was the political side of the Aenach; but it was also an occasion of literary, artistic, and social enjoyment, and an opportunity for the selling and buying of wares. Recitation of poetry, music, dancing, feats at arms, horse-racing, athletic sports—all these took place; and prizes were awarded by the king, who had charge of the fair, to the best competitor in each accomplishment. The bards came to the Aenach, and used it, not only as a literary stimulus, but also as an occasion for the interchange and comparison of ideas, thus helping to keep the historic traditions pure by the test of agreement. The smiths and skilful artificers, the weavers of woollen goods and others, came to show their wares and sell. The young people came to see and hear, and to enjoy one another's society; it was a time for marrying and giving in marriage. The serious came to hear the latest politics. All came to enjoy the music and poetry, the sports and the competitions. And so important a feature in the national life was the Aenach, that it was regulated by the strictest bye-laws, the breach of some of which was even punishable by death.

The only fragment of the Aenach left is in the selling and buying of wares and the social enjoyment of an Irish fair; but, with the exception, curiously enough, of this fragment, the whole non-political part of the institution is preserved in its main idea as the National Eisteddfod of Wales. That the custom was a general Celtic custom, and indeed not unknown to the Germanic peoples is certain. But there is, nevertheless, evidence to show that its revival in Wales in 1180, by Griffith ap Conan, was directly due to his observation of the practice in the neighbouring country of Ireland, and thus that the Eisteddfod of Wales is historically continuous with the Irish Fair.

Each kind of assembly might be held for the transaction of tribal, provincial, or national business. The celebrated Feast of Tara was the meeting of the council of the High King of Erin, followed by the Tocomrach, which was its natural sequel, and accompanied no doubt by the popular fair of which we have accounts reaching back to a very early period in Irish history. The Fair of Tara, occurring triennially, represented indeed, as has already been pointed out, the traditional unity of the Irish nation, and the High King was High King because he was chosen to convene and preside over that National Fair. To the Feast of Tara came the kings and the ollamhs of Ireland, and to the Fair came the people from all quarters.

It is not unlikely that the fall of Tara in the sixth and seventh centuries had an evil effect on the development of Irish political unity, since it left the country henceforth without a fixed political centre; and that fall itself may have been due to the change that had come over the religious traditions and associations of the people after the conversion to Christianity.

This account of early Irish institutions would be incomplete without further remark on the widespread custom of fosterage, and its development as literary fosterage into an educational system. Fosterage pure and simple, the giving and taking of children for nurture, existed in all the early Aryan communities; but in Ireland the practice became extraordinarily prevalent, and was carefully regulated by the law. It was quite usual, till very late times, that children of noble birth should be fostered by the lowlier dependents of their families, and this custom has no doubt contributed to intensify the sentiment of affection between the different ranks of the sept or clan. It has supplied the idea of foster-kindred when that of kindred was obscure. But it is with the use of the fosterage idea in spiritual, intellectual, and industrial relationships that we are more specially concerned. In a society organized under the idea of kindred, it is natural that every relationship should be assimilated to the family relationship. So we find in Ireland the family of the saint and spiritual fosterage or gossipred, the fraternity of the craftsmen and industrial fosterage, the family of the teacher, whether bard or brehon, and literary fosterage, besides the military fosterchildren of the great warriors. It is about literary fosterage that we read most in the Brehon law tracts, which give under this title the law of the relation between teacher and pupil. An entire subtract in the Senchus Mor is devoted to the subject of fosterage, and sets out with the utmost minuteness the rights and duties attaching to all parties concerned. And it is plain that the brehon's conception of the relation between foster-child and foster-family is a slight variation of that which regulates the relation between the child and its natural family, the child owing certain duties to the family, and the family bearing certain responsibilities for the child.

Out of this conception of fosterage grew the law regulating the relation of pupil to teacher—the literary foster-father. "However it may surprise us," says Sir Henry Maine, "that the connection between pupil and teacher was regarded as peculiarly sacred by the ancient Irish, and as closely resembling natural fatherhood, the Brehon tracts leave no room for doubt on the point. It is expressly laid down that it created the same *Patria Potestas* as actual paternity; and the literary foster-father, though he teaches gratuitously, has a claim through life upon portions of the property of the literary foster-son. Thus the brehon, with his pupils constituted not a school in our sense, but a true family. While the ordinary foster-father was bound by the law to give education of some kind to his foster-children—to the sons of chiefs instruction in riding, shooting with the bow, swimming, and chess-playing, and instruction to their daughters in sewing, cutting out, and embroidery—the brehon trained his foster-sons in learning of the highest dignity, the lore of the chief literary profession. He took payment, but it was the law which settled it for him. It was part of his status, and not the result of a bargain." *

Remembering that the natural family was in a measure responsible for the ill-deeds of its members, we look for some definition of the tutor's more limited responsibility for his pupils. The following passage from the laws makes this point clear, and gives us, at the same time, a pleasant picture of the educational system at work.

"The poet (or tutor) commands his pupils. The man from whom education is received is free from the crimes of his pupils if they be the children of natives, even though he feeds and clothes them and that they pay him for their learning. He is free, even though it be a stranger he instructs, feeds, and clothes, provided it is not for pay but for God that he does it. If he feeds and instructs a stranger *for pay*, it is then he is accountable for his crimes." †

The dual play of ideas in this passage gives us a sudden insight into the ideal life of the times. On the one hand, there is the tribal idea of the citizen's strict responsibility to the State for those he may

---

* Sir Henry Maine's " Early History of Institutions," Lecture viii. p. 242.
† O'Curry's "Manners and Customs of the Ancient Irish," vol. ii. p. 79.

introduce into the community. On the other hand, this idea is annulled by the permission to exercise free hospitality without limit. We know, too, that it was customary for the neighbours of the mediæval schools to exercise their hospitality for the support of the strangers who flocked as students to the schools. The "poor scholar," dependent on the charity of the neighbours for his living, as on the kindness of the teachers for his learning, was as familiar a feature of Irish society as the bard and the brehon themselves. The entertainment of strange students was in fact regarded by the people and by the law as a duty of national hospitality.

The children of the Irish upper classes paid for their education in the ordinary way, and the sons of the poorer classes who were educated at the same college were provided for by an arrangement similar to that of the modern though now old-fashioned sizarship. They waited on the wealthier students, and received educational benefits in return. The scholars who belonged to the neighbourhood lived in their homes; and those who were pensioners lived in the humble-looking group of dwellings called the college; while others coming from remote or foreign districts lived in their own huts adjoining the college and were supplied with provisions by the neighbours. The living doubtless was plain indeed, but of high thinking there was no lack.

The whole educational system was a spontaneous

growth over which the law threw its mantle of authority as it grew, regulating it by careful definition of those ideas of the right and desirable which were already more than half expressed in the national consciousness. Thus the aspiration after knowledge and intellectual activity which is of the very essence of Irish character, fulfilled itself at an early period of political development by institutions which embody the essential idea of Irish social life—the idea of kinship natural and voluntary as the source of mutual duties and joint responsibilities which it is the business of the law to define rather than to enforce.

Since then, the Dark Ages have been in Ireland, times when the education of all save a small ascendant class was made penal by law, followed by a period during which it was subject to serious discouragement only. But ideas that have once had a long and vigorous spell of practice seldom die, and so the old habit of spontaneous educational activity was never in the darkest times quite suspended in the ancient Isle of Saints. So between the national schoolmaster of to-day and the bardic tutor of the distant past, we see the gap partly filled by the quaint pedagogue of the hedge school in the penal times, who taught his scholars, though it was against the law, and was paid by odd little miscellaneous offerings of potatoes, turf-sods, and occasional eggs. Now, in these better days, the old impulse is fast restoring itself to its full activity, and has made the Intermediate

Education Act and the Royal University such successes as without it they could not possibly have been. Learning grows up in remote out-of-the-way places in Ireland without any appropriate educational appliances as it grows up nowhere else. And to the modern Irish Catholic Church all honour should be given, for the zeal and energy with which it has built up its own system of higher schools and colleges, without recognition—much less endowments—at first, and without direct endowment even now.

CHAPTER VII.

THE ARTS IN ERIN.

SOME last words are due to the subject of Irish Art. The history of early Ireland, in all its aspects, presents us with a picture of social development, under the influence of noble instincts and high ideals, in a people brave, affectionate, faithful, with a keen logical wit, a quick artistic sense, and a tendency to take the poetic view of Nature and of life. The history of later Ireland shows us, as plainly as history can show, the arrest of all this development; and, on the whole, it leaves us little in the dark as to the causes of this arrest. Ireland was highly organized, after her own manner, when the Norman invasion came; but she was not at all organized to protect herself from such an invasion. Nor could she, by her temperament, submit to the result—as the Greeks submitted to the Roman conquest—and afterwards teach the lessons she had learned to her conquerors. So the long conflict began that is not over yet; and, between the evils of perpetual war—war very different from that which used to be waged among the Irish tribes—and the greater evil of English legislation, Ireland came apparently to a social standstill. Yet it still remains for the future to show what noble lessons she has added to the lessons of olden times for the development of the nation in the times that are to come. There can be no real arrest of development for a nation that keeps its vitality amid desolating storms; but the development is inward, not outward—a development of the human spirit, though unexpressed, as the individual genius of that nation determines it.

In nothing, however, is the arrest of outward development more apparent than in the matter of Irish art. Here the evidence is not in historical records, but in the things themselves—the remains of Irish art that have come down to us through the centuries, the exquisite metal-work, the illuminated manuscripts, the sculptured monuments, the architecture just achieving its development into the beautiful Irish Romanesque style. Up to the middle of the twelfth century there is development, resulting in work of rare beauty. Soon afterwards, production almost ceases; the land is no longer a place for beautiful things to be made in it.

Metal Work.

The Irish bardic tales are full of allusions to the "smiths of Erin," and to their work in ornaments of silver and gold even more than to their work in forging weapons of war. Some specimens of this pagan metal-work remain, and it is evident that quantities of it must have been destroyed or lost in the Danish, even more than in the Norman, wars. There are some fragments of a pagan horned or radiated crown in the Petrie Museum, which may be taken as typical of this early work;* and these are said by experts to show in a very marked degree the two important characteristics of (1) complete mastery over the arts of tempering, stamping, and engraving, and (2) exquisite skill in design and execution. The most famous example, perhaps, of Irish metal-work is the brooch known as the Tara brooch, which was picked up on the seashore in the year 1850. We have no means of ascertaining the date of this fine specimen, but the nature of the patterns on it denote considerable antiquity no less than extraordinary skill, and, as we know that the royal brooch was an important part of the High King's regalia, it may very well be that this is really a Tara brooch, belonging to pagan times. Some of the work is so fine that it cannot be seen without a magnifying glass.

In Christian times, the art of the smith was employed to make costly shrines for books and bells, besides crosiers and chalices. In connection with these shrines and crosiers, we find a characteristic little bit of Irish sentiment. In other countries

---

* "Early Christian Art in Ireland," by Margaret Stokes, p. 53, *et seq.*, for full description.

valuable books had costly bindings bestowed on them as art developed. Shrines, too, for the rude bells of the early missionaries are unknown out of Ireland, with the exception of two in Scotland. But Irish sentiment seemed to have regarded the book itself as something too sacred to be re-bound, and so made for it a shrine, adorned with gold, silver, enamel, gems, and the finest work of the smith. So also it enshrined the bell; and it is an interesting fact that the shrine of St. Patrick's bell, made in the year 1091, has never been lost sight of since. It always had a special keeper, and we know exactly where it has been for these eight centuries. It is now in the Irish Royal Academy. Again, when we turn to the crosiers, we find that they are really shrines, containing the old walking-stick, with its crooked handle, which has been preserved in memory of some early saint. The object of poetic value is the old stick which supported the good man in his declining years; all the lavish material splendour of the shrine has its special spiritual interest as an expression of the zeal with which the relic is preserved.

"It would appear," says Dr. Petrie, "from the number of references to shrines in the Irish annals, that previously to the irruption of the Northmen in the eighth and ninth centuries, there were few if any of the distinguished churches in Ireland which had not costly shrines." It is clear, however, that such costly shrines would be the most appropriate prey

that Irish art could offer to the barbarian invader;
and this reflection makes it easy to understand the
fact that, though the work of the smith was more
ancient in Ireland than that of the scribe, the examples
left to us of the smith's work in ecclesiastical
articles belong to a later date than that of the fine
illuminated manuscripts. The churches and monasteries
were special objects of the Danish attack; none
of any considerable importance escaped.

The first pagan attack came to an end about 875;
and the peace that ensued till 916 appears to have
been used as a time of architectural restoration, and
equipment to meet future troubles with greater powers
of defence. Round towers were built for belfries
to the monasteries, but they were made of such
dimensions and strength as fitted them to be used
as places of safety for the monks and their treasure
in case of attack. In the entries of the annalists
regarding the earliest Norse attacks, from 789 to 845,
it is recorded that the clergy fled to the woods for
safety; and it may be that on one of these occasions
the beautiful chalice of Ardagh was buried for safety
in the place where it was afterwards found, the place
having been missed by the monks who concealed it
there. From 950 on, however, we read of the "tower
of a bell" as being the special object of Danish attack,
and it is very easy to imagine the much greater
security for works of art brought about by the erection
of these solid monasterial keeps. The earliest

literary reference to a round tower states that the bell-tower at Slane was burnt in the year 951.

It is impossible not to connect these events with the fact that no fine specimen of Christian art in metal-work has been found to which a date earlier than the tenth century can be definitely assigned. The earliest we have is the bell shrine of Maelbridge, which may be referred to the year 954, applying the usual and certain test of observing the names inscribed on the shrine and noting the dates under which any of the persons so named are mentioned in the annals. On most of the Irish works of art we find the name of the king, abbot, or bishop, by whom the work was ordered, and also that of the artist who carried it out; while not unseldom the request of a prayer for their souls is quaintly added. This practice makes it possible to fix dates with precision in many cases.

A much earlier dated example of fine metal-work, in the easily identified Irish style, is the silver chalice of Kremmünster in Lower Austria. The date of this is as early as between 757 and 781. It should be noticed, however, that in Ireland itself the metal chalice appears to have been less essential than the bell, crosier and book. Glass chalices were very often used, the one famous example of the engraved metallic chalice being the undated chalice of Ardagh, which is one of the most exquisite of all our memorials of early Irish art.

The first book-shrine of which we *hear* is that of the Book of Durrow, made between 877 and 916. The earliest we *have* is that of Molaise's Gospels, the date of which lies between 1001 and 1025, and falls about the second period of cessation in the struggle with the Danes, when the genius and valour of Brian Boru had restored peace to Ireland, confirming it by that last great struggle at Clontarf (1014). The earliest dated crosier is that of Kells (967), which falls within the second period of struggle when the means of defence had decidedly improved.

On shrines and crosiers alike the work is of the finest kind, and shows no less a delicate sense of artistic fitness than perfect skill in design and execution. The characteristic of Irish design in this, as in all other departments of Irish art, lies in the conservatism with which the artist clings to the fundamental forms of the old native patterns, and weaves in with them, as if growing out of them, all new designs that have been found elsewhere or that may have occurred to native invention working out its primary ideas. In art, as in politics and religion, Ireland seems to have been a land where ideas, once planted, live and grow on for ever, or, if they die, die hard. The fact has, there can be little doubt, as much to do with geography as it has with race.

One of the best known pieces of metal-work is the cross of Cong, which was made in the twelfth century, for the purpose of enshrining a supposed portion of the true cross. It is a processional cross, two feet six inches high, and the inscription asks a prayer for the king who caused it to be made, for the Bishop of Tuam for whom it was made, and for the artist who made it. There is no difficulty in assigning it, by these names, to the year 1123, in the first quarter of that fatal twelfth century after which Irish art-production came suddenly to an end. The latest of its products is the shrine of St. Manchan, dated the year 1166, three years before the Norman first set his foot on Irish shores.

Illumination.

Let us turn now to that later birth of art, the illuminated manuscripts, of which we have earlier examples in Christian art. These are judged to belong to a period extending from 460 to 1390;[*] but the earlier date is very uncertain, and the books approaching the later date are not to be compared with those of earlier centuries as works of art. Manuscripts are not so easy to date as metal-work, sculpture and architecture; but, by observing the version of Scripture used, the orthography, the style of writing, the nature of the vellum, and the kind of ink, very close approximation to accuracy may be made, and other tests occasionally present themselves. For example, the Book of Durrow, which for beauty

---

[*] For discussion of these dates, see "Early Christian Art in Ireland," chap. ii.

is only surpassed by the famous Book of Kells, is probably earlier than 718, because the Roman tonsure in the shape of a crown was then introduced, and the book has an illustration of a priest with the Irish tonsure across the top of the head from ear to ear, after the manner of St. Patrick. The Book of Kells is referred to an earlier date, between the years 650 and 690.

The art of illumination spread from Ireland to the Irish foundations of Iona, Melrose, and Lindisfarne. Thus, the style coming to be practised to some extent in England, Englishmen and others, in later times, fell into the error of calling it Anglo-Saxon. Its genesis in Ireland and progress through the Irish mission-stations can, however, be quite clearly traced. Nor was it to Britain only that the Irish art of illumination spread. Bound up as fine writing was with the life of the Irish monk, he carried his art with him wherever he went, and manuscripts illuminated in the Irish style are scattered throughout Europe in the tracks of his footsteps.* There are Irish manuscripts now in Italy, in the libraries of Milan, Turin, and Naples, all of which are said to have been brought from Bobbio, the monastery founded by St. Columbanus in the sixth century. We know, too, that the Irish missionary influence must have been strong at Reichenau, from the prevalence of the Irish style of writing in the manuscripts there.

The general character of the illuminated designs

* "Early Christian Art in Ireland," by Margaret Stokes, chap. iii.

is similar to that of those on the metal-work. The earliest forms are to be found on the pagan bronzes, and on the walls of the stone tumuli on the Boyne. These are decorated with spirals, zigzags, lozenges, circles, dots, and with a peculiar spiral form of double lines that diverge and twist again and again, and of which no traces, or scarcely any, can be found on the Continent. The uses to which the monastic scribes put this divergent spiral is extraordinary, and to it they added, with a skill and variety all their own, the interlacings and conventional forms found also in other countries though differently used.

Sculpture.

The main result of Irish sculpture is embodied in forty-five high crosses of the well-known characteristic shape—like a Greek cross with the arms projecting—which combines the Greek and the Latin forms. The Irish crosses are covered richly with fine sculpture, and it is noticeable that in the artistic treatment of the scriptural subjects sculptured on them, the same combination of Byzantine with Latin influences is shown as in their shape. These crosses date, speaking generally, from 914 to 1123.

The Christian stones of Ireland include, besides the high crosses, two hundred stones inscribed in ogam characters, two hundred and fifty tombstones, seven pillar-stones, and four altar-stones,* the greater

* "Early Christian Art in Ireland," p. 117, *et seq.*

number of the inscriptions being in Gaelic—not in Latin, as was customary elsewhere. About the tenth century the Irish cross becomes characteristic of the country, the old divergent spiral pattern reappears to decorate it, and the formula of inscription settles down to "*Oroit do*," that request to pray for the soul of the dead which, among early Christian inscriptions, is almost peculiar to Ireland.

In Scotland, Wales, and the Isle of Man, similar early Christian memorial stones are to be found ; and the ideas of ornamentation used in the sculpture of them are quite similar to those found in Ireland, belonging, it is clear, to a style which overspread the three countries in the ninth and tenth centuries. But in the use made of these ideas the difference between the Irish and British sculptured stones is great, a difference that lies mainly in the Irish artist's keener sense of fitness in abstinence from ornament as well as in its use The same ideas "attained," to quote Miss Stokes, "a more beautiful result in Ireland because in the hands of a people possessed of a fine artistic instinct."[*] Perhaps this fine artistic instinct is little more than a reverential attitude of mind towards the thing decorated, and to the idea of which therefore all its decorations should express subservience. Perhaps it is the same instinct that found another outlet in the production of book shrines rather than costly book bindings.

[*] "Early Christian Art in Ireland," p. 142.

Architecture.

The remains of early Irish architecture derive a special interest from the fact that they supply material for the continuous illustration of the development of the art in a way which is almost peculiar to the country. In Ireland, less than elsewhere, has the old been pulled down to build up the new; and we are, therefore, the better enabled to observe the Irish conservative instinct at work engrafting new ideas on old, till at last there was developed the style of architecture known as the Irish Romanesque. The history of that style was cut short in very early days, with its promise of nobler things all unfulfilled; but in one century it accomplished results of a very beautiful character, which may now be studied in Cormac's chapel on the Rock of Cashel, in parts of Killaloe and Tuam cathedrals, in the Abbey of Clonfert (1167), in Queen Dervorgila's church at Clonmacnoise (1167), and elsewhere. Two years only before the landing of Fitzstephen in Wexford, the two last of these churches were built, and they are almost the last examples of pure native Irish architecture that have been produced in Ireland.

The earliest stone buildings of Ireland are tombs or other monuments to the dead. Of these there are two kinds, the cromlech or dolmen, and the tumuli. The first of these show in Ireland signs of greater antiquity than the finest specimens of the latter, as in the entire absence of any attempt at sculptural decoration, however rude, while in the tumuli such decorations are plentiful. A cromlech consists of several large upright stones, with another large stone placed on the top of them like a roof; and sometimes it is surrounded by upright stones placed in a circle. The largest cromlechs of Ireland are in the east and north, and they decrease steadily in size from east to west; so that, whereas the average length of a roofing stone in Ulster is twenty-five feet, in Connaught it runs from eight to ten feet only.

A tumulus is a dome-shaped building, constructed without cement, and with a passage leading to the interior chamber. The most noticeable examples are to be found in the pagan royal cemeteries of New Grange, Dowth, Teltown, and Rathkenny; and it is on the walls and roofs of these that we find the earliest attempts at carving. In all the tumuli hitherto examined urns are to be found, indicating the custom of cremation, and the same remark applies to the chambered cairns or barrows of Scotland, whether round or long and horned; while in South Britain the barrows contain bones more commonly than ashes. If the ethnological argument in Chapter I. be correct, the royal cemeteries on the Boyne began to be built by that race which we have seen reason to identify with the Tuatha Dé Danann, and to associate vaguely with the Caledonian Picts—the large-limbed red-haired men described by Tacitus, and thought by him to be more like the Germans than were the Celts of Gaul. And Irish tradition bears this idea out; the Bruigh on the Boyne is sacred to the Tuatha Dé Danann, although it is there that the Milesian kings were laid to rest. It is interesting to note, in connection with the decoration of the walls and roofs of these great sepulchres, that superior knowledge of the arts is, by the Irish legend, ascribed to the mysterious Tuatha.

On the race that built the dolmens less light has as yet been shed. Twenty-three of these have been excavated, and while bones have been found in all, urns have been found in four only. They were not, therefore, built by the cremating tribes of Ireland and Scotland. There are no literary traditions about them, and all that the folk-lore of the people reveals is that in Ireland, as elsewhere, they are associated with the idea of giants' graves. Thus it appears that the race which built them has left no impression on the literature of the Gael. This is evidence, if it were necessary, that they cannot be regarded as strictly Gaelic monuments. The traditional Firbolg might have been their builder, and, if so, his identity with the dolmen-building people of Cornwall and Wales would become highly probable. But on this subject enough has been already said.

The dwelling-houses of the ancient Irish appear to have been mainly of two primitive kinds.* Either

* O'Curry's Lectures on "Manners and Customs."

they built for themselves quadrilateral houses of clay or of logs set on end close together, or they built cylindrical houses of wickerwork with a cup-shaped roof. The latter form appears to have been more generally used; and a homestead would consist of a group of such houses. The dwelling of a chief might be a considerable group, including the house for the women set apart and protected by a stake fence, and the grianan or sun-house, placed on a pleasant eminence to serve as a sort of Arcadian drawing-room. Lime appears to have been much used for whitening the walls of the houses, as it was also among the ancient Germans.

The smaller homesteads were generally surrounded by a fence or a bank with a quickset hedge; but the chief's dwelling would need a more effective protection, and it is in the construction of the protecting wall of earth or of stone that the character of the dwelling as a dun or a cathair consisted. A circular wall of earth, whether single, double, or treble, made the dwelling a rath, and a deep trench of water between the walls made it a dun, as defined in one of the law tracts. But the word "dun" is ordinarily used in a very general sense to include all kinds of fortified places. The city of Tara, for instance, is said to have consisted of seven duns, with a large group of houses inside each, besides the foradh or mound of Tara, round which the fair was held, and on which, no doubt, the Tocomrach of the High King met.

Cathairs and cashels were stone raths; and the building of cathairs—stone duns, as they are generally called in the west of Ireland—was the first step taken towards architecture proper unconnected with tombs. These stone forts are thought to belong to the last two hundred years before Christ, and they are found on the western shores of Kerry, Clare, Galway, and Sligo, with occasional examples in Mayo, Donegal, and Antrim. The most important are in Kerry, and in the islands of Arran off the coast of Galway. Twenty-four of these forts were examined by Lord Dunraven, and descriptions of these, with photographs, are given in his "Notes on Irish Architecture," edited by Miss Stokes. They are all large amphitheatres, encircled by outer walls, some of which are eighteen feet thick and twenty feet high. The walls are built without mortar, and with undressed stones, which are nevertheless fitted together with much skill and accuracy. The centre is of rubble, faced on either side by a thick stone structure; and chambers, as well as passages, occur in these walls, which are also marked by the existence of real doorways, very different from the gaps in the bank which do duty for doors in the British forts. Within the amphitheatre are sometimes found, clustered together, the remains of little circular and elongated huts—the first stone dwelling-houses in Ireland.

The word "cathair," Dr. Sullivan tells us, is

almost exclusively confined to the south and west of Ireland; and it is in the south-west also that these stone forts are at their best, while their extent is practically limited to the south and west coasts, with the single notable exception of Aileach, near Derry. The same observer also points out that in the south-west are found the greatest number of ogam inscriptions: there are none in Ulster, and only two in Leinster. Ogams cut on wood there may have been; for only the stone ogams would have been likely to be preserved.

The stone forts of Western Ireland are quite peculiar to it within these islands; and the fact is certainly a very significant one. They appear in that part of the country which is most accessible to Southern Europe, and open to influences, as well as immigrations, coming thence. That part is also the part to which tradition refers the landing of the Milesian immigrants from the south. The strong fort is a sign of conflict in the region where the strong fort is found, whether built by the invader as a help to secure his footing, or by the defender to prevent the same. The last supposition is not so likely in this case, as such huge structures could hardly have been thrown up by builders quite new to the work while the enemy was even upon them. It is impossible, therefore, to avoid suggesting the inference, uncertain though it be, that the cathairs were the work of the invading Milesians, or Scots, of tradition, and that their existence where they are is one more link in the chain of evidence corroborating the accuracy of that tradition. There is, indeed, a legend to the effect that the same forts, especially those on the Arran Isles, were built as a last defence by subject tribes who, hunted out of Britain, failed to find an asylum in Ireland, and were driven finally to this uttermost western coast. But it seems impossible to overcome the inherent improbability of this explanation; for why should not a race with such exceptional architectural skill have entrenched themselves similarly amid the mountain heights and passes of North Wales, where there is certainly no dearth of stone for building?

From the cathair we come to the cashel, a similar circular wall within which the early monks built their beehive cells or clochans, their little oratories, and, later, their belfry towers. Cashels, with their primitive belongings, are to be found in all parts of the country, reaching back to the sixth and seventh centuries. The picturesque situations in which many of these are to be found, especially in the islands on the west coast, reflects upon them a singular beauty, and an interest somewhat more than that of archæological inquiry. The most remarkable perhaps is the monastery on St. Michael's Rock, twelve miles off the coast of Kerry, in the stormy Atlantic ocean, where the monastic wall runs along a great precipice overlooking the sea.

We have already considered the practical motive which led to the almost universal addition of a round tower to the monastic group of buildings. The idea of the round tower, and of church towers in general, can be shown very clearly to have originated in Syria; and recent investigators have been able to trace the type, from its entrance into the Western world at Ravenna, across Europe to Ireland.* The Irish Celt, with his preference for round forms, and under the impulse communicated by the Danish attacks,† made much of the cylindrical tower, and preserved more carefully than other peoples his buildings generally. And so it is not surprising that we should find one hundred and eighteen of these towers now in Ireland, while only twenty-two examples can be found abroad. The Irish towers are, moreover, peculiar in this respect, that they are not attached to the churches, but stand alone; and there can be no doubt that they owe much of their solemn picturesque effect to this circumstance. In fact, they began to be built before churches large enough to bear them came into existence. And, indeed, the preference for small churches persisted long in the country, having behind it the support of a tradition referred to St. Patrick.

The towers are assigned by competent judges to

---

* Dunraven's "Notes on Irish Architecture," vol. ii. p. 180, *et seq.*, and Stokes's "Early Christian Art in Ireland," p. 176.

† See Map at end of Dunraven's "Notes, etc."

three periods (1) from 890 to 927; (2) from 973 to 1013; and (3) from 1170 to 1238. It is hardly necessary to point out that the first two were periods of cessation in the struggle with the Danes. The three types of towers belonging to these periods mark distinctly three stages in the progress of architecture from the primitive form of the entablature, shown in the horizontal lines of the doorways and windows, to that of the decorated Romanesque arch. In the later towers the beauty and number of the arched windows increase, and the signs are manifest of an approaching development from the solemn monotony of strong grey walls, suitable to the monastic keep of troubled times, into the storied variety of a fine church tower standing in a land of peace. That promised future of the round tower is still unfulfilled; but, with the recent spread in Ireland of knowledge about things Irish, and enthusiasm for them, it may not now be long delayed, and once more the Irish cylindrical bell-house may rise, majestic and apart, as in the olden times, but with all the added beauty of which its form is susceptible, while free from that vice of excessive decoration of which Irish art was never guilty.

The earliest Irish churches were the little oratories built without cement and with rounded roof, which are still found standing, with the beehive cells, within the monastic cashel. Churches, as distinguished from oratories, stand alone; but the first churches are of the very simplest kind—mere barns, with no distinction of nave and chancel, and no attempt, however rudimentary, to construct an arch. Presently, however, decoration begins, while still all the doorways are horizontal. The artist bethinks him to repeat in stone the designs of the illuminated manuscripts and the early metal-work. Then comes the addition of the chancel and the chancel arch; and the arch, once found, takes gradually more and more hold of the artistic consciousness, till arched doorways and windows become the rule. Nevertheless, the idea of horizontal extension still holds its own with a truly Irish vitality. We see it in the long level entablature uniting the tops of the columns, in place of the separate capitals which belong to the Romanesque style elsewhere.

This horizontal entablature is the most characteristic detail of the Irish Romanesque style, which is in general marked by blending in a thoroughly artistic harmony the two great architectural styles of the entablature and the arch. The development from simple entablature to the mixed type is well seen in the doorways of Maghera and Banagher, in Londonderry. As presenting examples of decorated pure entablature these doorways are almost unique. The native character of their ornamentation and its rich delicacy mark, indeed, the second characteristic of church architecture in the Irish style.

Another important point remains to be noticed.

The high, steep roof of such buildings as Cormac's chapel at Cashel, and others of the twelfth century, can hardly escape the eye of the most ordinary observer. These roofs are of stone, and so steep as to include an angle of about sixty-five degrees only. This result is obtained by the invention on the part of Irish architects of a double vault, the lower arch being circular, like a barrel, and the other pointed, as seen from the inside. The pointed arch is then roofed over with flat stones in the shape of a double inclined plane, the spaces between the arch and the plane being filled up by rubble. The desirability of the steep stone roof may have been suggested by climate; but, however that may be, it gives to the churches one characteristic of their appearance, and, while its construction was an invention which may yet have a future as well as a past in the way of roofs,* it implied a use of the pointed arch which would, in the natural course of things, soon have found its way into the body of later Irish churches.

The church of St. Caimin at Iniscaltra, erected in 1016, two years after the battle of Clontarf, marks the transition from the horizontal to the enriched round-arch style of Ireland. This was fifty years before Romanesque appeared in England, on the building of Westminster Abbey by Edward the Confessor, in 1066. From that date there was no halt in the progress of architecture till the end of the next century,

---

* The question is, how far it could have been used for larger buildings.

and a considerable number of churches were erected. The finest examples belong naturally to the twelfth century. Such are the tomb of Murlough O'Brien in Killaloe cathedral, the present chancel arch and east window of the cathedral at Tuam (1128–1150)— the interlaced patterns on the mouldings of which are very fine—the doorway and east window in the abbey at Clonfert (1167), the nun's church at Clonmacnoise (1167), and Cormac's chapel on the Rock of Cashel (1127).*

But, while churches abound, castles are nonexistent. That fact may have been significant in the twelfth century, both as expressing the Irish past and as a sign of the near future. Warlike as the old Irish were, they had as little idea of entrenching themselves behind strong walls as they had of covering their bodies with armour. Nevertheless, they had been successful in their struggle with the mailed Norsemen, and had won peace for their Scottish neighbours, as well as themselves, by that success. Now, however, they were to encounter another less terrible-seeming but much more dangerous enemy. The Norman was not only a mailed and fort-building foe; he was a foe that had made everything else in his social organization subservient to his urgent desire to win lands and to rule over others by the sword. To do this had been his work in history, and he had

* See "Early Christian Art in Ireland," M. Stokes, chap. vi., for excellent accounts of all these.

learned to do it well. Capable nations, or persons, always learn to do well that which their souls are most bent on doing. The Norseman tried his "prentice hand" on Ireland in the days of Danish struggle; but with all his military genius—and it was far from contemptible—and with all his true Norse worship for the naked sword, he was driven out once, and settled eventually as a colony subject to the Irish king. When the Norseman came again as Norman, he was educated in the art of conquest as well as in the art of war. He had conquered two countries before he took this one in hand. Yet in three centuries he failed to conquer it, while it failed also to drive him out or subjugate him. The suzerainty of England—in itself a harmless thing—was used amiss, merely for the benefit of fresh immigrants, whose sympathies were naturally supposed to be keenest for the English government; and so the true government of the country was disordered more and more, the people's peace of mind gone, development arrested at every point. No words could describe that arrest of development so eloquently or so lucidly as the facts of Irish art-history. "Since then," says Miss Stokes, "the native character of Ireland has best found expression in her music. No work of purely Celtic art, whether in illumination of the sacred writings, or in gold, or bronze, or stone was wrought by Irish hands after that century."

Music.

Music survived. The habits of musical expression were so wrought in upon the popular mind by the practice of the art from times beyond the reach of the historian's longest vision, and so bound up with the poetry in which the popular traditions were enshrined, and music is so easily and naturally preserved by a people as far advanced in musical appreciation as the Irish must have been, that no matter of surprise can be found in the undoubted fact that very old Irish music has been preserved to our own times, and is now written down and thus made safe, though not all generally accessible. Nevertheless, it would hardly be correct to say that music had survived in the sense of continuing to develop towards its natural future. As with other arts, so with this art, it is more than probable that a future was dawning for it seven centuries ago, which was then postponed, and is still in a sense before it. There can, however, be no doubt that the seven centuries were by no means barren of true native production in music as they were barren in other arts; and so the Irish have always been classed with their kindred, the Welsh and the Scotch, as a nation with unmistakable popular genius in music. A lyrical genius it was, however, as fitted the circumstances of the seven centuries; and for strictly lyrical work in music and poetry it must be admitted that the character of those centuries was not altogether unfavourable. It has not been favourable to work on a larger scale; and so the production of great Irish opera and cantata belongs to the future of that Irish Renaissance when the ancient epics will be sung once more by Irish poets, while the minstrels of Ireland will live again in her modern composers to weave round the epics a more complex structure of music—a structure that shall be Irish as well as modern.

The Irish annals and stories show that several musical instruments were used in old times; but of all these the harp is by far the most important. It was customary for the bards to recite their poems to the accompaniment of the harp, and this custom continued down to the eighteenth century. The race of the popular Irish harpers is now extinct; but Mr. Bunting, in his work on the "Ancient Music of Ireland," written in 1840, describes a great meeting of harpers at Belfast in 1792, the performance at which was conducted according to the traditional rules of Irish harp-playing, the music being played with rapidity, spirit, and liveliness, quite different from the slow manner which many persons imagine suitable to the Irish airs. It is interesting to notice the agreement of these facts with the observation of Cambrensis at the time of the Norman invasion. The slanders of Cambrensis, looking through his hostile spectacles, on the Irish people, are proverbial, and can now be read very conveniently in Strongbow's "Conquest of Ireland," in the series of "English History from Contemporary Writers." Once, and once only, he finds something pleasant to say. "It is only in instrumental music that I find any commendable diligence in this nation; but in that art they incomparably excel every other nation that I have met. For their execution is not, like that which we hear in Britain, slow and laboured, but adroit and sprightly; while their tone is full, and the refrain of their melodies sweet and gay." And in another place he tells us something of their manner. "They enter into a movement so sportively, and conclude it in so delicate a manner, and play the little notes so sportively under the blunter sounds of the bass strings, enlivening with wanton levity, or communicating a deeper internal sensation of pleasure, so that the perfection of their art appears in the concealment of it."

This reference to the bass and the little notes makes it clear that the old Irish made some use of the principles of harmony; and there is good reason also to think that singing in parts was practised in some of the Irish monasteries. St. Jerome refers to the choral service of the Scots at Bangor, county Down, in the seventh century, and both Bede and Cambrensis refer to part singing in one of the Northumbrian monasteries which was connected with Bangor. There is some indication, too, of part-singing in Iona; and, as another piece of evidence, a reference occurs in the Book of Leccan to the "harmony of strings," which, if the word is used accurately, would certainly show that some use of polyphonal music was made at the time to which the reference occurs. Moreover, the Irish "burdoon," or refrain at the end of each verse of a song, was almost certainly sung in harmony.

Nevertheless, it would be absurd to claim for old Irish musicians either knowledge or practice of the principles of harmony proper. The real development of harmonious music belongs to the fifteenth and sixteenth centuries; and these were centuries of darkness in Ireland, centuries in which the conditions necessary for the growth of harmonious music were absolutely non-existent. Moreover, the characteristics of Irish music were such as to favour highly melodic combinations, while they placed difficulties in the way of choral composition. This will become more evident presently.

Down to the end of the eighteenth century a complete native musical vocabulary was in use. This is given by Mr. Bunting, and is of much interest from the picturesqueness of the terms. For instance, the names of the first, second, and fifth of the scale as applied to the harp-strings, are "sisters"—two strings lying together for the first—"servant to the sisters," and "the string of the leading sirens," or "string of melody," while all the octaves upwards and downwards are called by two Irish names which he translates as "answering" and "response" respectively. All the other strings have names of a similar kind. Then again, for the rates of execution indicated by the Italian words *adagio, larghetto, andante, allegro*, we have the beautiful and very racy Irish equivalents, " dirge time," " lamentation time," " heroic time," " lesson time," while a quicker pace is indicated as " trebly rapid," or jig time.

On the characteristics of old Irish musical composition a few words must suffice. There can be no doubt that one characteristic lies in the fact that many Irish airs of decided antiquity are composed in a key of five notes only, the fourth and seventh of the diatonic scale being omitted. One has only to play or sing this quinquegrade scale to be reminded forcibly, though vaguely, of Irish and Scotch music. The antiquity of Irish ideas, and their persistence— though not to the exclusion of new ones—is well illustrated by this characteristic use of a scale which is as antique and natural as it seems to us curious and quaint. The first musical scale was, no doubt, the tetrachord 1 3 5 8, knowledge of which appears to have been at an early time universal. It is easy to see how the second note of the common scale would be discovered from this; for the fifth of the fifth gives the octave of the second. Again, the fifth of the second gives similarly the sixth. Thus the quinquegrade scale emerges 1 2 3 5 6 8, the conception of which may be readily formed by playing a scale on the piano with omission of the fourth and seventh. This was almost certainly the first musical scale for all ancient Asiatic and European peoples, and it is still to be found in China and elsewhere.

The old diatonic scale was completed by the discovery of the fourth as the fifth below, and of the seventh as the fifth of the third. The whole can be exhibited as a series of fifths thus—

$$\overset{.}{4} \quad 1 \quad 5 \quad \overset{.}{2} \quad \overset{.}{6} \quad \overset{.}{3} \quad \overset{..}{7},$$

the dot below the number indicating the lower, and dots above, the higher octaves. The complete scale, obtained in this way, was that used for the church music of the Middle Ages; and it differs from the modern diatonic scale, to which the great composers of the fifteenth and sixteenth centuries bound all future music, in the exact values of the third, fourth, and sixth notes of the scale. In the old scale the value of the notes are as follows :—

$$1, \tfrac{9}{8}, \tfrac{81}{64}, \tfrac{4}{3}, \tfrac{3}{2}, \tfrac{27}{16}, \tfrac{243}{128}, 2,$$

while in the modern scale they run thus—

$$1, \tfrac{9}{8}, \tfrac{5}{4}, \tfrac{4}{3}, \tfrac{3}{2}, \tfrac{5}{3}, \tfrac{15}{8}, 2,$$

and the scale cannot be exhibited as a chain of fifths. The true antique quinquegrade scale is exactly the same as the old scale with the fourth and seventh left out, and differs, therefore, from its reproduction on a modern piano in this respect, that its third and sixth are both slightly sharpened.

The old diatonic scale was inevitably introduced into Ireland with the church music of the monasteries, and was not without its effects on the secular music outside. So, while the genuine old Irish and Scotch airs are in the quinquegrade scale, later music had no reason to be without the additional notes of the septigrade scale. But by that time Irish music had acquired a character, and Irish taste a habit, which affected all later production and made it seem racy of the soil.

Irish music, and the old church music, whether naturalized in Ireland or not, had this common characteristic, that any note in the scale might in its turn be used as a tonic. Thus, instead of being limited, like the modern musician, to the simple alternative of the major and minor keys, these old musicians had the choice of five different keys in the one case, and seven in the other, according to the note which they chose as tonic. The variety of the church scales had given rise to much confusion when the great composers reformed the diatonic scale, and settled the lines of development by their splendid work. But something may have been lost for the future in the reform, greatly as it simplified the problem of musical composition in harmony.

Irish airs are written in all the five Irish keys, and those in the key of G with a flat seventh introduced are common. The flat seventh, indeed, occurs in four out of the five Irish keys, while, with characteristic conservatism, the introduction of the additional note is not allowed to involve departure from composition in the antique scale which had wrought itself into the Irish musical taste.

The Highland Scotch music differs in no respect from the Irish. This we should expect; but it is, perhaps, a little surprising to find that Lowland Scotch music is Gaelic too, though much more modernized in its present form than either of the other two Gaelic branches. That Welsh music was much influenced by Irish music at one period there is no doubt, but as we have it now the music of Wales is evidently, from its structure, a good deal more modern than that of the western island.

In the Irish manuscripts the harp is referred to under the name of "crut," and it is likely that in early times the instrument had few strings, and was similar in this respect to the primitive harps of which we find traces in the history of so many other countries. The first picture of a true harp of the modern type occurs in a St. Blain manuscript of the ninth century, as a "Cithara Anglica," and this is one indication among several that the modern harp had its origin in the British Isles. Thus we hear that in the twelfth century British harps were said to be much superior to French. Between the eighth and the fourteenth centuries, Irish crut-players wandered over Europe after the Irish manner; and, on Dante's authority, Vincenzo Galilei[*] says that the harp—the modern harp, no doubt, he means—was introduced into

---

[*] "Discorso della Musica antica et moderna." Fiorenze, 1581.

Italy from Ireland. From this and similar evidence, it appears that the genesis of the true harp may be associated with the British Isles, and especially with Ireland, in which country, it is quite evident from the general musical history of the two countries, it had the best chance of being invented. A picture of the Irish harp occurs on a reliquary made about 1370, with thirty strings, and this appears to have been the typical number at that time.

The last fair of Carman was held in the year 718, and a poem descriptive of it dates from the twelfth century. In this, there is a list of the musical instruments used at the fair, among which we find the "fidel" mentioned. This was, no doubt, the same as the mediæval "vièle" on the Continent, the bowed instrument which was the progenitor of the modern fiddle or violin. The fiddle, like the bagpipe, which is also enumerated among the instruments at the fair, appears to have been in use chiefly among the peasantry, and neither are admitted to any such place in the literature as is accorded to the royal and aristocratic harp.

It is certain, however, that in later times the Irish bagpipe, which was identical with that now used in Scotland, was a very noted and favourite instrument, and chiefly relied on for military purposes till the time of the treaty of Limerick. In the sixteenth century, the Italian Galilei, in writing of the bagpipe, says, "It is much used by the Irish;

to its sound this unconquered, fierce, and warlike people march their armies and encourage each other to deeds of valour. With it also they accompany their dead to the grave, making such mournful sounds as invite, nay almost force, the bystanders to weep."

Irish music survived the twelfth century in Ireland, and, if this had not been the case, it had at any rate a direct descendant in Scotland, and found a second home in Wales, where a kindred race with kindred ideas, tastes, and customs, was at this very time disposed to look to Ireland for advice and assistance. So, in 1180, through the agency of Griffith ap Conan, the Welsh Eisteddfod was revived in the presence, at least, of Irish influences, and the Welsh musical canon was regulated by Irish harpers.* The Welsh vocabulary of musical terms is manifestly connected with the Irish, and some of it is Irish, thus marking the close approximation of the two peoples musically at this time of Welsh national revival. From the time of Griffith ap Conan, the Welsh Eisteddfodic institution never died out, and its steady persistence expresses a resolve of which Welshmen may well be proud that the national life should not die in those inner movements which are of its very essence, whatever the political fortunes of the nation might be. And so to-day popular musical education—so popular that children catch the taste and faculty for song like an infection—is a living reality in Wales as it is

* Sullivan's Introduction, p. 625.

nowhere else in these two islands. Ireland, ere long, perhaps, will relight her popular torch of music at the altar where she helped to rekindle a dying blaze, and, taking up the line of a popular musical culture at the point to which Wales has brought it, make every Irish town and hamlet ring with the music of an educated choir.

Nor is such a revival and development of the popular taste for song the most that may be hoped. The song itself, with all its characteristic marks of melody and rhythm, is not lost. It remains for the musical genius of Irishmen to study, to feel, and to reproduce it, with all the developments of which it is capable and which the general progress of the art has made possible. In music, as in poetry and the other arts, an Irish Renaissance is at hand, a time when the living thought of Irish artists, instinct with all the knowledge-gain that is humanity's common heritage from the past, will infuse new powers of life, growth, and development into those old forms of expression and ideas of beauty which are the national heritage of every Irishman.

INDEX.

A

Aenach, or fair, 168
—— of Tara, 170
Aicill, Book of, 79, 139, 141
Aileach, 193
Airechts, or Courts of Justice, 159, etc.
Aires, or nobles, 142
—— Echtai, 158
——, Elective, 154
—— Fine, 167
—— Forgaill, Tuisi, Ard, Cosraing, 157
Architecture, 188
——, Irish Romanesque, 197–199
Ardagh, Chalice of, 181, 182
Ard Macha, *i.e.* Armagh, foundation of royal seat, 31
—— Primacy, 117, 129, 130
—— See founded by Patrick, 113
Argyle, 43
Army, Cormac's national, 71, 73
——, its failure, 76, etc.
Arran, Stone forts in, 192, 194
Art, Character of Irish design in, 183, 186
Art, Effect of Norman invasion on Irish, 180, 199
Artisans, position in tribe, 153
Artistic instinct, Irish, 179, 180, 187
Assembly, Hills of, 70, 122
——, Edmund Spenser's description, 71
——, Tribal, origin of Parliaments and Courts of Justice, 133
——, Various kinds of, 164, etc.
Attecotti, 3, 33

B

Bagpipe, 209
Banshee, 100, 101
Bardic competition, 84
—— preparation of the Irish for Christianity, xii., xiii., 104, 113
Bards, Influence of, xiii., 77
—— in danger, 122
——, Migratory habits of, 81
——, Poets' "Pot of Avarice," 82
——, qualifications of, xi., 84
——, Satire of, 83
——, Tutorial habits of, 82
——, Two classes of, xiii., 81

Barristers, 81, 160
Barrows, Long, of Stone Age, 3
——, Round, of Bronze Age, 4
Belgae, 5
Bo-aire, *i.e.* cow-nobleman, 142
Book of Durrow, 184
—— of Kells, 185
Bothachs, 146
Boyne, Brugh on the, 6, 80, 100, 189
Brehon, Moral influence of the, 77, 78
——, Antiquity of the, 81
—— law. *See* Land, Fosterage, Tenants, Women, etc.
——, revision by Cormac Mac Art, 69
Brian Boru, 125, 128
Brigit, St., 86
—— of the Judgments, 87
Britain, Irish attack on Roman, 34, 35
——, Irish settlements in West, 35, etc.
——, Tribute paid to Irish kings in South-West, 38, 39
Bronze Age men, 4, 17
Bruigh, the borough, village, guild, 154, 155
——, Germs of local government in, 165
Bruighfer, the borough magistrate, 154
——, election of king in his house, 141, 155
——, probable convener of the Tocomrach, 167
——, relation to directly representative system, 155
Bruigh rechta, bye-laws of the borough, 154, 155

C

Cairbré Cinn Cait, 33
Caledonians, 5, 13, 19, 190
Carman, 168
——, Last fair of, 209
Cashel, 194
Cathair, 191, 192
Ceilé. *See* Tenant
Cemeteries, Royal, 6, 97, 189
Chalice of Ardagh, 181, 182
—— of Kremmünster, 182
Christianity, Irish *v.* Roman, 48, 54, 64
——, Decadence of Roman, from fourth century, 60
——, Irish, in Europe, 60, etc.
——, Roman Church organization prevails, and Irish influence abroad declines, 64, 66, 67
Church, Tribal organization of Irish, 115
——, advantages of this, 116
——, centralization and union with Rome of Irish, in the twelfth century, 117-119, 129-131
Circles of stone, 6
Classes, System of, 141
Clochan, 194
Compurgators, 161
Connor Mac Nessa, 73
Contracts, King's power of making, 142-143
—— of strangers with manorial lords, 148
Cormac Mac Art, 35, 68, etc.
Coronation stone, 47, 53
Council of the Alehouse, 167
Courts of law. *See* Airecht
Cremation, 2, 188
Crimes. *See* Torts

INDEX. 215

Crimes, Responsibility of family for member's, 140, 160
——, Responsibility of tutor for pupil's, 173
Cromlech. *See* Dolmens
Crosses, Irish stone, 186, 187
Cruithuigh, or Picts, in Ireland, 11

D

Dae, a family policeman, 158
Dal, tribal assembly dealing with finance, 165
Dalaradia and Dalriada, 43
Danes, Pagan crusade of, 58, 125, etc.
——, Confederation of, overthrown at Clontarf, 128
Danish attacks on churches, 181
—— cities in Ireland, and parliaments, 127
—— Church, 129-130
——, First, bishop, 128
—— kingdom of Dublin, 126
Davies, Sir J., on law-abiding character of Irish, 78
Dolmens, 188-189
——, Distribution of, 6
——, Ethnology of their builders, 8
Downpatrick, 127
Druid, 83, 133
Duns, or forts, 191
——, Stone, 28, 192, 193

E

Education, Laws regulating. *See* Fosterage
——, Natural growth of system of, 174-175
——, Physical, 76

Elective kings, 141, 155-156
—— nobles, 153
Eric of king and aires, 142
Erigena Joannes, 57
Ethnic traditions, Irish, 16
Executive government, 156-158

F

Fair. *See* Aenach
Fairies, 100-102
Family ("Fine"), Structure of Irish, 136, etc.
—— assembly, or Mathluagh, 164
——, Foster, 171
——, Industrial, 154
——, Religious, 114
Fasting on a creditor, 163
Feast (Feis) of Tara, 31, 70, 170
Feni of Erin, 73, 79
Fergus Mac Erc, 43
Feudalism and tribalism, 144, 150-152
"Fidel," *i.e.* "fiddle," at fair of Carman, 209
Fuidirs, 146, 148
—— and modern Irish tenants, 149
"Fine." *See* Family
Finn Mac Cumhal, 73, 75
Firbolgs, 16, 19, 20, 24, 25, 190
Flaths, or Lords, 154, 155
Fodhla Ollamh, 69
Fomorians possibly pure Ugrian, 18
Forts. *See* Duns

G

Gaelic language in Aquitaine, 28
—— —— and Picts, 11, 12
—— physical type, xiv., 13, 21

Gavelkind, 134
Geilfine, 136-139
Germanus of Auxerre in Wales, 40, 41
―― and Patrick's mission, 108
Gods and goddesses, Irish, 31, 98, 99
Gossipred, 171
Greek in Irish monasteries, 56
Guilds, Origin of, 153
Gwyddel and Gwyddel Ffichti, 10

H

Hallelujah Victory, 40
Harmony, Limited knowledge of, in Ireland, 203
Harp, Probable origin of modern, 208, 209
Historian, Duties of Irish, xi., 81, 160
History, Materials of Irish, x., etc.
Honour-price of king and aires, 142
Houses of ancient Irish, 190, 191

I

Iberian stock, 13, 19, 20
Ideals, Irish, of heroism, xiii.
Idols, 104
Iona, 44, 47
Illuminated MSS., Dates of, 184
Illumination, Irish art of, 184
――, abroad, 185

J

Judges. *See* Brehon
Judicial system. *See* Airecht
Jury, Germs of trial by, 162

K

Kenneth Mac Alpine, 45-47
Kimbay Mac Fiontann, 30
Kindred, Solidarity of, 168
――, Artificial group of, 154
――, Foster, and nationality, 98, 149
――, Idea of foster, and religion of nature, 101-103
King, Election of, 141, 155, 156
――, High, of Erin, 31, 32, 156
――, Limited privileges of, 142, 143, 151
Kremmünster, Chalice of, 182

L

Land, Tribal tenure of, 133, 134
――, English law applied to Irish, 136, 148
――, Fixity of family tenure of, how secured, 139, 140
――, Law of succession in, 134
――, Private ownership in, 135
Landlordism, Origin of genuine, 146-148
Laoghaire, 110
Law, Criminal. *See* Torts
――, Civil, 162, 163
――, Common, a common inheritance in Britain and Ireland, 162
Learning, Ireland mission home of, in dark ages, 61, 65
――, Mission centres become homes of, 119, 120
Legislatures, Source of, 133, 163
――, Irish. *See* Tocomrach
Libraries containing Irish MSS., xv., xvi., 185

Lindisfarne, 48
Literature, when written, xv.

M

Mac Erc, 97
Magistrates, 80, 155, 159
Malachy O'Morgair, 130
Manuscripts. *See* Libraries
Mathluagh, 164, 167
Metal-work in Petrie Museum, 179
———, how dated, 181
Milesians from the South, 27, 193
———, Four families of, 31
———, Physical type of, 21, 23
Missions, Irish, to Picts, 44
———, to English, 48
———, to Germany, 63
———, to Northern Isles, 55
———, to Western Europe, 55, 61, etc.
Mithal Flatha, 164
——— Tuātha, 164
Monasteries, Irish, abroad, 44, 47, 48, 62
———, at home. *See* Schools
Music, Irish, 201
———, Cambrensis on, 203
———, Scotch and Irish, 208
———, Welsh and Irish, 208, 210
Musical scales, 205-207

N

Naas, 112
National Irish assembly, 69
——— unity, bardic, 77
Nemidh, Story of the children of, 25
Niall of the Nine Hostages, 35, 39

Normans and the four nations, 49
——— and Irish development, 177-178, 199-200

O

Ogams, Stone, in south-west, 193
Oratories, 196

P

Paganism, Irish, 90
——— gods as Tuatha or Sidhe, 99-102
———, fairy fosterage, modern form, 103
———, four great pagan festivals, 91, 92
———, homage to ancestral dead, 93, 97
———, homage to national heroes, 98
———, sun and fire worship, 95
——— two great religious ideas, 96

R

Races, Tradition of three Celtic, in Ireland, 16
———, Celtic, fair, 19
———, Mac Firbis's three types, 23
———, mixed types, 5, 20
———, two modern types contrasted, 21
Rath, 190
Red Branch of Emania, 73
Rent, Origin of, 143
———, "fair rent" and "rack rent" distinguished in laws, 148
———, Judicial, 144
Round towers, 181, 195-196

S

Sabaid Cuirimtigi, 167
Saints, Irish: Finnian of Clonard, 42, 119
——, Brigit, 86
——, Columba, 45, 47, 120
——, Columbanus, 54, 61, 124, etc.
——, Cummian of Durrow, 118
——, Finnian of Moville, 121
——, Gallus, 62, 123
—— Kilian, 63
Saul, 109, 113
Schools, Monastic, in Ireland: Clonard, 42, 119, 120
——, Armagh Lismore, 59
——, Bangor, 57, 124
——, British students in these, 59, 65
——, Clonmacmoise, Mayo, Clonfert, Glasnevin, Lough Erne, 120
——, Cormac Mac Art's three, of Law, Literature, War, 79
——, Hedge, 175
——, Moville, 124
——, Secular, instituted, 122
Scotland, Early connection of, with Ireland, 43, etc.
——, Kingdom of, develops, 46
Sculpture, 186
Senchus Mor on fosterage, 172
Sencleith, 146
Sept, Formation of, 138
——, Religious, 114, 115
Shrines, 179
—— Earliest, in existence, 183
——, early examples probably destroyed by Danes, 180, 181
Sidhe, 17
——, Irish worshipped the, 99, 100
Silures, 3, 13, 40

Sizars, Ancient, 174
Skene on Picts, 12
Spain, Migrations from, to British Isles, 7
Stock, Irish custom of taking, 143, 144
Strangers absorbed into tribe, 149, 150

T

Tailltè, 98
Tanistry, 140, 141
Tara, the capital, 31
—— brooch, 179
——, City of, 191
——, Decline of, 71, 155
Taxation (power of purse), 166
Tenants, Saer and daer stock, 144, 145
——, Manorial, of various grades, 146-148
——, Law of lord and, 144, 145, 148
——, Modern Irish, 149
Tocomrach, 166, 167, 190
Torts, Law of, 160, etc.
——, Chief Baron Gilbert on, 161
——, Refinements of Irish, 162
Tribalism and feudalism, 145, 150-152
Tribe and land, 133
——, Classes outside, 145, etc.
Tribesmen, common, 143, 148
Tuatha Dè Danann, 16
—— and cemetery on the Boyne, 190
——, connection with Caledonians, 20
——, connection with North, 17, 19
——, Double character of, 17, 99
Tumuli, 4, 189

U

Ugrian races, 5, 18
Ulster, Early military organization in, 30, 73
Usnagh, Synod of, 130

V

Vièle (modern violin), 209

W

Wales and Ireland, 35, 210, 211

Welsh music, 208, 210
—— Eisteddfod, 170, 210
—— Gorsedd, 84
—— saints and scholars, 42
Whitby, Council at, 48
Witness and bail of kings and aires, 142
—— of lords for fuidir tenant, 148
—— of tenants, 145
Women in battle, 72, 85, 86, 122
——, German, 85
——, Laws affecting marriage of, 88
——, Laws affecting property of, 87
——, Law-writer's ideal of, 90
——, Learned Irish, 86

THE END.

there were four, if we count the several varieties of the man of law as constituting one class. The ancient Irishman had all the modern appliances of legal advice when he went to law, besides judges of several grades, from the ollamh or chief judge attached to the king's court down to the common judges in the inferior courts; nor was Irish society quite without magistrates of more kinds than one. He had his attorney, moreover, as also had the Welsh, who called him the "guider," and the Irish barrister was called "the burnisher," who brightened up his client's case. These varieties may however have been of later development than the third century. But the Brehon is probably as old as Miledh himself, or older.

The literary class had two branches—the poet who represented more particularly the ancient bard, and the historian whose was the practical duty of acting as a book of reference on all points of genealogy and of territorial rights as constituted by contract. In the inter-territorial courts, for example, the historian sat on the judicial bench. He, like the brehon, indeed, was a professional person with definite duties attached to the court, and had not the wide-spreading influence of his wandering poetic brother.

For the poets wandered a good deal. They knew every inch of Irish ground, and attached all their stories to definite localities with the utmost precision. Every event in bardic literature happens in a real space, and thus the bards have covered the whole of

the land with a living mantle of Irish romance.* The
bard tells his tale, as the general plans his battle, with
the place of it visibly before his mind. The wanderings of the poets had other uses : it brought them into
communication with one another, and, as they always
had an historical intention in their story-telling, this
contact with other minds was clearly important. To
them the national and provincial parliaments were of
great consequence. On such occasions they met one
another, and they also got good audiences for their
recitations.

When a poet travelled he took a band of pupils
with him, teaching them whenever he found it convenient,—sometimes indoors, but oftener in the open
air. His rank as poet entitled him to be received
with a certain number of his company at a respectable
house, and when his company was too numerous the
neighbours were glad to entertain the excess. The
chief poet was generally accompanied by assistants of
various degrees, who had not yet attained the highest
rank.

In this aspect the poet appears as a schoolmaster,
occasionally travelling with his pupils from place to
place. But he had a well-understood duty to the
community which supported him and showed him
honour. He and his fellows entertained their hosts
with music, song and recitation. In wealthy houses

---

* See Standish O'Grady's "Early Bardic Literature, Ireland," p. 3.
et seq.

it was the custom to give the bard some handsome reward for his special services on such occasions, generally a reward which he named himself. It is said, indeed, that the poets were sometimes avaricious, and once or twice, when they became very numerous and exacting, the popular feeling rose against them. Thus we hear that the vessel in which they collected their fees was called the " Poets' Pot of Avarice," and once a bard went so far as to demand from the high king of Erin, in reward for his recitation, the golden brooch of Tara, an event which might have led to the suppression of the bardic order had it not been for the intervention of St. Columba. The avarice of the poet was the more objectionable because a refusal to satisfy it was followed, or might be, by the poet's satire. This the sensitive Irishman greatly dreaded: it seemed to his imagination that the terrible satire must bring evil to pass by the mere effective utterance of the idea of such evil. The poet's satire was, indeed, a sort of literary curse into which the poet threw all his force of language and his dramatic instinct.

Like other academic classes, the bards of Ireland had, no doubt, their faults, begotten of privilege and the pride of intellect ; but they were, nevertheless, in all probability, the truest benefactors that Ireland ever had. Under their influence was developed in the Irish people that vivid imagination, dramatic taste, and literary capacity which distinguishes the

Irish peasant of our own time, and of the inborn tendency to which the Irish bards are themselves the result.

Side by side, and often identified with the literary classes, was the Druid, "the man of *science*" as the stories often call him. He it was who aspired to know and have power over Nature,—the would-be man of science, as we might truly call him, for his object was exactly the same, and his logical methods not quite different from those of scientific men in all ages. He aimed at ruling Nature for the service of men, and he experimented on Nature with his magical arts. The difference is that he did not criticise his ideas, . nor did the people who reverenced him for his power to work good or ill. So he conjured contentedly with his "druidical wand," and "druidical mists" or "druidical storms" arose ; or, if they did not, the explanation of another druid in opposition, or the wrath of the Tuatha Dé Danann, the gods of the country—these were manifestly satisfactory explanations.

It is probable that admission to the professions was, from an early period, consequent on the attainment of a recognized quantity of learning and perhaps some original composition; but whether the graduation of a candidate was dependent on election by several poets, or was by the decree of his teacher only, we do not know. Probably both methods had their time. It is certain, however, that for important posts, such as that of chief poet in a king's court, the candidates displayed their knowledge and skill in a competitive contest, and the most successful was chosen by general consent. The idea of a bardic degree and the bardic competition is still preserved, though somewhat faintly, among other good old Celtic ideas, by the Welsh Gorsedd.

Perhaps there is no question more important in the general inquiry as to the social ideas and condition of a people than that of the position assigned to women. The stories are on this point quite as useful as the histories and the laws ; and the stories, as well as the laws, reveal a state of the national mind and manners worthy in this respect of the courteous modern Irish peasant's ancestors. If Irishmen have nothing else to be proud of, they might at least be proud of this, that in all times Irish women have been treated with the chivalry, not merely of tenderness, but of genuine respect ; and Irish women may, too, be proud that they have always been ready to take a part in their brothers' work, and be real comrades to their husbands. Most of us have heard of the surprise experienced by the Romans on observing the position of respect in which the women of the German tribes were held, a surprise only equalled by that which moved them on finding that these women were accustomed occasionally to take the field of battle with the men. Well, the Celtic tribes of Ireland exhibit the same two phenomena from the earliest times. The *will* of the woman, be she wife or daughter, is treated with respect, even though the daughter may be very capricious about marrying the suitable prince. And, on the other hand, while there are bardic championesses like the Ultonian Macha, and that queen of the ragged isle who was foster mother-in-arms to the champion Cuculain, and while there are powerful queens like the celebrated Meave who led the three provinces of Ireland against Ulster about nineteen hundred years ago, the fact that Irish women later were not slow to fight in time of war is plain, since a law restraining them from military service was passed as late as the year 697, by the influence of the Columban monk, Adamnan.

The warlike women were, however, manifestly exceptional. The point to be noticed is that they were permitted and held in high regard. In ancient Ireland women stayed for the most part in their own " sphere " : there was more of that special sphere then than there is now, and the general subordination of individual to family life is specially effective in limiting the activity of women. Nevertheless, there were exceptions, and in other fields more suitable, as doubtless we should think, than that of war: the traditional list of the Tuatha Dé Danann historians contains the names of two women and four men ; and the names of women occur not unseldom in the lists of judges and expounders of the law. We also hear of " learned women " as druidesses. All these eminent pagan women are precursors of the celebrated St. Brigit, the contemporary of St. Patrick, who seems to have been a decidedly strong-minded person, abbess of the Kildare monastery, with a bishop under her, and in perfectly good-fellowship with her comrades of the other sex in the work of learning and the Church.* These instances, and others, do not prove more, but they prove this, first that there was a clear tradition, to which custom corresponded, in favour of allowing women to come out of their "sphere," if they wanted to come, and secondly that Irishmen were not slow to award them the honours they might reap in other fields.

It is also certain that they held by no means a servile place in that sphere. This is proved by the marriage laws on the one hand, and the woman's property laws on the other.

At a woman's marriage her father, or her family if he were dead, conferred on her a portion—in the case of one daughter usually a third—of her father's personal property. Her husband also gave her a bridal gift, and these constituted her *separate property for her own use.* As regards inheritance of the right to use land, it is manifest that the Irish tribal custom and tribal ownership of land would lead in the first instance to the principle of inheritance in the male line only. Indeed, if a woman married into another

---

* For references see O'Curry's "Manuscript Materials of Ancient Irish History," p. 339, *et seq.*

tribe, it was evidently impossible that she should ever in tribal times be allowed to share in the land of her own tribe. Nevertheless, we find it stated, as a reform of older law, that a father might give one third of his lands to his daughter if there were no sons; and ultimately daughters could inherit all. This right of daughters to inherit is said to have been completely established by a legal decision in the case of a certain Ulster woman, Brigit Ambui, known as Brigit of the Judgments, who pleaded the cause of "women's rights" in the time of the Ulster king Conor Mac Nessa, at the beginning of the Christian era. It would seem probable on the face of it, however, that so long as tribal ownership prevailed in its purity, this law could only have been quite effective for women not married out of the tribe, though, later, it would naturally apply to all.

The marriage laws show a singular ease of divorce, which proves at once that they are not of Christian origin. What concerns us here is, in the first place, the careful manner in which the interests and dignity of the woman are protected by the divorce laws. For no less than seven different causes it was lawful for her to separate from her husband, taking with her the whole, or in certain cases part, of her marriage portion and her husband's bridal gift, obtaining, moreover, compensation for the injury done her. It will suffice to mention the three minor of these causes: (1) if a blemish ever so slight were inflicted on her, by beating or otherwise maltreating her; (2) if she were rendered the subject of ridicule by her husband; (3) if full rights in domestic and other social matters were not given her. "Every noble woman," says the law tract, commenting on this last condition, "is entitled to the exercise of her free will." Let us hope the women of Erin did not abuse their privileges.

Another part of the marriage law is still more suggestive. This deals with the respective rights of the two contracting parties in three carefully distinguished cases:—(1) the marriage of equal rank, when the wealth and social position of the two persons are such as to make them social equals; (2) the marriage of unequal rank, when the husband's property is the support of the household; (3) the similar marriage, when the wealth belongs to the wife.

In the first case, the equal rights of the two parties are plainly laid down. "What each gives the other is *equally* forfeited"—her wealth to him no more than his to her. And to carry out this principle of equality, it is decreed that "a contract made by either party is not a *lawful* contract without the consent of the other, except in case of contracts tending equally to the welfare of both." Again, we are told—and I quote this as an index of the Brehonic view on the subject—"The woman may oppose the evidence of the man . . . for it is a law of headship that is between them, and though the law cedes the headship to the man, because of his manhood and nobility, he has not the greater power of proof upon the woman on that account, for it is only a contract that is between them."

In the marriage of unequal rank, the two parties have—and this is consistent with the whole social system—status and rights proportionate to their property. The wealthier member has the greater privilege; and the law takes no account of sex. The man supported by the woman's wealth is on the same footing as the woman supported by the man's. After describing minutely the regulations for the latter case, the writer of the tract begins his treatment of the former by the simple statement that in this case "*the man goes in the place of the woman and the woman in the place of the man.*" *

Nor does it appear that this somewhat prosaic equalization before the law was at all destructive of the romantic tendency to idealize the typical man and typical woman as different, however similar. Even the law-writer betrays himself quaintly in the derivation he gives of the Irish words, for women "ben," and for man "fer." Thus they are called, he tells us, "from the *kindliness* of a woman and the *dignity* of a man, and *to reach these qualities they exist.*"

The law tract from which this and the other quotations are taken was undoubtedly written in Christian times; but I have dealt with the subject

* See " Law of Social Connexions " in " Brehon Laws," vol. ii. p. 391.

in this place because it is evident from the whole tenor of early Irish history, and the internal evidence of the legal definition of rights here considered, that the ideas reflected are those of Irish paganism. And, indeed, it takes little knowledge of European history to make manifest that the *early* Christianity of each country assumed, with modifications, the ethical character of the paganism which preceded it.

Having now some general conception of the main social ideas and instincts of pagan Ireland, no inquiry can be more interesting than one into the religious ideas lying behind them. Few subjects of inquiry are beset with greater difficulties. An adequate treatment of it would require careful study, not only of Irish bardic literature and the legendary lore still lingering among the Irish peasantry, with a view to discovery of the pagan customs as well as pagan ideas which they imply, but also a similar study of such similar materials as exist—much more scantily in most cases—for other nations. To understand the Irish non-Christian tradition and worship, we should understand the corresponding tradition and worship, and their history, for all the peoples that issued from the same Aryan home, and grew to express themselves by diverse modifications of their original habits feelings ideas and languages, in accordance with the diversity of the circumstances in which they lived and grew.

Here, however, we must be content with a much

narrower range, and a very incomplete idea. Yet a few facts may be stated showing the connection of Irish with Aryan tradition generally, and indicating also the tenacious hold which the Irish imagination has of its past. The memory of four great pagan festivals lingers on all soil that Aryan races have trod, but it is most vivid and clear in Ireland. The first is the feast of Beltine, on May Day, when in ancient times the sacred fire was lit at Tara, while no light was allowed to be visible that night on all the surrounding plain: and, just as in those times a lighted brand from that fire was used to kindle all the fires around, so even now in remote places, if the fire goes out in a peasant's house before the morning of the first of May, a lighted sod from the *priest's* house to kindle it is highly esteemed. The second great festival is on Midsummer Eve, when the bonfires are still lighted on the Irish hills, and it is still "lucky" for the young people to jump over the flames or for the cattle to pass between two fires; at least, the tradition lingers where the superstition is practically extinct. It should be noted, however, that of this and the Midwinter festival we read comparatively little in the old literature. It is the other two that stand out as having national importance, and there is not the faintest indication of any druidical rites of sacrifice having ever been practised in connection with the Midsummer fires during bardic times. The third festival is that of Samhain, or

November Eve, with which occasion was associated the great popular assembly and national council of the kings at Tara, and which now, as then, connects itself with the idea of mirth and sociability though no longer politics. There is, however, a superstition about November Eve, familiar to the Irish peasantry, which may have an important bearing on the historical fact that Samhain was the time originally associated with the national assembly. November Eve is sacred to the spirits of the dead. In the Western Isles the old superstitions are dying very hard, and tradition is still well alive. It is "dangerous" to be out on November Eve, because it is the one night in the year when the dead come out of their graves to dance with the fairies on the hills, and as it is their night, they do not like to be disturbed. Now, if Samhain were always sacred to the ancestral dead, which is likely, then the choice of Samhain as the time of a national assembly may have been due to the fact that one primary purpose of the assembly originally was to pay homage to the sacred dead of Erin. The passionate love of kindred that still characterizes the Celtic Irish makes it probable that homage to the dead must have constituted a marked feature in any system of national worship they may have had, while it is certain, from the evidence of the literature, that they did believe in the existence and protecting power of their dead heroes. So it seems very possible that the national significance of the festival at Tara was bound up with the recognition of the heroic dead who were sacred, not merely each to his own tribe, but to the nation. The fourth festival is that of Midwinter, the memory of which still flourishes everywhere in the festivities of Christmas Day, though the pagan meaning has been wholly forgotten, the vitality of the custom being now entirely due to its Christian associations.

These four festivals are supposed to be connected with the worship of the sun and moon,* and the various practices associated with them, in Ireland and elsewhere, to be significant of ideas relative to that worship. We need not, however, dwell on this subject, because, not only have the ideas themselves now vanished from the Irish mind, but apparently they had vanished in bardic times and left no trace behind. A general reverence for Nature we find, indeed, and plenty of it—a sense of sacredness in fountains lakes and hills, in the winds of Ireland and her encircling seas. Every aspect of Nature has a personality—poetic, however, rather than superstitious—lovable, sympathetic, as when the waves of Ireland roar in sympathy with the shield of her king which had been forged by fairy smiths beneath the sea. And the only clear idea we can gather of a druid's priestly function, which some imagine to

---

* This applies, no doubt, more especially to the Midsummer and Midwinter festivals, and these are the two of which the bardic literature tells us least.

have involved a definite ceremonial and sacrificial rites, is that, by his magical arts — corresponding, doubtless, sometimes to artistic and scientific skill — he acquired influence over Nature and bent her to his will. Of any such limitation to this vague Nature-worship as the Persian sun-and-fire worship implies, no trace whatever can be found except the popular observance of the festivals and the peasant's belief in the luckiness of fire. Indeed, the picture of the Irish druid, as painted by the bards, is altogether inconsistent with the notion that he should limit his magical activity to dealings with the sun, that least hopeful of all objects, or to the one element of fire. The druid has a true dash of scientific aspiration in him. He does not want merely to influence the popular mind, but to work an effect — or imagine that he does — on Nature. Probably the fact that the druidic profession was open to all students, and that the country was full of the active bardic intellect, contributed to make and keep this aspiration purer than it could have been kept had the druids become either a caste or the only learned class in the country. The bardic influence, too — and druids are frequently bards themselves — must have contributed directly to prevent any limitation of Nature-reverence; for to the poet there is as much soul in the glistening of the dew on the grass, or the moan of the sea on the shore, as in the journey of the sun across the heavens day by day.

Let us note now this curious fact. There is more trace of sun-and-fire worship in the peasant's superstition lingering among us to-day than in the bardic literature of the remote Irish past. The explanation that suggests itself is on the surface. The druids and bards of those far-reaching bardic times were practically heretics with respect to the more ancient forms of religious idea, which linger without meaning in the Irish peasant's tenacious memory, or adhere to his habits by the bare persistence of conservative instinct. At some very early date, Irish religious conceptions began to develop along a line quite different from that of the solar myth, giving scope, on the one hand, for the bardic imagination and the druidic ambition for Nature-control, and, on the other hand, for the people's moral and religious sentiments, bound up as these were with the idea of kindred.

For the satisfaction of these something much more catholic than sun-worship was necessary. All objects of possible religious reverence come under two great heads—the Idea of Nature and the Idea of Humanity—and a *moral religion is one which associates these objects of reverence with the idea of human activity in relation to them.* Now, the most conspicuous fact about the Irish intellect is its vividness of imagination, and the closeness with which that imagination works in relation to the external nature familiar to it: Irish poetry and Irish poetic feeling are "racy of the soil" in a way that is quite extraordinary.

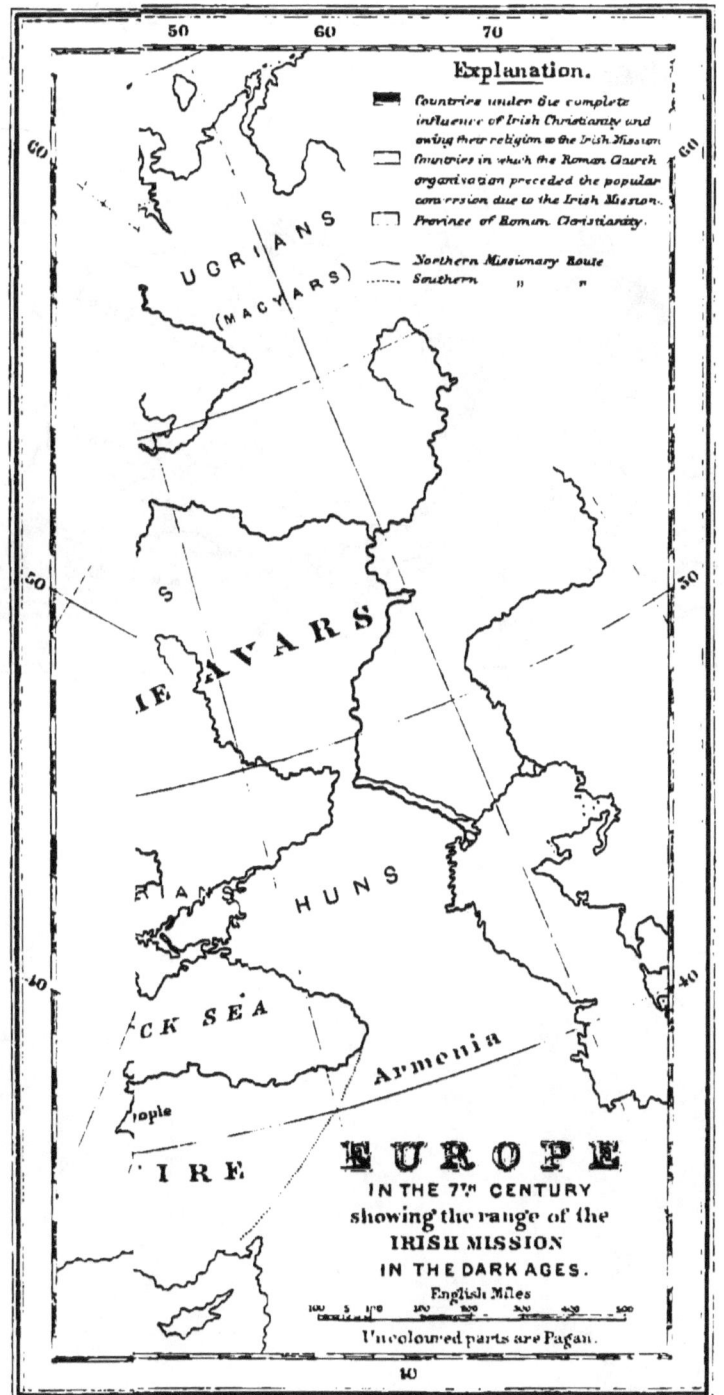

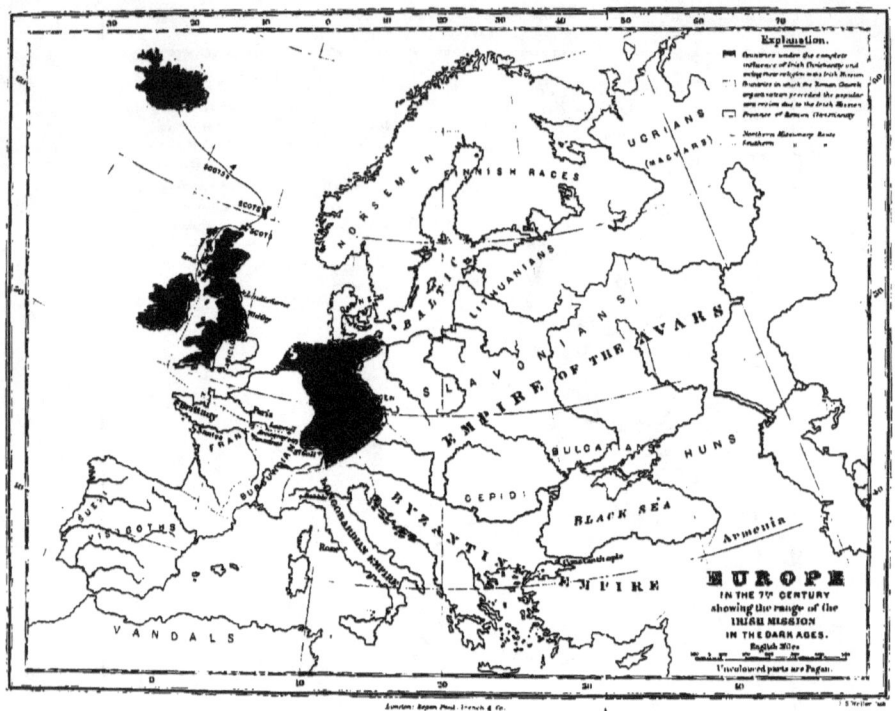

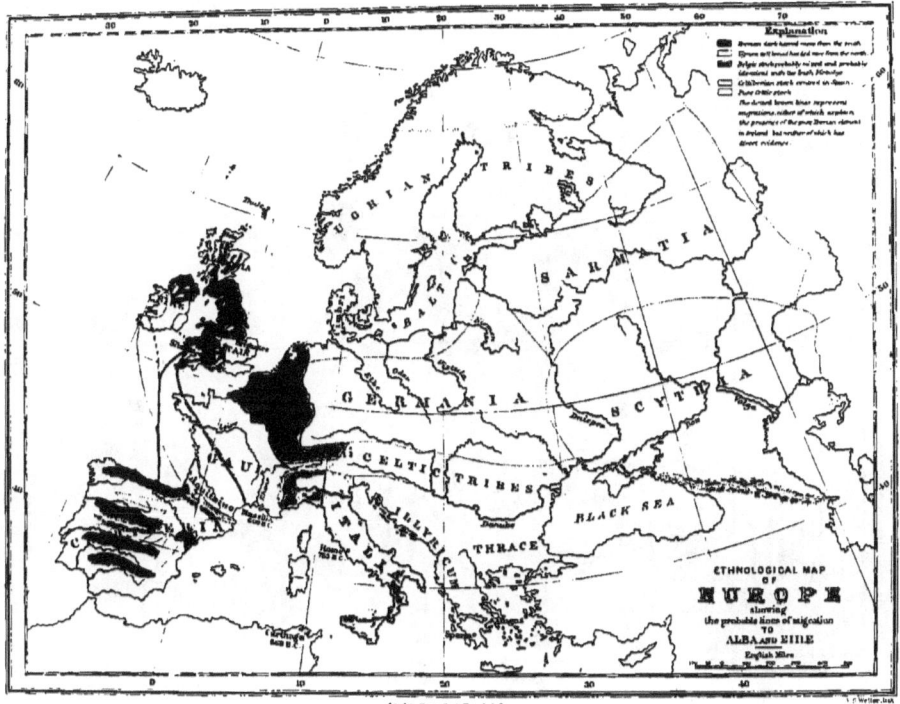

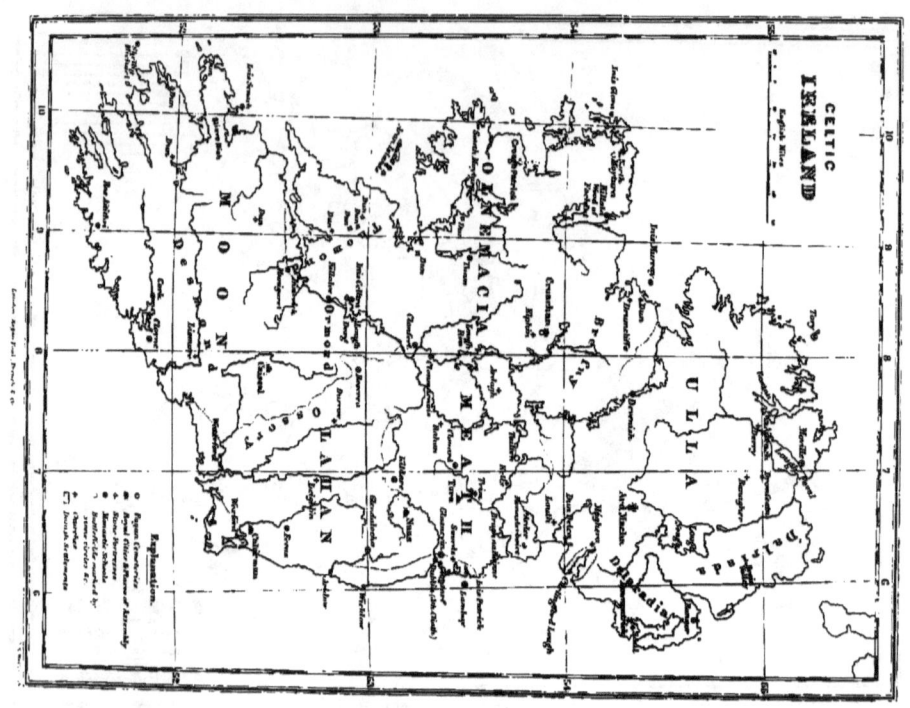

A LIST OF
KEGAN PAUL, TRENCH & CO.'S PUBLICATIONS.

3.89

1, *Paternoster Square,*
London.

A LIST OF
KEGAN PAUL, TRENCH & CO.'S
PUBLICATIONS.

CONTENTS.

	PAGE		PAGE
GENERAL LITERATURE .	2	MILITARY WORKS .	33
PARCHMENT LIBRARY .	18	POETRY .	34
PULPIT COMMENTARY .	20	NOVELS AND TALES .	39
INTERNATIONAL SCIENTIFIC SERIES .	29	BOOKS FOR THE YOUNG	41

GENERAL LITERATURE.

AINSWORTH, W. F.—**Personal Narrative of the Euphrates Expedition.** 2 vols. Demy 8vo, 32*s*.

A. K. H. B.—**From a Quiet Place.** A Volume of Sermons. Crown 8vo, 5*s*.

ALEXANDER, William, D.D., Bishop of Derry.—**The Great Question, and other Sermons.** Crown 8vo, 6*s*.

ALLIES, T. W., M.A.—**Per Crucem ad Lucem.** The Result of a Life. 2 vols. Demy 8vo, 25*s*.

A Life's Decision. Crown 8vo, 7*s*. 6*d*.

AMHERST, Rev. W. J.—**The History of Catholic Emancipation and the Progress of the Catholic Church in the British Isles (chiefly in England) from 1771-1820.** 2 vols. Demy 8vo, 24*s*.

AMOS, Professor Sheldon.—**The History and Principles of the Civil Law of Rome.** An aid to the Study of Scientific and Comparative Jurisprudence. Demy 8vo, 16*s*.

Are Foreign Missions doing any Good? An Enquiry into their Social Effects. Crown 8vo, 1*s*.

ARISTOTLE.—**The Nicomachean Ethics of Aristotle.** Translated by F. H. Peters, M.A. Third Edition. Crown 8vo, 6*s*.

AUBERTIN, J. J.—**A Flight to Mexico.** With 7 full-page Illustrations and a Railway Map of Mexico. Crown 8vo, 7s. 6d.

Six Months in Cape Colony and Natal. With Illustrations and Map. Crown 8vo, 6s.

A Fight with Distances. Illustrations and Maps. Crown 8vo, 7s. 6d.

Aucassin and Nicolette. Edited in Old French and rendered in Modern English by F. W. BOURDILLON. Fcap 8vo, 7s. 6d.

BADGER, *George Percy*, D.C.L.—**An English-Arabic Lexicon.** In which the equivalent for English Words and Idiomatic Sentences are rendered into literary and colloquial Arabic. Royal 4to, 80s.

BAGEHOT, *Walter.*—**The English Constitution.** Fifth Edition. Crown 8vo, 7s. 6d.

Lombard Street. A Description of the Money Market. Ninth Edition. Crown 8vo, 7s. 6d.

Essays on Parliamentary Reform. Crown 8vo, 5s.

Some Articles on the Depreciation of Silver, and Topics connected with it. Second Edition. Demy 8vo, 5s.

BAGOT, *Alan*, C.E.—**Accidents in Mines:** their Causes and Prevention. Crown 8vo, 6s.

The Principles of Colliery Ventilation. Second Edition, greatly enlarged. Crown 8vo, 5s.

The Principles of Civil Engineering as applied to Agriculture and Estate Management. Crown 8vo, 7s. 6d.

BAKER, *Ella.*—**Kingscote Essays and Poems.** Fcap 8vo. 2s. 6d.

BALDWIN, *Capt. J. H.*—**The Large and Small Game of Bengal and the North-Western Provinces of India.** With 20 Illustrations. New and Cheaper Edition. Small 4to, 10s. 6d.

BALL, *John*, F.R.S.—**Notes of a Naturalist in South America.** With Map. Crown 8vo, 8s. 6d.

BALLIN, *Ada S. and F. L.*—**A Hebrew Grammar.** With Exercises selected from the Bible. Crown 8vo, 7s. 6d.

BASU, *K. P.*, M.A.—**Students' Mathematical Companion.** Containing problems in Arithmetic, Algebra, Geometry, and Mensuration, for Students of the Indian Universities. Crown 8vo, 6s.

BAUR, *Ferdinand, Dr. Ph.*—**A Philological Introduction to Greek and Latin for Students.** Translated and adapted from the German, by C. KEGAN PAUL, M.A., and E. D. STONE, M.A. Third Edition. Crown 8vo, 6s.

Becket, Thomas, Martyr Patriot. By R. A. THOMPSON, M.A. Crown 8vo. 6s.

BENSON, A. C.—William Laud, sometime Archbishop of Canterbury. A Study. With Portrait. Crown 8vo, 6s.

BLOOMFIELD, The Lady.—Reminiscences of Court and Diplomatic Life. New and Cheaper Edition. With Frontispiece. Crown 8vo, 6s.

BLUNT, The Ven. Archdeacon. — The Divine Patriot, and other Sermons. Preached in Scarborough and in Cannes. New and Cheaper Edition. Crown 8vo, 4s. 6d.

BLUNT, Wilfrid S.—The Future of Islam. Crown 8vo, 6s.

Ideas about India. Crown 8vo. Cloth, 6s.

BOWEN, H. C., M.A.—Studies in English. For the use of Modern Schools. Tenth Thousand. Small crown 8vo, 1s. 6d.

English Grammar for Beginners. Fcap. 8vo, 1s.

Simple English Poems. English Literature for Junior Classes. In four parts. Parts I., II., and III., 6d. each. Part IV., 1s. Complete, 3s.

BRADLEY, F. H.—The Principles of Logic. Demy 8vo, 16s.

Bradshaw, Henry: Memoir. By G. W. PROTHERO. With Portrait and Facsimile. Demy 8vo. 16s.

BRIDGETT, Rev. T. E.—History of the Holy Eucharist in Great Britain. 2 vols. Demy 8vo, 18s.

BROOKE, Rev. Stopford A.—The Fight of Faith. Sermons preached on various occasions. Fifth Edition. Crown 8vo, 7s. 6d.

The Spirit of the Christian Life. Third Edition. Crown 8vo, 5s.

Theology in the English Poets.—Cowper, Coleridge, Wordsworth, and Burns. Sixth Edition. Post 8vo, 5s.

Christ in Modern Life. Seventeenth Edition. Crown 8vo, 5s.

Sermons. First Series. Thirteenth Edition. Crown 8vo, 5s.

Sermons. Second Series. Sixth Edition. Crown 8vo, 5s.

BROWN, Horatio F.—Life on the Lagoons. With 2 Illustrations and Map. Crown 8vo, 6s.

Venetian Studies. Crown 8vo, 7s. 6d.

BROWN, Rev. J. Baldwin.—The Higher Life. Its Reality, Experience, and Destiny. Seventh Edition. Crown 8vo, 5s.

Doctrine of Annihilation in the Light of the Gospel of Love. Five Discourses. Fourth Edition. Crown 8vo, 2s. 6d.

The Christian Policy of Life. A Book for Young Men of Business. Third Edition. Crown 8vo, 3s. 6d.

BURKE, *The Late Very Rev. T. N.*—His Life. By W. J. FITZ-PATRICK. 2 vols. With Portrait. Demy 8vo, 30s.

BURTON, *Lady.*—The Inner Life of Syria, Palestine, and the Holy Land. Post 8vo, 6s.

BURY, *Richard de.*—Philobiblon. Edited by E. C. THOMAS. Crown 8vo. 10s. 6d.

CANDLER, *C.*—The Prevention of Consumption. A Mode of Prevention founded on a New Theory of the Nature of the Tubercle-Bacillus. Demy 8vo, 10s. 6d.

CARPENTER, *W. B.*—The Principles of Mental Physiology. With their Applications to the Training and Discipline of the Mind, and the Study of its Morbid Conditions. Illustrated. Sixth Edition. 8vo, 12s.

> Nature and Man. With a Memorial Sketch by the Rev. J. ESTLIN CARPENTER. Portrait. Large crown 8vo, 8s. 6d.

Catholic Dictionary. Containing some Account of the Doctrine, Discipline, Rites, Ceremonies, Councils, and Religious Orders of the Catholic Church. Edited by THOMAS ARNOLD, M.A. Third Edition. Demy 8vo, 21s.

Charlemagne. A History of Charles the Great. By J. I. MOMBERT, D.D. Medium 8vo. 15s.

CHARLES, *Rev. R. H.*—Forgiveness, and other Sermons. Crown 8vo, 4s. 6d.

CHEYNE, *Canon.*—The Prophecies of Isaiah. Translated with Critical Notes and Dissertations. 2 vols. Fifth Edition. Demy 8vo, 25s.

> Job and Solomon; or, the Wisdom of the Old Testament. Demy 8vo, 12s. 6d.

> The Psalms; or, Book of The Praises of Israel. Translated with Commentary. Demy 8vo. 16s.

Churgress, The. By "THE PRIG." Fcap. 8vo, 3s. 6d.

CLAIRAUT.—Elements of Geometry. Translated by Dr. KAINES. With 145 Figures. Crown 8vo, 4s. 6d.

CLAPPERTON, *Jane Hume.*—Scientific Meliorism and the Evolution of Happiness. Large crown 8vo, 8s. 6d.

CLODD, *Edward, F.R.A.S.*—The Childhood of the World: a Simple Account of Man in Early Times. Eighth Edition. Crown 8vo, 3s.
> A Special Edition for Schools. 1s.

> The Childhood of Religions. Including a Simple Account of the Birth and Growth of Myths and Legends. Eighth Thousand. Crown 8vo, 5s.
>> A Special Edition for Schools. 1s. 6d.

CLODD, *Edward, F.R.A.S.—continued.*

    Jesus of Nazareth. With a brief sketch of Jewish History to the Time of His Birth. Second Edition. Small crown 8vo, 6s.
      A Special Edition for Schools. In 2 parts. Each 1s. 6d.

COGHLAN, *J. Cole, D.D.*—**The Modern Pharisee**, and other Sermons. Edited by the Very Rev. H. H. DICKINSON, D.D., Dean of Chapel Royal, Dublin. New and Cheaper Edition. Crown 8vo, 7s. 6d.

COLERIDGE, *The Hon. Stephen.*—**Demetrius.** Crown 8vo, 5s.

CONNELL, *A. K.*—**Discontent and Danger in India.** Small crown 8vo, 3s. 6d.

    The Economic Revolution of India. Crown 8vo, 4s. 6d.

CORR, *the late Rev. T. J., M.A.*—**Favilla**: Tales, Essays, and Poems. Crown 8vo, 5s.

CORY, *William.*—**A Guide to Modern English History.** Part I.—MDCCCXV.-MDCCCXXX. Demy 8vo, 9s. Part II.—MDCCCXXX.-MDCCCXXXV., 15s.

COTTON, *H. J. S.*—**New India, or India in Transition.** Third Edition. Crown 8vo, 4s. 6d.; Cheap Edition, paper covers, 1s.

COWIE, *Right Rev. W. G.*—**Our Last Year in New Zealand.** 1887. Crown 8vo, 7s. 6d.

COX, *Rev. Sir George W., M.A., Bart.*—**The Mythology of the Aryan Nations.** New Edition. Demy 8vo, 16s.

    Tales of Ancient Greece. New Edition. Small crown 8vo, 6s.

    A Manual of Mythology in the form of Question and Answer. New Edition. Fcap. 8vo, 3s.

    An Introduction to the Science of Comparative Mythology and Folk-Lore. Second Edition. Crown 8vo, 7s. 6d.

COX, *Rev. Sir G. W., M.A., Bart., and JONES, Eustace Hinton.*—**Popular Romances of the Middle Ages.** Third Edition, in 1 vol. Crown 8vo, 6s.

COX, *Rev. Samuel, D.D.*—**A Commentary on the Book of Job.** With a Translation. Second Edition. Demy 8vo, 15s.

    Salvator Mundi; or, Is Christ the Saviour of all Men? Twelfth Edition. Crown 8vo, 2s. 6d.

    The Larger Hope. A Sequel to "Salvator Mundi." Second Edition. 16mo, 1s.

    The Genesis of Evil, and other Sermons, mainly expository. Third Edition. Crown 8vo, 6s.

    Balaam. An Exposition and a Study. Crown 8vo, 5s.

    Miracles. An Argument and a Challenge. Crown 8vo, 2s. 6d.

CRAVEN, Mrs.—A Year's Meditations. Crown 8vo, 6s.

CRAWFURD, Oswald.—Portugal, Old and New. With Illustrations and Maps. New and Cheaper Edition. Crown 8vo, 6s.

Cross Lights. Crown 8vo. 5s.

CRUISE, Francis Richard, M.D.—Thomas à Kempis. Notes of a Visit to the Scenes in which his Life was spent. With Portraits and Illustrations. Demy 8vo, 12s.

Dante: The Banquet (Il Convito). Translated by KATHARINE HILLARD. Crown 8vo. 7s. 6d.

DARMESTETER, Arsene.—The Life of Words as the Symbols of Ideas. Crown 8vo, 4s. 6d.

DAVIDSON, Rev. Samuel, D.D., LL.D.—Canon of the Bible: Its Formation, History, and Fluctuations. Third and Revised Edition. Small crown 8vo, 5s.

The Doctrine of Last Things contained in the New Testament compared with the Notions of the Jews and the Statements of Church Creeds. Small crown 8vo, 3s. 6d.

DAWSON, Geo., M.A. Prayers, with a Discourse on Prayer. Edited by his Wife. First Series. Tenth Edition. Small Crown 8vo, 3s. 6d.

Prayers, with a Discourse on Prayer. Edited by GEORGE ST. CLAIR, F.G.S. Second Series. Small Crown 8vo, 3s. 6d.

Sermons on Disputed Points and Special Occasions. Edited by his Wife. Fourth Edition. Crown 8vo, 6s.

Sermons on Daily Life and Duty. Edited by his Wife. Fifth Edition. Small Crown 8vo, 3s. 6d.

The Authentic Gospel, and other Sermons. Edited by GEORGE ST. CLAIR, F.G.S. Third Edition. Crown 8vo, 6s.

Every-day Counsels. Edited by GEORGE ST. CLAIR, F.G.S. Crown 8vo, 6s.

Biographical Lectures. Edited by GEORGE ST. CLAIR, F.G.S. Third Edition. Large crown 8vo, 7s. 6d.

Shakespeare, and other Lectures. Edited by GEORGE ST. CLAIR, F.G.S. Large crown 8vo, 7s. 6d.

DE JONCOURT, Madame Marie.—Wholesome Cookery. Fifth Edition. Crown 8vo, cloth, 1s. 6d; paper covers, 1s.

DENT, H. C.—A Year in Brazil. With Notes on Religion, Meteorology, Natural History, etc. Maps and Illustrations. Demy 8vo, 18s.

DOWDEN, Edward, LL.D.—Shakspere: a Critical Study of his Mind and Art. Ninth Edition. Post 8vo, 12s.

DOWDEN, Edward, LL.D.—continued.

    Studies in Literature, 1789-1877. Fourth Edition. Large post 8vo, 6s.

    Transcripts and Studies. Large post 8vo. 12s.

Drummond, Thomas, Under Secretary in Ireland, 1835-40. Life and Letters. By R. BARRY O'BRIEN. Demy 8vo. 14s.

Dulce Domum. Fcap. 8vo, 5s.

DU MONCEL, Count.—**The Telephone, the Microphone, and the Phonograph.** With 74 Illustrations. Third Edition. Small crown 8vo, 5s.

DUNN, H. Percy.—**Infant Health.** The Physiology and Hygiene of Early Life. Crown 8vo. 3s. 6d.

DURUY, Victor.—**History of Rome and the Roman People.** Edited by Prof. MAHAFFY. With nearly 3000 Illustrations. 4to. 6 vols. in 12 parts, 30s. each vol.

Education Library. Edited by Sir PHILIP MAGNUS:—

    An Introduction to the History of Educational Theories. By OSCAR BROWNING, M.A. Second Edition. 3s. 6d.

    Industrial Education. By Sir PHILIP MAGNUS. 6s.

    Old Greek Education. By the Rev. Prof. MAHAFFY, M.A. Second Edition. 3s. 6d.

    School Management. Including a general view of the work of Education, Organization, and Discipline. By JOSEPH LANDON. Seventh Edition. 6s.

EDWARDES, Major-General Sir Herbert B.—**Memorials of his Life and Letters.** By his Wife. With Portrait and Illustrations. 2 vols. Demy 8vo, 36s.

Eighteenth Century Essays. Selected and Edited by AUSTIN DOBSON. Cheap Edition. Cloth 1s. 6d.

ELSDALE, Henry.—**Studies in Tennyson's Idylls.** Crown 8vo, 5s.

Emerson's (Ralph Waldo) Life. By OLIVER WENDELL HOLMES. English Copyright Edition. With Portrait. Crown 8vo, 6s.

EYTON, Rev. Robert.—**The True Life,** and other Sermons. Crown 8vo, 7s. 6d.

Five o'clock Tea. Containing Receipts for Cakes, Savoury Sandwiches, etc. Seventh Thousand. Fcap. 8vo, cloth, 1s. 6d.; paper covers, 1s.

FLINN, D. Edgar.—**Ireland: its Health-Resorts and Watering-Places.** With Frontispiece and Maps. Demy 8vo, 5s.

Forbes, Bishop: A Memoir. By the Rev. DONALD J. MACKAY. With Portrait and Map. Crown 8vo, 7s. 6d.

FOTHERINGHAM, *James.*—Studies in the Poetry of Robert Browning. Second Edition. Crown 8vo, 6s.

Franklin (Benjamin) as a Man of Letters. By J. B. MACMASTER. Crown 8vo, 5s.

FREWEN, Moreton.—The Economic Crisis. Crown 8vo, 2s. 6d.

From World to Cloister; or, My Novitiate. By BERNARD. Crown 8vo, 5s.

FULLER, Rev. Morris.—Pan-Anglicanism: What is It? or, The Church of the Reconciliation. Crown 8vo. 5s.

GARDINER, Samuel R., and J. BASS MULLINGER, M.A.—Introduction to the Study of English History. Second Edition. Large crown 8vo, 9s.

GEORGE, Henry.—Progress and Poverty. An Inquiry into the Causes of Industrial Depressions, and of Increase of Want with Increase of Wealth. The Remedy. Fifth Library Edition. Post 8vo, 7s. 6d. Cabinet Edition. Crown 8vo, 2s. 6d. Also a Cheap Edition. Limp cloth, 1s. 6d.; paper covers, 1s.

Protection, or Free Trade. An Examination of the Tariff Question, with especial regard to the Interests of Labour. Second Edition. Crown 8vo, 5s. Cheap Edition, limp cloth, 1s. 6d.; paper covers, 1s.

Social Problems. Fourth Thousand. Crown 8vo, 5s. Cheap Edition, paper covers, 1s.; cloth, 1s. 6d.

GILBERT, Mrs.—Autobiography, and other Memorials. Edited by JOSIAH GILBERT. Fifth Edition. Crown 8vo, 7s. 6d.

GILLMORE, Parker.—Days and Nights by the Desert. Illustrated. Demy 8vo, 10s. 6d.

GLANVILL, Joseph.—Scepsis Scientifica; or, Confest Ignorance, the Way to Science; in an Essay of the Vanity of Dogmatizing and Confident Opinion. Edited, with Introductory Essay, by JOHN OWEN. Elzevir 8vo, printed on hand-made paper, 6s.

GLASS, H. A.—The Story of the Psalters. A History of the Metrical Versions from 1549 to 1885. Crown 8vo, 5s.

Glossary of Terms and Phrases. Edited by the Rev. H. PERCY SMITH and others. Second and Cheaper Edition. Medium 8vo, 7s. 6d.

GLOVER, F., M.A.—Exempla Latina. A First Construing Book, with Short Notes, Lexicon, and an Introduction to the Analysis of Sentences. Second Edition. Fcap. 8vo, 2s.

GOODCHILD, John A. Chats at St. Ampelio. Crown 8vo. 5s.

GOODENOUGH, *Commodore J. G.*—Memoir of, with Extracts from his Letters and Journals. Edited by his Widow. With Steel Engraved Portrait. Third Edition. Crown 8vo, 5*s*.

GORDON, *Major-General C. G.*—**His Journals at Kartoum.** Printed from the original MS. With Introduction and Notes by A. EGMONT HAKE. Portrait, 2 Maps, and 30 Illustrations. Two vols., demy 8vo, 21*s*. Also a Cheap Edition in 1 vol., 6*s*.

Gordon's (General) Last Journal. A Facsimile of the last Journal received in England from GENERAL GORDON. Reproduced by Photo-lithography. Imperial 4to, £3 3*s*.

Events in his Life. From the Day of his Birth to the Day of his Death. By Sir H. W. GORDON. With Maps and Illustrations. Second Edition. Demy 8vo, 7*s*. 6*d*.

GOSSE, *Edmund.*—**Seventeenth Century Studies.** A Contribution to the History of English Poetry. Demy 8vo, 10*s*. 6*d*.

GOUGH, *E.*—**The Bible True from the Beginning.** Vol. I. Demy 8vo, 16*s*.

GOULD, *Rev. S. Baring, M.A.*—**Germany, Present and Past.** New and Cheaper Edition. Large crown 8vo, 7*s*. 6*d*.

GOWAN, *Major Walter E.*—**A. Ivanoff's Russian Grammar.** (16th Edition.) Translated, enlarged, and arranged for use of Students of the Russian Language. Demy 8vo, 6*s*.

GOWER, *Lord Ronald.* **My Reminiscences.** MINIATURE EDITION, printed on hand-made paper, limp parchment antique, 10*s*. 6*d*.

Bric-à-Brac. Being some Photoprints illustrating art objects at Gower Lodge, Windsor. With descriptions. Super royal 8vo. 15*s*.; extra binding, 21*s*.

Last Days of Mary Antoinette. An Historical Sketch. With Portrait and Facsimiles. Fcap. 4to, 10*s*. 6*d*.

Notes of a Tour from Brindisi to Yokohama, 1883-1884. Fcap. 8vo, 2*s*. 6*d*.

GRAHAM, *William, M.A.*—**The Creed of Science,** Religious, Moral, and Social. Second Edition, Revised. Crown 8vo, 6*s*.

The Social Problem, in its Economic, Moral, and Political Aspects. Demy 8vo, 14*s*.

GRIMLEY, *Rev. H. N., M.A.*—**Tremadoc Sermons,** chiefly on the Spiritual Body, the Unseen World, and the Divine Humanity. Fourth Edition. Crown 8vo, 6*s*.

The Temple of Humanity, and other Sermons. Crown 8vo, 6*s*.

GURNEY, *Alfred.*—**Our Catholic Inheritance in the Larger Hope.** Crown 8vo, 1*s*. 6*d*.

Wagner's Parsifal. A Study. Fcap. 8vo, 1*s*. 6*d*.

HADDON, Caroline.—The Larger Life, Studies in Hinton's Ethics. Crown 8vo, 5*s.*

HAECKEL, Prof. Ernst.—The History of Creation. Translation revised by Professor E. RAY LANKESTER, M.A., F.R.S. With Coloured Plates and Genealogical Trees of the various groups of both Plants and Animals. 2 vols. Third Edition. Post 8vo, 32*s.*

The History of the Evolution of Man. With numerous Illustrations. 2 vols. Post 8vo, 32*s.*

A Visit to Ceylon. Post 8vo, 7*s.* 6*d.*

Freedom in Science and Teaching. With a Prefatory Note by T. H. HUXLEY, F.R.S. Crown 8vo, 5*s.*

Hamilton, Memoirs of Arthur, B.A., of Trinity College, Cambridge. Crown 8vo, 6*s.*

Handbook of Home Rule, being Articles on the Irish Question by Various Writers. Edited by JAMES BRYCE, M.P. Second Edition. Crown 8vo, 1*s.* sewed, or 1*s.* 6*d.* cloth.

HAWEIS, Rev. H. R., M.A.—Current Coin. Materialism—The Devil—Crime—Drunkenness—Pauperism—Emotion—Recreation—The Sabbath. Fifth Edition. Crown 8vo, 5*s.*

Arrows in the Air. Fifth Edition. Crown 8vo, 5*s.*

Speech in Season. Sixth Edition. Crown 8vo, 5*s.*

Thoughts for the Times. Fourteenth Edition. Crown 8vo, 5*s.*

Unsectarian Family Prayers. New Edition. Fcap. 8vo, 1*s.* 6*d.*

HAWTHORNE, Nathaniel.—Works. Complete in Twelve Volumes. Large post 8vo, 7*s.* 6*d.* each volume.

HEIDENHAIN, Rudolph, M.D.—Hypnotism, or Animal Magnetism. With Preface by G. J. ROMANES. Second Edition. Small crown 8vo, 2*s.* 6*d.*

HENDRIKS, Dom Lawrence.—The London Charterhouse: its Monks and its Martyrs. Illustrated. Demy 8vo, 14*s.*

HINTON, J.—Life and Letters. With an Introduction by Sir W. W. GULL, Bart., and Portrait engraved on Steel by C. H. Jeens. Sixth Edition. Crown 8vo, 8*s.* 6*d.*

Philosophy and Religion. Selections from the Manuscripts of the late James Hinton. Edited by CAROLINE HADDON. Second Edition. Crown 8vo, 5*s.*

The Law Breaker, and The Coming of the Law. Edited by MARGARET HINTON. Crown 8vo, 6*s.*

The Mystery of Pain. New Edition. Fcap. 8vo, 1*s.*

Homer's Iliad. Greek text, with a Translation by J. G. CORDERY. 2 vols. Demy 8vo, 24*s.*

HOOPER, Mary.—**Little Dinners: How to Serve them with Elegance and Economy.** Twenty-first Edition. Crown 8vo, 2s. 6d.

Cookery for Invalids, Persons of Delicate Digestion, and Children. Fifth Edition. Crown 8vo, 2s. 6d.

Every-day Meals. Being Economical and Wholesome Recipes for Breakfast, Luncheon, and Supper. Seventh Edition. Crown 8vo, 2s. 6d.

HOPKINS, Ellice.—**Work amongst Working Men.** Sixth Edition. Crown 8vo, 3s. 6d.

HORNADAY, W. T.—**Two Years in a Jungle.** With Illustrations. Demy 8vo, 21s.

HOSPITALIER, E.—**The Modern Applications of Electricity.** Translated and Enlarged by JULIUS MAIER, Ph.D. 2 vols. Second Edition, Revised, with many additions and numerous Illustrations. Demy 8vo, 25s.

HOWARD, Robert, M.A.—**The Church of England and other Religious Communions.** A course of Lectures delivered in the Parish Church of Clapham. Crown 8vo, 7s. 6d.

HYNDMAN, H. M.—**The Historical Basis of Socialism in England.** Large crown 8vo, 8s. 6d.

IDDESLEIGH, Earl of.—**The Pleasures, Dangers, and Uses of Desultory Reading.** Fcap. 8vo, 2s. 6d.

IM THURN, Everard F.—**Among the Indians of Guiana.** Being Sketches, chiefly anthropologic, from the Interior of British Guiana. With 53 Illustrations and a Map. Demy 8vo, 18s.

JEAFFRESON, Herbert H.—**The Divine Unity and Trinity.** Demy 8vo, 12s.

JENKINS, E., and RAYMOND, J.—**The Architect's Legal Handbook.** Fourth Edition, revised. Crown 8vo, 6s.

JENKINS, Rev. Canon R. C.—**Heraldry. English and Foreign.** With a Dictionary of Heraldic Terms and 156 Illustrations. Small crown 8vo, 3s. 6d.

Jerome, St., Life. By M. J. MARTIN. Crown 8vo, 6s.

JOEL, L.—**A Consul's Manual and Shipowner's and Shipmaster's Practical Guide in their Transactions Abroad.** With Definitions of Nautical, Mercantile, and Legal Terms; a Glossary of Mercantile Terms in English, French, German, Italian, and Spanish; Tables of the Money, Weights, and Measures of the Principal Commercial Nations and their Equivalents in British Standards; and Forms of Consular and Notarial Acts. Demy 8vo, 12s.

JOHNSTON, H. H., F.Z.S.—**The Kilima-njaro Expedition.**
A Record of Scientific Exploration in Eastern Equatorial Africa, and a General Description of the Natural History, Languages, and Commerce of the Kilima-njaro District. With 6 Maps, and over 80 Illustrations by the Author. Demy 8vo, 21s.

KAUFMANN, Rev. M., M.A.—**Socialism** its Nature, its Dangers, and its Remedies considered. Crown 8vo, 7s. 6d.

Utopias; or, Schemes of Social Improvement, from Sir Thomas More to Karl Marx. Crown 8vo, 5s.

Christian Socialism. Crown 8vo, 4s. 6d.

KAY, David, F.R.G.S.—**Education and Educators.** Crown 8vo. 7s. 6d.

Memory: what it is and how to improve it. Crown 8vo, 6s.

KAY, Joseph.—**Free Trade in Land.** Edited by his Widow. With Preface by the Right Hon. JOHN BRIGHT, M.P. Seventh Edition. Crown 8vo, 5s.

*** Also a cheaper edition, without the Appendix, but with a Review of Recent Changes in the Land Laws of England, by the RIGHT HON. G. OSBORNE MORGAN, Q.C., M.P. Cloth, 1s. 6d.; paper covers, 1s.

KELKE, W. H. H.—**An Epitome of English Grammar for the Use of Students.** Adapted to the London Matriculation Course and Similar Examinations. Crown 8vo, 4s. 6d.

KEMPIS, Thomas à.—**Of the Imitation of Christ.** Parchment Library Edition.—Parchment or cloth, 6s.; vellum, 7s. 6d. The Red Line Edition, fcap. 8vo, cloth extra, 2s. 6d. The Cabinet Edition, small 8vo, cloth limp, 1s.; cloth boards, 1s. 6d. The Miniature Edition, cloth limp, 32mo, 1s.; or with red lines, 1s. 6d.

*** All the above Editions may be had in various extra bindings.

Notes of a Visit to the Scenes in which his Life was spent. With numerous Illustrations. By F. R. CRUISE, M.D. Demy 8vo, 12s.

KENDALL, Henry.—**The Kinship of Men.** An argument from Pedigrees, or Genealogy viewed as a Science. With Diagrams. Crown 8vo, 5s.

KENNARD, Rev. R. B.—**A Manual of Confirmation.** 18mo. Sewed, 3d.; cloth, 1s.

KIDD, Joseph, M.D.—**The Laws of Therapeutics**; or, the Science and Art of Medicine. Second Edition. Crown 8vo, 6s.

KINGSFORD, Anna, M.D.—**The Perfect Way in Diet.** A Treatise advocating a Return to the Natural and Ancient Food of our Race. Third Edition. Small crown 8vo, 2s.

KINGSLEY, *Charles, M.A.*—**Letters and Memories of his Life.** Edited by his Wife. With two Steel Engraved Portraits, and Vignettes on Wood. Sixteenth Cabinet Edition. 2 vols. Crown 8vo, 12s.

※ Also a People's Edition, in one volume. With Portrait. Crown 8vo, 6s.

All Saints' Day, and other Sermons. Edited by the Rev. W. HARRISON. Third Edition. Crown 8vo, 7s. 6d.

True Words for Brave Men. A Book for Soldiers' and Sailors' Libraries. Sixteenth Thousand. Crown 8vo, 2s. 6d.

KNOX, *Alexander A.*—**The New Playground**; or, Wanderings in Algeria. New and Cheaper Edition. Large crown 8vo, 6s.

Lamartine, Alphonse de, Life. By Lady MARGARET DOMVILE. Large crown 8vo, 7s. 6d.

Land Concentration and Irresponsibility of Political Power, as causing the Anomaly of a Widespread State of Want by the Side of the Vast Supplies of Nature. Crown 8vo, 5s.

LANDON, *Joseph.*—**School Management**; Including a General View of the Work of Education, Organization, and Discipline. Seventh Edition. Crown 8vo, 6s.

LANG, *Andrew.*—**Lost Leaders.** Crown 8vo, 5s.

LAURIE, *S. S.*—**The Rise and Early Constitution of Universities.** With a Survey of Mediæval Education. Crown 8vo, 6s.

LEFEVRE, *Right Hon. G. Shaw.*—**Peel and O'Connell.** Demy 8vo, 10s. 6d.

Incidents of Coercion. A Journal of visits to Ireland. Third Edition. Crown 8vo, limp cloth, 1s. 6d.; paper covers, 1s.

Letters from an Unknown Friend. By the Author of "Charles Lowder." With a Preface by the Rev. W. H. CLEAVER. Fcap. 8vo, 1s.

LILLIE, *Arthur, M.R.A.S.*—**The Popular Life of Buddha.** Containing an Answer to the Hibbert Lectures of 1881. With Illustrations. Crown 8vo, 6s.

Buddhism in Christendom; or, Jesus the Essene. With Illustrations. Demy 8vo, 15s.

LITTLE, *E. A.*—**Log-Book Notes through Life.** Oblong. Illustrated. 6s.

LOCHER, *Carl.*—**An Explanation of Organ Stops,** with Hints for Effective Combinations. Demy 8vo, 5s.

LONGFELLOW, *H. Wadsworth.*—**Life.** By his Brother, SAMUEL LONGFELLOW. With Portraits and Illustrations. 3 vols. Demy 8vo, 42s.

LONSDALE, Margaret.—**Sister Dora**: a Biography. With Portrait. Thirtieth Edition. Small crown 8vo, 2s. 6d.

George Eliot: Thoughts upon her Life, her Books, and Herself. Second Edition. Small crown 8vo, 1s. 6d.

LOUNSBURY, Thomas R.—**James Fenimore Cooper.** With Portrait. Crown 8vo, 5s.

LOWDER, Charles.—**A Biography.** By the Author of "St. Teresa." Twelfth Edition. Crown 8vo. With Portrait. 3s. 6d.

LÜCKES, Eva C. E.—**Lectures on General Nursing**, delivered to the Probationers of the London Hospital Training School for Nurses. Third Edition. Crown 8vo, 2s. 6d.

LYTTON, Edward Bulwer, Lord.—**Life, Letters and Literary Remains.** By his Son, the EARL OF LYTTON. With Portraits, Illustrations, and Facsimiles. Demy 8vo. Vols. I. and II., 32s.

MACHIAVELLI, Niccolò. — **Life and Times.** By Prof. VILLARI. Translated by LINDA VILLARI. 4 vols. Large post 8vo, 48s.

Discourses on the First Decade of Titus Livius. Translated from the Italian by NINIAN HILL THOMSON, M.A. Large crown 8vo, 12s.

The Prince. Translated from the Italian by N. H. T. Small crown 8vo, printed on hand-made paper, bevelled boards, 6s.

MACNEILL, J. G. Swift.—**How the Union was carried.** Crown 8vo, cloth, 1s. 6d.; paper covers, 1s.

MAGNUS, Lady.—**About the Jews since Bible Times.** From the Babylonian Exile till the English Exodus. Small crown 8vo, 6s.

MAGNUS, Sir Philip.—**Industrial Education.** Crown 8vo, 6s.

Maintenon, Madame de. By EMILY BOWLES. With Portrait, Large crown 8vo, 7s. 6d.

Many Voices. A volume of Extracts from the Religious Writers of Christendom from the First to the Sixteenth Century. With Biographical Sketches. Crown 8vo, cloth extra, red edges, 6s.

MARKHAM, Capt. Albert Hastings, R.N.—**The Great Frozen Sea**: A Personal Narrative of the Voyage of the *Alert* during the Arctic Expedition of 1875-6. With 6 full-page Illustrations, 2 Maps, and 27 Woodcuts. Sixth and Cheaper Edition. Crown 8vo, 6s.

MARTINEAU, Gertrude.—**Outline Lessons on Morals.** Small crown 8vo, 3s. 6d.

MASON, Charlotte M.—**Home Education**: a Course of Lectures to Ladies. Crown 8vo, 3s. 6d.

MASSEY, Gerald. — **The Secret Drama of Shakspeare's Sonnets.** 4to. 12s. 6d.

Matter and Energy: An Examination of the Fundamental Conceptions of Physical Force. By B. L. L. Small crown 8vo, 2s.

MATUCE, H. Ogram. A Wanderer. Crown 8vo, 5s.

MAUDSLEY, H., M.D.—Body and Will. Being an Essay concerning Will, in its Metaphysical, Physiological, and Pathological Aspects. 8vo, 12s.

Natural Causes and Supernatural Seemings. Second Edition. Crown 8vo, 6s.

McGRATH, Terence.—Pictures from Ireland. New and Cheaper Edition. Crown 8vo, 2s.

McKINNEY, S. B. G.—Science and Art of Religion. Crown 8vo, 8s. 6d.

MILLER, Edward.—The History and Doctrines of Irvingism; or, The so-called Catholic and Apostolic Church. 2 vols. Large post 8vo, 15s.

MILLS, Herbert.—Poverty and the State; or, Work for the Unemployed. An Inquiry into the Causes and Extent of Enforced Idleness, with a Statement of a Remedy. Crown 8vo, 6s. Cheap Edition, limp cloth, 1s. 6d.; paper covers, 1s.

MINTON, Rev. Francis.—Capital and Wages. 8vo, 15s.

Mitchel, John, Life. By WILLIAM DILLON. 2 vols. 8vo. With Portrait. 21s.

MITCHELL, Lucy M.—A History of Ancient Sculpture. With numerous Illustrations, including 6 Plates in Phototype. Super-royal 8vo, 42s.

MIVART, St. George.—On Truth. Demy 8vo, 16s.

MOCKLER, E.—A Grammar of the Baloochee Language, as it is spoken in Makran (Ancient Gedrosia), in the Persia-Arabic and Roman characters. Fcap. 8vo, 5s.

MOHL, Julius and Mary.—Letters and Recollections of. By M. C. M. SIMPSON. With Portraits and Two Illustrations. Demy 8vo, 15s.

MOLESWORTH, Rev. W. Nassau, M.A.—History of the Church of England from 1660. Large crown 8vo, 7s. 6d.

MOORE, Aubrey L.—Science and the Faith: Essays on Apologetic Subjects. Crown 8vo, 6s.

MORELL, J. R.—Euclid Simplified in Method and Language. Being a Manual of Geometry. Compiled from the most important French Works, approved by the University of Paris and the Minister of Public Instruction. Fcap. 8vo, 2s. 6d.

MORISON, J. Cotter.—The Service of Man: an Essay towards the Religion of the Future. Crown 8vo, 5s.

MORRIS, Gouverneur, U.S. Minister to France.—Diary and Letters. 2 vols. Demy 8vo, 30s.

MORSE, E. S., Ph.D.—**First Book of Zoology.** With numerous Illustrations. New and Cheaper Edition. Crown 8vo, 2s. 6d.

My Lawyer: A Concise Abridgment of the Laws of England. By a Barrister-at-Law. Crown 8vo, 6s. 6d.

Natural History. "Riverside" Edition. Edited by J. S. KINGSLEY. 6 vols. 4to. 2200 Illustrations. £6 6s.

NELSON, J. H., M.A.—**A Prospectus of the Scientific Study of the Hindû Law.** Demy 8vo, 9s.

Indian Usage and Judge-made Law in Madras. Demy 8vo, 12s.

NEVILL, F.—**The Service of God.** Small 4to, 3s. 6d.

NEWMAN, Cardinal.—**Characteristics from the Writings of.** Being Selections from his various Works. Arranged with the Author's personal Approval. Eighth Edition. With Portrait. Crown 8vo, 6s.

⁂ A Portrait of Cardinal Newman, mounted for framing, can be had, 2s. 6d.

NEWMAN, Francis William.—**Essays on Diet.** Small crown 8vo, cloth limp, 2s.

Miscellanies. Vol. II. Essays, Tracts, and Addresses, Moral and Religious. Demy 8vo, 12s.

Reminiscences of Two Exiles and Two Wars. Crown 8vo, 3s. 6d.

New Social Teachings. By POLITICUS. Small crown 8vo, 5s.

NICOLS, Arthur, F.G.S., F.R.G.S.—**Chapters from the Physical History of the Earth:** an Introduction to Geology and Palæontology. With numerous Illustrations. Crown 8vo, 5s.

NOEL, The Hon. Roden.—**Essays on Poetry and Poets.** Demy 8vo, 12s.

NOPS, Marianne.—**Class Lessons on Euclid.** Part I. containing the First Two Books of the Elements. Crown 8vo, 2s. 6d.

Nuces: EXERCISES ON THE SYNTAX OF THE PUBLIC SCHOOL LATIN PRIMER. New Edition in Three Parts. Crown 8vo, each 1s.

⁂ The Three Parts can also be had bound together, 3s.

OATES, Frank, F.R.G.S.—**Matabele Land and the Victoria Falls.** A Naturalist's Wanderings in the Interior of South Africa. Edited by C. G. OATES, B.A. With numerous Illustrations and 4 Maps. Demy 8vo, 21s.

O'BRIEN, R. Barry.—**Irish Wrongs and English Remedies,** with other Essays. Crown 8vo, 5s.

OLIVER, Robert.—**Unnoticed Analogies.** A Talk on the Irish Question. Crown 8vo, 3s. 6d.

C

O'MEARA, Kathleen.—**Henri Perreyve and his Counsels to the Sick.** Small crown 8vo, 5s.

One and a Half in Norway. A Chronicle of Small Beer. By Either and Both. Small crown 8vo, 3s. 6d.

OTTLEY, H. Bickersteth.—**The Great Dilemma.** Christ His Own Witness or His Own Accuser. Six Lectures. Second Edition. Crown 8vo, 3s. 6d.

Our Priests and their Tithes. By a Priest of the Province of Canterbury. Crown 8vo, 5s.

Our Public Schools—Eton, Harrow, Winchester, Rugby, Westminster, Marlborough, The Charterhouse. Crown 8vo, 6s.

OWEN, F. M.—**Across the Hills.** Small crown 8vo, 1s. 6d.

PALMER, the late William.—**Notes of a Visit to Russia in 1840–1841.** Selected and arranged by JOHN H. CARDINAL NEWMAN, with Portrait. Crown 8vo, 8s. 6d.

Early Christian Symbolism. A Series of Compositions from Fresco Paintings, Glasses, and Sculptured Sarcophagi. Edited by the Rev. Provost NORTHCOTE, D.D., and the Rev. Canon BROWNLOW, M.A. With Coloured Plates, folio, 42s., or with Plain Plates, folio, 25s.

Parchment Library. Choicely Printed on hand-made paper, limp parchment antique or cloth, 6s. ; vellum, 7s. 6d. each volume.

Sartor Resartus. By THOMAS CARLYLE.

The Poetical Works of John Milton. 2 vols.

Chaucer's Canterbury Tales. Edited by A. W. POLLARD. 2 vols.

Letters and Journals of Jonathan Swift. Selected and edited, with a Commentary and Notes, by STANLEY LANE-POOLE.

De Quincey's Confessions of an English Opium Eater. Reprinted from the First Edition. Edited by RICHARD GARNETT.

The Gospel according to **Matthew, Mark,** and **Luke.**

Selections from the Prose Writings of Jonathan Swift. With a Preface and Notes by STANLEY LANE-POOLE and Portrait.

English Sacred Lyrics.

Sir Joshua Reynolds's Discourses. Edited by EDMUND GOSSE.

Selections from Milton's Prose Writings. Edited by ERNEST MYERS.

Parchment Library—*continued*.

The Book of Psalms. Translated by the Rev. Canon T. K. CHEYNE, M.A., D.D.

The Vicar of Wakefield. With Preface and Notes by AUSTIN DOBSON.

English Comic Dramatists. Edited by OSWALD CRAWFURD.

English Lyrics.

The Sonnets of John Milton. Edited by MARK PATTISON. With Portrait after Vertue.

French Lyrics. Selected and Annotated by GEORGE SAINTSBURY. With a Miniature Frontispiece designed and etched by H. G. Glindoni.

Fables by Mr. John Gay. With Memoir by AUSTIN DOBSON, and an Etched Portrait from an unfinished Oil Sketch by Sir Godfrey Kneller.

Select Letters of Percy Bysshe Shelley. Edited, with an Introduction, by RICHARD GARNETT.

The Christian Year. Thoughts in Verse for the Sundays and Holy Days throughout the Year. With Miniature Portrait of the Rev. J. Keble, after a Drawing by G. Richmond, R.A.

Shakspere's Works. Complete in Twelve Volumes.

Eighteenth Century Essays. Selected and Edited by AUSTIN DOBSON. With a Miniature Frontispiece by R. Caldecott.

Q. Horati Flacci Opera. Edited by F. A. CORNISH, Assistant Master at Eton. With a Frontispiece after a design by L. Alma Tadema, etched by Leopold Lowenstam.

Edgar Allan Poe's Poems. With an Essay on his Poetry by ANDREW LANG, and a Frontispiece by Linley Sambourne.

Shakspere's Sonnets. Edited by EDWARD DOWDEN. With a Frontispiece etched by Leopold Lowenstam, after the Death Mask.

English Odes. Selected by EDMUND GOSSE. With Frontispiece on India paper by Hamo Thornycroft, A.R.A.

Of the Imitation of Christ. By THOMAS À KEMPIS. A revised Translation. With Frontispiece on India paper, from a Design by W. B. Richmond.

Poems: Selected from PERCY BYSSHE SHELLEY. Dedicated to Lady Shelley. With a Preface by RICHARD GARNETT and a Miniature Frontispiece.

PARSLOE, Joseph.—**Our Railways.** Sketches, Historical and Descriptive. With Practical Information as to Fares and Rates, etc., and a Chapter on Railway Reform. Crown 8vo, 6s.

PASCAL, Blaise.—**The Thoughts of.** Translated from the Text of Auguste Molinier, by C. KEGAN PAUL. Large crown 8vo, with Frontispiece, printed on hand-made paper, parchment antique, or cloth, 12*s.*; vellum, 15*s.* New Edition. Crown 8vo, 6*s.*

PATON, W. A.—**Down the Islands.** A Voyage to the Caribbees. With Illustration. Medium 8vo, 16*s.*

PAUL, C. Kegan.—**Biographical Sketches.** Printed on hand-made paper, bound in buckram. Second Edition. Crown 8vo, 7*s.* 6*d.*

PEARSON, Rev. S.—**Week-day Living.** A Book for Young Men and Women. Second Edition. Crown 8vo, 5*s.*

PENRICE, Major J.—**Arabic and English Dictionary of the Koran.** 4to, 21*s.*

PESCHEL, Dr. Oscar.—**The Races of Man and their Geographical Distribution.** Second Edition. Large crown 8vo, 9*s.*

PIDGEON, D.—**An Engineer's Holiday**; or, Notes of a Round Trip from Long. 0° to 0°. New and Cheaper Edition. Large crown 8vo, 7*s.* 6*d.*

Old World Questions and New World Answers. Second Edition. Large crown 8vo, 7*s.* 6*d.*

Plain Thoughts for Men. Eight Lectures delivered at Forester's Hall, Clerkenwell, during the London Mission, 1884. Crown 8vo, cloth, 1*s.* 6*d*; paper covers, 1*s.*

PLOWRIGHT, C. B.—**The British Uredineæ and Ustilagineæ.** With Illustrations. Demy 8vo, 12*s.*

PRICE, Prof. Bonamy.—**Chapters on Practical Political Economy.** Being the Substance of Lectures delivered before the University of Oxford. New and Cheaper Edition. Crown 8vo, 5*s.*

Prigment, The. "The Life of a Prig," "Prig's Bede," "How to Make a Saint," "The Churgress." In 1 vol. Crown 8vo, 6*s.*

Prig's Bede: the Venerable Bede, Expurgated, Expounded, and Exposed. By "THE PRIG." Second Edition. Fcap. 8vo, 3*s.* 6*d.*

Pulpit Commentary, The. (*Old Testament Series.*) Edited by the Rev. J. S. EXELL, M.A., and the Very Rev. Dean H. D. M. SPENCE, M.A., D.D.

Genesis. By the Rev. T. WHITELAW, D.D. With Homilies by the Very Rev. J. F. MONTGOMERY, D.D., Rev. Prof. R. A. REDFORD, M.A., LL.B., Rev. F. HASTINGS, Rev. W. ROBERTS, M.A. An Introduction to the Study of the Old Testament by the Venerable Archdeacon FARRAR, D.D., F.R.S.; and Introductions to the Pentateuch by the Right Rev. H. COTTERILL, D.D., and Rev. T. WHITELAW, M.A. Ninth Edition. 1 vol., 15*s.*

Pulpit Commentary, The—*continued.*

Exodus. By the Rev. Canon RAWLINSON. With Homilies by Rev. J. ORR, D.D., Rev. D. YOUNG, B.A., Rev. C. A. GOODHART, Rev. J. URQUHART, and the Rev. H. T. ROBJOHNS. Fourth Edition. 2 vols., 9s. each.

Leviticus. By the Rev. Prebendary MEYRICK, M.A. With Introductions by the Rev. R. COLLINS, Rev. Professor A. CAVE, and Homilies by Rev. Prof. REDFORD, LL.B., Rev. J. A. MACDONALD, Rev. W. CLARKSON, B.A., Rev. S. R. ALDRIDGE, LL.B., and Rev. MCCHEYNE EDGAR. Fourth Edition. 15s.

Numbers. By the Rev. R. WINTERBOTHAM, LL.B. With Homilies by the Rev. Professor W. BINNIE, D.D., Rev. E. S. PROUT, M.A., Rev. D. YOUNG, Rev. J. WAITE, and an Introduction by the Rev. THOMAS WHITELAW, M.A. Fifth Edition. 15s.

Deuteronomy. By the Rev. W. L. ALEXANDER, D.D. With Homilies by Rev. C. CLEMANCE, D.D., Rev. J. ORR, D.D., Rev. R. M. EDGAR, M.A., Rev. D. DAVIES, M.A. Fourth edition. 15s.

Joshua. By Rev. J. J. LIAS, M.A. With Homilies by Rev. S. R. ALDRIDGE, LL.B., Rev. R. GLOVER, REV. E. DE PRESSENSÉ, D.D., Rev. J. WAITE, B.A., Rev. W. F. ADENEY, M.A.; and an Introduction by the Rev. A. PLUMMER, M.A. Fifth Edition. 12s. 6d.

Judges and Ruth. By the Bishop of BATH and WELLS, and Rev. J. MORISON, D.D. With Homilies by Rev. A. F. MUIR, M.A., Rev. W. F. ADENEY, M.A., Rev. W. M. STATHAM, and Rev. Professor J. THOMSON, M.A. Fifth Edition. 10s. 6d.

1 and 2 Samuel. By the Very Rev. R. P. SMITH, D.D. With Homilies by Rev. DONALD FRASER, D.D., Rev. Prof. CHAPMAN, and Rev. B. DALE. Seventh Edition. 15s. each.

1 Kings. By the Rev. JOSEPH HAMMOND, LL.B. With Homilies by the Rev. E. DE PRESSENSÉ, D.D., Rev. J. WAITE, B.A., Rev. A. ROWLAND, LL.B., Rev. J. A. MACDONALD, and Rev. J. URQUHART. Fifth Edition. 15s.

1 Chronicles. By the Rev. Prof. P. C. BARKER, M.A., LL.B. With Homilies by Rev. Prof. J. R. THOMSON, M.A., Rev. R. TUCK, B.A., Rev. W. CLARKSON, B.A., Rev. F. WHITFIELD, M.A., and Rev. RICHARD GLOVER. 15s.

Ezra, Nehemiah, and Esther. By Rev. Canon G. RAWLINSON, M.A. With Homilies by Rev. Prof. J. R. THOMSON, M.A., Rev. Prof. R. A. REDFORD, LL.B., M.A., Rev. W. S. LEWIS, M.A., Rev. J. A. MACDONALD, Rev. A. MACKENNAL, B.A., Rev. W. CLARKSON, B.A., Rev. F. HASTINGS, Rev. W. DINWIDDIE, LL.B., Rev. Prof. ROWLANDS, B.A., Rev. G. WOOD, B.A., Rev. Prof. P. C. BARKER, M.A., LL.B., and the Rev. J. S. EXELL, M.A. Seventh Edition. 1 vol., 12s. 6d.

Pulpit Commentary, The—*continued.*

    Isaiah. By the Rev. Canon G. RAWLINSON, M.A. With Homilies by Rev. Prof. E. JOHNSON, M.A., Rev. W. CLARKSON, B.A., Rev. W. M. STATHAM, and Rev. R. TUCK, B.A. Second Edition. 2 vols., 15s. each.

    Jeremiah. (Vol. I.) By the Rev. Canon T. K. CHEYNE, D.D. With Homilies by the Rev. W. F. ADENEY, M.A., Rev. A. F. MUIR, M.A., Rev. S. CONWAY, B.A., Rev. J. WAITE, B.A., and Rev. D. YOUNG, B.A. Third Edition. 15s.

    Jeremiah (Vol. II.) and Lamentations. By Rev. Canon T. K. CHEYNE, D.D. With Homilies by Rev. Prof. J. R. THOMSON, M.A., Rev. W. F. ADENEY, M.A., Rev. A. F. MUIR, M.A., Rev. S. CONWAY, B.A., Rev. D. YOUNG, B.A. 15s.

    Hosea and Joel. By the Rev. Prof. J. J. GIVEN, Ph.D., D.D. With Homilies by the Rev. Prof. J. R. THOMSON, M.A., Rev. A. ROWLAND, B.A., LL.B., Rev. C. JERDAN, M.A., LL.B., Rev. J. ORR, D.D., and Rev. D. THOMAS, D.D. 15s.

Pulpit Commentary, The. (*New Testament Series.*)

    St. Mark. By Very Rev. E. BICKERSTETH, D.D., Dean of Lichfield. With Homilies by Rev. Prof. THOMSON, M.A., Rev. Prof. J. J. GIVEN, Ph.D., D.D., Rev. Prof. JOHNSON, M.A., Rev. A. ROWLAND, B.A., LL.B., Rev. A. MUIR, and Rev. R. GREEN. Fifth Edition. 2 vols., 10s. 6d. each.

    St. Luke. By the Very Rev. H. D. M. SPENCE. With Homilies by the Rev. J. MARSHALL LANG, D.D., Rev. W. CLARKSON, and Rev. R. M. EDGAR. Vol. I., 10s. 6d.

    St. John. By Rev. Prof. H. R. REYNOLDS, D.D. With Homilies by Rev. Prof. T. CROSKERY, D.D., Rev. Prof. J. R. THOMSON, M.A., Rev. D. YOUNG, B.A., Rev. B. THOMAS, Rev. G. BROWN. Second Edition. 2 vols., 15s. each.

    The Acts of the Apostles. By the Bishop of BATH and WELLS. With Homilies by Rev. Prof. P. C. BARKER, M.A., LL.B., Rev. Prof. E. JOHNSON, M.A., Rev. Prof. R. A. REDFORD, LL.B., Rev. R. TUCK, B.A., Rev. W. CLARKSON, B.A. Fourth Edition. 2 vols., 10s. 6d. each.

    1 Corinthians. By the Ven. Archdeacon FARRAR, D.D. With Homilies by Rev. Ex-Chancellor LIPSCOMB, LL.D., Rev. DAVID THOMAS, D.D., Rev. D. FRASER, D.D., Rev. Prof. J. R. THOMSON, M.A., Rev. J. WAITE, B.A., Rev. R. TUCK, B.A., Rev. E. HURNDALL, M.A., and Rev. H. BREMNER, B.D. Fourth Edition. 15s.

    2 Corinthians and Galatians. By the Ven. Archdeacon FARRAR, D.D., and Rev. Prebendary E. HUXTABLE. With Homilies by Rev. Ex-Chancellor LIPSCOMB, LL.D., Rev. DAVID THOMAS, D.D., Rev. DONALD FRASER, D.D., Rev. R. TUCK, B.A., Rev. E. HURNDALL, M.A., Rev. Prof. J. R. THOMSON, M.A., Rev. R. FINLAYSON, B.A., Rev. W. F. ADENEY, M.A., Rev. R. M. EDGAR, M.A., and Rev. T. CROSKERY, D.D. Second Edition. 21s.

Pulpit Commentary, The—*continued.*

Ephesians, Philippians, and Colossians. By the Rev. Prof. W. G. BLAIKIE, D.D., Rev. B. C. CAFFIN, M.A., and Rev. G. G. FINDLAY, B.A. With Homilies by Rev. D. THOMAS, D.D., Rev. R. M. EDGAR, M.A., Rev. R. FINLAYSON, B.A., Rev. W. F. ADENEY, M.A., Rev. Prof. T. CROSKERY, D.D., Rev. E. S. PROUT, M.A., Rev. Canon VERNON HUTTON, and Rev. U. R. THOMAS, D.D. Second Edition. 21s.

Thessalonians, Timothy, Titus, and Philemon. By the Bishop of Bath and Wells, Rev. Dr. GLOAG, and Rev. Dr. EALES. With Homilies by the Rev. B. C. CAFFIN, M.A., Rev. R. FINLAYSON, B.A., Rev. Prof. T. CROSKERY, D.D., Rev. W. F. ADENEY, M.A., Rev. W. M. STATHAM, and Rev. D. THOMAS, D.D. 15s.

Hebrews and James. By the Rev. J. BARMBY, D.D., and Rev. Prebendary E. C. S. GIBSON, M.A. With Homiletics by the Rev. C. JERDAN, M.A., LL.B., and Rev. Prebendary E. C. S. GIBSON. And Homilies by the Rev. W. JONES, Rev. C. NEW, Rev. D. YOUNG, B.A., Rev. J. S. BRIGHT, Rev. T. F. LOCKYER, B.A., and Rev. C. JERDAN, M.A., LL.B. Second Edition. 15s.

PUSEY, Dr.—**Sermons for the Church's Seasons from Advent to Trinity.** Selected from the Published Sermons of the late EDWARD BOUVERIE PUSEY, D.D. Crown 8vo, 5s.

QUEKETT, Rev. W.—**My Sayings and Doings.** With Reminiscences of my Life. With Illustrations. Demy 8vo, 18s.

RANKE, Leopold von.—**Universal History.** The oldest Historical Group of Nations and the Greeks. Edited by G. W. PROTHERO. Demy 8vo, 16s.

Remedy (The) for Landlordism; or, Free Land Tenure. Small crown 8vo, 2s. 6d.

RENDELL, J. M.—**Concise Handbook of the Island of Madeira.** With Plan of Funchal and Map of the Island. Fcap. 8vo, 1s. 6d.

REYNOLDS, Rev. J. W.—**The Supernatural in Nature.** A Verification by Free Use of Science. Third Edition, Revised and Enlarged. Demy 8vo, 14s.

The Mystery of Miracles. Third and Enlarged Edition. Crown 8vo, 6s.

The Mystery of the Universe our Common Faith. Demy 8vo, 14s.

The World to Come: Immortality a Physical Fact. Crown 8vo, 6s.

RIBOT, Prof. Th.—**Heredity**: A Psychological Study of its Phenomena, its Laws, its Causes, and its Consequences. Second Edition. Large crown 8vo, 9s.

RICHARDSON, Austin.—"**What are the Catholic Claims?**" With Introduction by Rev. LUKE RIVINGTON. Crown 8vo, 3s. 6d.

RIVINGTON, Luke.—**Authority, or a Plain Reason for joining the Church of Rome.** Fifth Edition. Crown 8vo, 3s. 6d.

ROBERTSON, The late Rev. F. W., M.A.—**Life and Letters of.** Edited by the Rev. STOPFORD BROOKE, M.A.
    I. Two vols., uniform with the Sermons. With Steel Portrait. Crown 8vo, 7s. 6d.
    II. Library Edition, in Demy 8vo, with Portrait. 12s.
    III. A Popular Edition, in 1 vol. Crown 8vo, 6s.

Sermons. Five Series. Small crown 8vo, 3s. 6d. each.

Notes on Genesis. New and Cheaper Edition. Small crown 8vo, 3s. 6d.

Expository Lectures on St. Paul's Epistles to the Corinthians. A New Edition. Small crown 8vo, 5s.

Lectures and Addresses, with other Literary Remains. A New Edition. Small crown 8vo, 5s.

An Analysis of Tennyson's " In Memoriam." (Dedicated by Permission to the Poet-Laureate.) Fcap. 8vo, 2s.

The Education of the Human Race. Translated from the German of GOTTHOLD EPHRAIM LESSING. Fcap. 8vo, 2s. 6d.

*** A Portrait of the late Rev. F. W. Robertson, mounted for framing, can be had, 2s. 6d.

ROGERS, William.—**Reminiscences.** Compiled by R. H. HADDEN. With Portrait. Crown 8vo, 6s. Cheap Edition, 2s. 6d.

ROMANES, G. J.—**Mental Evolution in Animals.** With a Posthumous Essay on Instinct by CHARLES DARWIN, F.R.S. Demy 8vo, 12s.

Mental Evolution in Man: Origin of Human Faculty. Demy 8vo, 14s.

ROSMINI SERBATI, Antonio.—**Life.** By the REV. W. LOCKHART. 2 vols. With Portraits. Crown 8vo, 12s.

ROSS, Janet.—**Italian Sketches.** With 14 full-page Illustrations. Crown 8vo, 7s. 6d.

RULE, Martin, M.A.—**The Life and Times of St. Anselm, Archbishop of Canterbury and Primate of the Britains.** 2 vols. Demy 8vo, 32s.

SANTIAGOE, Daniel.—**The Curry Cook's Assistant.** Fcap. 8vo, cloth. 1s. 6d.; paper covers, 1s.

SAVERY, C. E.—**The Church of England; an Historical Sketch.** Crown 8vo, 1s. 6d.

SAYCE, *Rev. Archibald Henry.*—Introduction to the Science of Language. 2 vols. Second Edition. Large post 8vo, 21s.

SCOONES, *W. Baptiste.*—Four Centuries of English Letters: A Selection of 350 Letters by 150 Writers, from the Period of the Paston Letters to the Present Time. Third Edition. Large crown 8vo, 6s.

Selwyn, Bishop, *of New Zealand and of Lichfield.* A Sketch of his Life and Work, with Further Gleanings from his Letters, Sermons, and Speeches. By the Rev. Canon CURTEIS. Large crown 8vo, 7s. 6d.

SEYMOUR, *W. Digby, Q.C.,*—Home Rule and State Supremacy. Crown 8vo, 3s. 6d.

Shakspere's Macbeth. With Preface, Notes, and New Renderings. By MATTHIAS MULL. Demy 8vo, 6s.

Shakspere's Works. The Avon Edition, 12 vols., fcap. 8vo, cloth, 18s.; in cloth box, 21s.; bound in 6 vols., cloth, 15s.

Shakspere's Works, an Index to. By EVANGELINE O'CONNOR. Crown 8vo, 5s.

SHELLEY, *Percy Bysshe.*—Life. By EDWARD DOWDEN, LL.D. 2 vols. With Portraits. Demy 8vo, 36s.

SHILLITO, *Rev. Joseph.*—Womanhood: its Duties, Temptations, and Privileges. A Book for Young Women. Third Edition. Crown 8vo, 3s. 6d.

Shooting, Practical Hints on. Being a Treatise on the Shot Gun and its Management. By "20 Bore." With 55 Illustrations. Demy 8vo, 12s.

Sister Augustine, Superior of the Sisters of Charity at the St. Johannis Hospital at Bonn. Authorized Translation by HANS THARAU, from the German "Memorials of AMALIE VON LASAULX." Cheap Edition. Large crown 8vo, 4s. 6d.

SKINNER, *James.*—A Memoir. By the Author of "Charles Lowder." With a Preface by the Rev. Canon CARTER, and Portrait. Large crown, 7s. 6d.

** Also a cheap Edition. With Portrait. Fourth Edition. Crown 8vo, 3s. 6d.

SMITH, *L, A.*—The Music of the Waters: Sailor's Chanties and Working Songs of the Sea. Demy 8vo, 12s.

Spanish Mystics. By the Editor of "Many Voices." Crown 8vo, 5s.

Specimens of English Prose Style from Malory to Macaulay. Selected and Annotated, with an Introductory Essay, by GEORGE SAINTSBURY. Large crown 8vo, printed on handmade paper, parchment antique or cloth, 12s.; vellum, 15s.

STRACHEY, *Sir John, G.C.S.I.*—India. With Map. Demy 8vo, 15s.

Stray Papers on Education, and Scenes from School Life. By B. H. Second Edition. Small crown 8vo, 3s. 6d.

STRECKER-WISLICENUS.—**Organic Chemistry.** Translated and Edited, with Extensive Additions, by W. R. HODGKINSON, Ph.D., and A. J. GREENAWAY, F.I.C. Second and cheaper Edition. Demy 8vo, 12s. 6d.

Suakin, 1885: being a Sketch of the Campaign of this year. By an Officer who was there. Second Edition. Crown 8vo, 2s. 6d.

SULLY, James, M.A.—**Pessimism:** a History and a Criticism. Second Edition. Demy 8vo, 14s.

SWEDENBORG, Eman.—**De Cultu et Amore Dei ubi Agitur de Telluris ortu, Paradiso et Vivario, tum de Primogeniti Seu Adami Nativitate Infantia, et Amore.** Crown 8vo, 6s.

> **On the Worship and Love of God.** Treating of the Birth of the Earth, Paradise, and the Abode of Living Creatures. Translated from the original Latin. Crown 8vo, 7s. 6d.

> **Prodromus Philosophiæ Ratiocinantis de Infinito, et Causa Finali Creationis:** deque Mechanismo Operationis Animæ et Corporis. Edidit THOMAS MURRAY GORMAN, M.A. Crown 8vo, 7s. 6d.

TARRING, C. J.—**A Practical Elementary Turkish Grammar.** Crown 8vo, 6s.

TAYLOR, Rev. Canon Isaac, LL.D.—**The Alphabet.** An Account of the Origin and Development of Letters. With numerous Tables and Facsimiles. 2 vols. Demy 8vo, 36s.

> **Leaves from an Egyptian Note-book.** Crown 8vo, 5s.

TAYLOR, Reynell, C.B., C.S.I. **A Biography.** By E. GAMBIER PARRY. With Portait and Map. Demy 8vo, 14s.

TAYLOR, Sir Henry.—**The Statesman.** Fcap. 8vo, 3s. 6d.

THOM, J. Hamilton.—**Laws of Life after the Mind of Christ.** Two Series. Crown 8vo, 7s. 6d. each.

THOMPSON, Sir H.—**Diet in Relation to Age and Activity.** Fcap. 8vo, cloth, 1s. 6d.; paper covers, 1s.

> **Modern Cremation.** Crown 8vo, 2s. 6d.

TODHUNTER, Dr. J.—**A Study of Shelley.** Crown 8vo, 7s.

TOLSTOI, Count Leo.—**Christ's Christianity.** Translated from the Russian. Large crown 8vo, 7s. 6d.

TRANT, William.—**Trade Unions: Their Origin, Objects, and Efficacy.** Small crown 8vo, 1s. 6d.; paper covers, 1s.

TRENCH, The late R. C., *Archbishop*.—**Letters and Memorials.** By the Author of "Charles Lowder." With two Portraits. 2 vols. 8vo, 21s.

Notes on the Parables of Our Lord. 8vo, 12s. Cheap Edition. Fifty-sixth Thousand. 7s. 6d.

Notes on the Miracles of Our Lord. 8vo, 12s. Cheap Edition. Forty-eighth Thousand. 7s. 6d.

Studies in the Gospels. Fifth Edition, Revised. 8vo, 10s. 6d.

Brief Thoughts and Meditations on Some Passages in Holy Scripture. Third Edition. Crown 8vo, 3s. 6d.

Synonyms of the New Testament. Tenth Edition, Enlarged. 8vo, 12s.

Sermons New and Old. Crown 8vo, 6s.

Westminster and other Sermons. Crown 8vo, 6s.

On the Authorized Version of the New Testament. Second Edition. 8vo, 7s.

Commentary on the Epistles to the Seven Churches in Asia. Fourth Edition, Revised. 8vo, 8s. 6d.

The Sermon on the Mount. An Exposition drawn from the Writings of St. Augustine, with an Essay on his Merits as an Interpreter of Holy Scripture. Fourth Edition, Enlarged. 8vo, 10s. 6d.

Shipwrecks of Faith. Three Sermons preached before the University of Cambridge in May, 1867. Fcap. 8vo, 2s. 6d.

Lectures on Mediæval Church History. Being the Substance of Lectures delivered at Queen's College, London. Second Edition. 8vo, 12s.

English, Past and Present. Thirteenth Edition, Revised and Improved. Fcap. 8vo, 5s.

On the Study of Words. Twentieth Edition, Revised. Fcap. 8vo, 5s.

Select Glossary of English Words used Formerly in Senses Different from the Present. Sixth Edition, Revised and Enlarged. Fcap. 8vo, 5s.

Proverbs and Their Lessons. Seventh Edition, Enlarged. Fcap. 8vo, 4s.

Poems. Collected and Arranged anew. Tenth Edition. Fcap. 8vo, 7s. 6d.

Poems. Library Edition. 2 vols. Small crown 8vo, 10s.

Sacred Latin Poetry. Chiefly Lyrical, Selected and Arranged for Use. Third Edition, Corrected and Improved. Fcap. 8vo, 7s.

TRENCH, The late R. C., Archbishop—continued.

 A Household Book of English Poetry. Selected and Arranged, with Notes. Fourth Edition, Revised. Extra fcap. 8vo, 5s. 6d.

 An Essay on the Life and Genius of Calderon. With Translations from his "Life's a Dream" and "Great Theatre of the World." Second Edition, Revised and Improved. Extra fcap. 8vo, 5s. 6d.

 Gustavus Adolphus in Germany, and other Lectures on the Thirty Years' War. Third Edition, Enlarged. Fcap. 8vo, 4s.

 Plutarch: his Life, his Lives, and his Morals. Second Edition, Enlarged. Fcap. 8vo, 3s. 6d.

 Remains of the late Mrs. Richard Trench. Being Selections from her Journals, Letters, and other Papers. New and Cheaper Issue. With Portrait. 8vo, 6s.

TUTHILL, C. A. H.—**Origin and Development of Christian Dogma.** Crown 8vo, 3s. 6d.

Two Centuries of Irish History. By various Writers. Edited by Prof. J. BRYCE. Demy 8vo, 16s.

UMLAUFT, Prof. F.—**The Alps.** Illustrations and Maps. 8vo, 25s.

VAL d'EREMAO, Rev. J. P.—**The Serpent of Eden.** A Philological and Critical Essay. Crown 8vo, 4s. 6d.

VOLCKXSOM, E. W. v.—**Catechism of Elementary Modern Chemistry.** Small crown 8vo, 3s.

WALLER, C. B.—**Unfoldings of Christian Hope.** Second Edition. Crown 8vo, 3s. 6d.

WALPOLE, Chas. George.—**A Short History of Ireland from the Earliest Times to the Union with Great Britain.** With 5 Maps and Appendices. Third Edition. Crown 8vo, 6s.

WARD, Wilfrid.—**The Wish to Believe.** A Discussion Concerning the Temper of Mind in which a reasonable Man should undertake Religious Inquiry. Small crown 8vo, 5s.

WARD, William George, Ph.D.—**Essays on the Philosophy of Theism.** Edited, with an Introduction, by WILFRID WARD. 2 vols. Demy 8vo, 21s.

WARTER, J. W.—**An Old Shropshire Oak.** 2 vols. Demy 8vo, 28s.

WEDMORE, Frederick.—**The Masters of Genre Painting.** With Sixteen Illustrations. Post 8vo, 7s. 6d.

WHIBLEY, Charles.—**In Cap and Gown.** Crown 8vo.

WHITMAN, Sidney.—**Conventional Cant: its Results and Remedy.** Crown 8vo, 6s.

WHITNEY, *Prof. William Dwight.*—**Essentials of English Grammar,** for the Use of Schools. Second Edition. Crown 8vo, 3s. 6d.

WHITWORTH, *George Clifford.*—**An Anglo-Indian Dictionary:** a Glossary of Indian Terms used in English, and of such English or other Non-Indian Terms as have obtained special meanings in India. Demy 8vo, cloth, 12s.

Wilberforce, Bishop, *of Oxford and Winchester.* Life. By his Son REGINALD WILBERFORCE. Crown 8vo, 6s.

WILSON, *Mrs. R. F.*—**The Christian Brothers.** Their Origin and Work. With a Sketch of the Life of their Founder, the Ven. JEAN BAPTISTE, de la Salle. Crown 8vo, 6s.

WOLTMANN, *Dr. Alfred, and* WOERMANN, *Dr. Karl.*—**History of Painting.** With numerous Illustrations. Medium 8vo. Vol. I. Painting in Antiquity and the Middle Ages. 28s.; bevelled boards, gilt leaves, 30s. Vol. II. The Painting of the Renascence. 42s.; bevelled boards, gilt leaves, 45s.

Words of Jesus Christ taken from the Gospels. Small crown 8vo, 2s. 6d.

YOUMANS, *Edward L., M.D.*—**A Class Book of Chemistry,** on the Basis of the New System. With 200 Illustrations. Crown 8vo, 5s.

YOUMANS, *Eliza A.*—**First Book of Botany.** Designed to cultivate the Observing Powers of Children. With 300 Engravings. New and Cheaper Edition. Crown 8vo, 2s. 6d.

THE INTERNATIONAL SCIENTIFIC SERIES.

I. **Forms of Water in Clouds and Rivers, Ice and Glaciers.** By J. Tyndall, LL.D., F.R.S. With 25 Illustrations. Ninth Edition. 5s.

II. **Physics and Politics**; or, Thoughts on the Application of the Principles of "Natural Selection" and "Inheritance" to Political Society. By Walter Bagehot. Eighth Edition. 5s.

III. **Foods.** By Edward Smith, M.D., LL.B., F.R.S. With numerous Illustrations. Ninth Edition. 5s.

IV. **Mind and Body: the Theories of their Relation.** By Alexander Bain, LL.D. With Four Illustrations. Eighth Edition. 5s.

V. **The Study of Sociology.** By Herbert Spencer. Fourteenth Edition. 5s.

VI. **The Conservation of Energy.** By Balfour Stewart, M.A., LL.D., F.R.S. With 14 Illustrations. Seventh Edition. 5*s*.

VII. **Animal Locomotion**; or, Walking, Swimming, and Flying. By J. B. Pettigrew, M.D., F.R.S., etc. With 130 Illustrations. Third Edition. 5*s*.

VIII. **Responsibility in Mental Disease.** By Henry Maudsley, M.D. Fourth Edition. 5*s*.

IX. **The New Chemistry.** By Professor J. P. Cooke. With 31 Illustrations. Ninth Edition. 5*s*.

X. **The Science of Law.** By Professor Sheldon Amos. Sixth Edition. 5*s*.

XI. **Animal Mechanism**: a Treatise on Terrestrial and Aerial Locomotion. By Professor E. J. Marey. With 117 Illustrations. Third Edition. 5*s*.

XII. **The Doctrine of Descent and Darwinism.** By Professor Oscar Schmidt. With 26 Illustrations. Seventh Edition. 5*s*.

XIII. **The History of the Conflict between Religion and Science.** By J. W. Draper, M.D., LL.D. Twentieth Edition. 5*s*.

XIV. **Fungi: their Nature, Influences, and Uses.** By M. C. Cooke, M.A., LL.D. Edited by the Rev. M. J. Berkeley, M.A., F.L.S. With numerous Illustrations. Fourth Edition. 5*s*.

XV. **The Chemistry of Light and Photography.** By Dr. Hermann Vogel. With 100 Illustrations. Fifth Edition. 5*s*.

XVI. **The Life and Growth of Language.** By Professor William Dwight Whitney. Fifth Edition. 5*s*.

XVII. **Money and the Mechanism of Exchange.** By W. Stanley Jevons, M.A., F.R.S. Eighth Edition. 5*s*.

XVIII. **The Nature of Light.** With a General Account of Physical Optics. By Dr. Eugene Lommel. With 188 Illustrations and a Table of Spectra in Chromo-lithography. Fifth Edition. 5*s*.

XIX. **Animal Parasites and Messmates.** By P. J. Van Beneden. With 83 Illustrations. Third Edition. 5*s*.

XX. **On Fermentation.** By Professor Schützenberger. With 28 Illustrations. Fourth Edition. 5*s*.

XXI. **The Five Senses of Man.** By Professor Bernstein. With 91 Illustrations. Fifth Edition. 5*s*.

XXII. **The Theory of Sound in its Relation to Music.** By Professor Pietro Blaserna. With numerous Illustrations. Third Edition. 5*s*.

XXIII. **Studies in Spectrum Analysis.** By J. Norman Lockyer, F.R.S. With six photographic Illustrations of Spectra, and numerous engravings on Wood. Fourth Edition. 6*s*. 6*d*.

XXIV. **A History of the Growth of the Steam Engine.** By Professor R. H. Thurston. With numerous Illustrations. Fourth Edition. 5s.

XXV. **Education as a Science.** By Alexander Bain, LL.D. Seventh Edition. 5s.

XXVI. **The Human Species.** By Professor A. de Quatrefages. Fourth Edition. 5s.

XXVII. **Modern Chromatics.** With Applications to Art and Industry. By Ogden N. Rood. With 130 original Illustrations. Second Edition. 5s.

XXVIII. **The Crayfish:** an Introduction to the Study of Zoology. By Professor T. H. Huxley. With 82 Illustrations. Fifth Edition, 5s.

XXIX. **The Brain as an Organ of Mind.** By H. Charlton Bastian, M.D. With numerous Illustrations. Third Edition. 5s.

XXX. **The Atomic Theory.** By Prof. Wurtz. Translated by E. Cleminshaw, F.C.S. Fifth Edition. 5s.

XXXI. **The Natural Conditions of Existence as they affect Animal Life.** By Karl Semper. With 2 Maps and 106 Woodcuts. Third Edition. 5s.

XXXII. **General Physiology of Muscles and Nerves.** By Prof. J. Rosenthal. Third Edition. With 75 Illustrations. 5s.

XXXIII. **Sight:** an Exposition of the Principles of Monocular and Binocular Vision. By Joseph le Conte, LL.D. Second Edition. With 132 Illustrations. 5s.

XXXIV. **Illusions:** a Psychological Study. By James Sully. Third Edition. 5s.

XXXV. **Volcanoes: what they are and what they teach.** By Professor J. W. Judd, F.R.S. With 96 Illustrations on Wood. Fourth Edition. 5s.

XXXVI. **Suicide:** an Essay on Comparative Moral Statistics. By Prof. H. Morselli. Second Edition. With Diagrams. 5s.

XXXVII. **The Brain and its Functions.** By J. Luys. With Illustrations. Second Edition. 5s.

XXXVIII. **Myth and Science:** an Essay. By Tito Vignoli. Third Edition. With Supplementary Note. 5s.

XXXIX. **The Sun.** By Professor Young. With Illustrations. Third Edition. 5s.

XL. **Ants, Bees, and Wasps:** a Record of Observations on the Habits of the Social Hymenoptera. By Sir John Lubbock, Bart., M.P. With 5 Chromo-lithographic Illustrations. Ninth Edition. 5s.

XLI. **Animal Intelligence.** By G. J. Romanes, LL.D., F.R.S. Fourth Edition. 5s.

XLII. **The Concepts and Theories of Modern Physics.** By J. B. Stallo. Third Edition. 5s.

XLIII. **Diseases of Memory**: An Essay in the Positive Psychology. By Prof. Th. Ribot. Third Edition. 5s.

XLIV. **Man before Metals.** By N. Joly, with 148 Illustrations. Fourth Edition. 5s.

XLV. **The Science of Politics.** By Prof. Sheldon Amos. Third Edition. 5s.

XLVI. **Elementary Meteorology.** By Robert H. Scott. Fourth Edition. With Numerous Illustrations. 5s.

XLVII. **The Organs of Speech and their Application in the Formation of Articulate Sounds.** By Georg Hermann Von Meyer. With 47 Woodcuts. 5s.

XLVIII. **Fallacies.** A View of Logic from the Practical Side. By Alfred Sidgwick. Second Edition. 5s.

XLIX. **Origin of Cultivated Plants.** By Alphonse de Candolle. Second Edition. 5s.

L. **Jelly-Fish, Star-Fish, and Sea-Urchins.** Being a Research on Primitive Nervous Systems. By G. J. Romanes. With Illustrations. 5s.

LI. **The Common Sense of the Exact Sciences.** By the late William Kingdon Clifford. Second Edition. With 100 Figures. 5s.

LII. **Physical Expression : Its Modes and Principles.** By Francis Warner, M.D., F.R.C.P., Hunterian Professor of Comparative Anatomy and Physiology, R.C.S.E. With 50 Illustrations. 5s.

LIII. **Anthropoid Apes.** By Robert Hartmann. With 63 Illustrations. 5s.

LIV. **The Mammalia in their Relation to Primeval Times.** By Oscar Schmidt. With 51 Woodcuts. 5s.

LV. **Comparative Literature.** By H. Macaulay Posnett, LL.D. 5s.

LVI. **Earthquakes and other Earth Movements.** By Prof. John Milne. With 38 Figures. Second Edition. 5s.

LVII. **Microbes, Ferments, and Moulds.** By E. L. Trouessart. With 107 Illustrations. 5s.

LVIII. **Geographical and Geological Distribution of Animals.** By Professor A. Heilprin. With Frontispiece. 5s.

LIX. **Weather.** A Popular Exposition of the Nature of Weather Changes from Day to Day. By the Hon. Ralph Abercromby. Second Edition. With 96 Illustrations. 5s.

LX. **Animal Magnetism.** By Alfred Binet and Charles Féré. Second Edition. 5s.

LXI. **Manual of British Discomycetes,** with descriptions of all the Species of Fungi hitherto found in Britain included in the Family, and Illustrations of the Genera. By William Phillips, F.L.S. 5s.

LXII. **International Law.** With Materials for a Code of International Law. By Professor Leone Levi. 5s.

LXIII. **The Geological History of Plants.** By Sir J. William Dawson. With 80 Figures. 5s.

LXIV. **The Origin of Floral Structures through Insect and other Agencies.** By Rev. Prof. G. Henslow. With 88 Illustrations. 5s.

LXV. **On the Senses, Instincts, and Intelligence of Animals.** With special Reference to Insects. By Sir John Lubbock, Bart., M.P. 100 Illustrations. Second Edition. 5s.

LXVI. **The Primitive Family: Its Origin and Development.** By C. N. Starcke.

MILITARY WORKS.

BRACKENBURY, Col. C. B., R.A.—**Military Handbooks for Regimental Officers.**

I. **Military Sketching and Reconnaissance.** By Col. F. J. Hutchison and Major H. G. MacGregor. Fifth Edition. With 16 Plates. Small crown 8vo, 4s.

II. **The Elements of Modern Tactics Practically applied to English Formations.** By Lieut.-Col. Wilkinson Shaw. Sixth Edition. With 25 Plates and Maps. Small crown 8vo, 9s.

III. **Field Artillery.** Its Equipment, Organization and Tactics. By Major Sisson C. Pratt, R.A. With 12 Plates. Third Edition. Small crown 8vo, 6s.

IV. **The Elements of Military Administration.** First Part: Permanent System of Administration. By Major J. W. Buxton. Small crown 8vo, 7s. 6d.

V. **Military Law: Its Procedure and Practice.** By Major Sisson C. Pratt, R.A. Fourth Edition. Revised. Small crown 8vo, 4s. 6d.

VI. **Cavalry in Modern War.** By Major-General F. Chenevix Trench. Small crown 8vo, 6s.

BRACKENBURY, Col. C. B., R.A.—continued.
> VII. **Field Works.** Their Technical Construction and Tactical Application. By the Editor, Col. C. B. Brackenbury, R.A. Small crown 8vo, in 2 parts, 12s.

BROOKE, Major, C. K.—**A System of Field Training.** Small crown 8vo, cloth limp, 2s.

Campaign of Fredericksburg, November—December, 1862. A Study for Officers of Volunteers. By a Line Officer. With 5 Maps and Plans. Second Edition. Crown 8vo, 5s.

CLERY, C. Francis, Col.—**Minor Tactics.** With 26 Maps and Plans. Eighth Edition, Revised. Crown 8vo, 9s.

COLVILE, Lieut.-Col. C. F.—**Military Tribunals.** Sewed, 2s. 6d.

CRAUFURD, Capt. H. J.—**Suggestions for the Military Training of a Company of Infantry.** Crown 8vo, 1s. 6d.

HAMILTON, Capt. Ian, A.D.C.—**The Fighting of the Future.** 1s.

HARRISON, Col. R.—**The Officer's Memorandum Book for Peace and War.** Fourth Edition, Revised throughout. Oblong 32mo, red basil, with pencil, 3s. 6d.

Notes on Cavalry Tactics, Organisation, etc. By a Cavalry Officer. With Diagrams. Demy 8vo, 12s.

PARR, Col. H. Hallam, C.M.G.—**The Dress, Horses, and Equipment of Infantry and Staff Officers.** Crown 8vo, 1s.
> **Further Training and Equipment of Mounted Infantry.** Crown 8vo, 1s.

SCHAW, Col. H.—**The Defence and Attack of Positions and Localities.** Fourth Edition. Crown 8vo, 3s. 6d.

STONE, Capt. F. Gleadowe, R.A.—**Tactical Studies from the Franco-German War of 1870-71.** With 22 Lithographic Sketches and Maps. Demy 8vo, 10s. 6d.

WILKINSON, H. Spenser, Capt. 20th Lancashire R.V.—**Citizen Soldiers.** Essays towards the Improvement of the Volunteer Force. Crown 8vo, 2s. 6d.

POETRY.

ALEXANDER, William, D.D., Bishop of Derry.—**St. Augustine's Holiday,** and other Poems. Crown 8vo, 6s.

AUCHMUTY, A. C.—**Poems of English Heroism:** From Brunanburh to Lucknow; from Athelstan to Albert. Small crown 8vo, 1s. 6d.

BARNES, William.—**Poems of Rural Life, in the Dorset Dialect.** New Edition, complete in one vol. Crown 8vo, 6s.

BAYNES, Rev. Canon H. R.—**Home Songs for Quiet Hours.** Fourth and Cheaper Edition. Fcap. 8vo, cloth, 2s. 6d.

BEVINGTON, L. S.—**Key Notes.** Small crown 8vo, 5s.

BLUNT, Wilfrid Scawen.—**The Wind and the Whirlwind.** Demy 8vo, 1s. 6d.

The Love Sonnets of Proteus. Fifth Edition. Elzevir 8vo, 5s.

In Vinculis. With Portrait. Elzevir 8vo; 5s.

BOWEN, H. C., M.A.—**Simple English Poems.** English Literature for Junior Classes. In Four Parts. Parts I., II., and III., 6d. each, and Part IV., 1s. Complete, 3s.

BRYANT, W. C.—**Poems.** Cheap Edition, with Frontispiece. Small crown 8vo, 3s. 6d.

Calderon's Dramas: the Wonder-Working Magician—Life is a Dream—the Purgatory of St. Patrick. Translated by DENIS FLORENCE MACCARTHY. Post 8vo, 10s.

Camoens' Lusiads.—Portuguese Text, with Translation by J. J. AUBERTIN. Second Edition. 2 vols. Crown 8vo, 12s.

CHRISTIE, Albany J.—**The End of Man.** Fourth Edition. Fcap. 8vo, 2s. 6d.

COLERIDGE, Hon. Stephen.—**Fibulæ.** Small crown 8vo, 4s. 6d.

COXHEAD, Ethel.—**Birds and Babies.** With 33 Illustrations. Imp. 16mo, 1s.

Dante's Divina Commedia. Translated in the *Terza Rima* of Original, by F. K. H. HASELFOOT. Demy 8vo, 16s.

DENNIS, J.—**English Sonnets.** Collected and Arranged by. Small crown 8vo, 2s. 6d.

DE VERE, Aubrey.—**Poetical Works.**
    I. THE SEARCH AFTER PROSERPINE, etc. 3s. 6d.
    II. THE LEGENDS OF ST. PATRICK, etc. 3s. 6d.
    III. ALEXANDER THE GREAT, etc. 3s. 6d.

The Foray of Queen Meave, and other Legends of Ireland's Heroic Age. Small crown 8vo, 3s. 6d.

Legends of the Saxon Saints. Small crown 8vo, 3s. 6d.

Legends and Records of the Church and the Empire. Small crown 8vo, 3s. 6d.

DOBSON, Austin.—**Old World Idylls,** and other Verses. Eighth Edition. Elzevir 8vo, gilt top, 6s.

DOBSON, Austin—continued.

    At the Sign of the Lyre. Sixth Edition. Elzevir 8vo, gilt top, 6s.

DOWDEN, Edward, LL.D.—**Shakspere's Sonnets.** With Introduction and Notes. Large post 8vo, 7s. 6d.

DURANT, Héloïse.—**Dante.** A Dramatic Poem. Small crown 8vo, 5s.

DUTT, Toru.—**A Sheaf Gleaned in French Fields.** New Edition. Demy 8vo, 10s. 6d.

    Ancient Ballads and Legends of Hindustan. With an Introductory Memoir by EDMUND GOSSE. Second Edition, 18mo. Cloth extra, gilt top, 5s.

ELLIOTT, Ebenezer, The Corn Law Rhymer.—**Poems.** Edited by his son, the Rev. EDWIN ELLIOTT, of St. John's, Antigua. 2 vols. Crown 8vo, 18s.

English Verse. Edited by W. J. LINTON and R. H. STODDARD. 5 vols. Crown 8vo, cloth, 5s. each.
    I. CHAUCER TO BURNS.
    II. TRANSLATIONS.
    III. LYRICS OF THE NINETEENTH CENTURY.
    IV. DRAMATIC SCENES AND CHARACTERS.
    V. BALLADS AND ROMANCES.

GOSSE, Edmund.—**New Poems.** Crown 8vo, 7s. 6d.

    Firdausi in Exile, and other Poems. Second Edition. Elzevir 8vo, gilt top, 6s.

GURNEY, Rev. Alfred.—**The Vision of the Eucharist,** and other Poems. Crown 8vo, 5s.

    A Christmas Faggot. Small crown 8vo, 5s.

HARRISON, Clifford.—**In Hours of Leisure.** Second Edition. Crown 8vo, 5s.

KEATS, John.—**Poetical Works.** Edited by W. T. ARNOLD. Large crown 8vo, choicely printed on hand-made paper, with Portrait in *eau-forte.* Parchment or cloth, 12s.; vellum, 15s. New Edition, crown 8vo, cloth, 3s. 6d.

KING, Mrs. Hamilton.—**The Disciples.** Tenth Edition. Small crown 8vo, 5s.; Elzevir Edition, cloth extra, 6s.

    A Book of Dreams. Third Edition. Crown 8vo, 3s. 6d.

    The Sermon in the Hospital (From "The Disciples"). Fcap. 8vo, 1s. Cheap Edition for distribution 3d., or 20s. per 100.

LANG, A.—**XXXII. Ballades in Blue China.** Elzevir 8vo, 5s.

    Rhymes à la Mode. With Frontispiece by E. A. Abbey. Second Edition. Elzevir 8vo, cloth extra, gilt top, 5s.

LARMINIE, W.—Glanlua, and other Poems. Small crown 8vo, 3s. 6d.

Living English Poets MDCCCLXXXII. With Frontispiece by Walter Crane. Second Edition. Large crown 8vo. Printed on hand-made paper. Parchment or cloth, 12s.; vellum, 15s.

LOCKER, F.—**London Lyrics.** Tenth Edition. With Portrait, Elzevir 8vo. Cloth extra, gilt top, 5s.

LUSTED, C. T.—Semblance, and other Poems. Small crown 8vo, 3s. 6d.

MAGNUSSON, Eirikr, M.A., and PALMER, E. H., M.A.—Johan Ludvig Runeberg's Lyrical Songs, Idylls, and Epigrams. Fcap. 8vo, 5s.

MEREDITH, Owen [The Earl of Lytton].—**Lucile.** New Edition. With 32 Illustrations. 16mo, 3s. 6d. Cloth extra, gilt edges, 4s. 6d.

MORISON, Jeanie.—**Gordon.** An Our-Day Idyll. Crown 8vo, 3s. 6d.

MORRIS, Lewis.—**Poetical Works of.** New and Cheaper Editions, with Portrait. In 4 vols., 5s. each.
   Vol. I. contains "Songs of Two Worlds." Thirteenth Edition.
   Vol. II. contains "The Epic of Hades." Twenty-third Edition.
   Vol. III. contains "Gwen" and "The Ode of Life." Seventh Edition.
   Vol. IV. contains "Songs Unsung" and "Gycia." Fifth Edition.

   Songs of Britain. Third Edition. Fcap. 8vo, 5s.

   The Epic of Hades. With 16 Autotype Illustrations, after the Drawings of the late George R. Chapman. 4to, cloth extra, gilt leaves, 21s.

   The Epic of Hades. Presentation Edition. 4to, cloth extra, gilt leaves, 10s. 6d.

   The Lewis Morris Birthday Book. Edited by S. S. COPEMAN, with Frontispiece after a Design by the late George R. Chapman. 32mo, cloth extra, gilt edges, 2s.; cloth limp, 1s. 6d.

MORSHEAD, E. D. A.—**The House of Atreus.** Being the Agamemnon, Libation-Bearers, and Furies of Æschylus. Translated into English Verse. Crown 8vo, 7s.

   The Suppliant Maidens of Æschylus. Crown 8vo, 3s. 6d.

MULHOLLAND, Rosa.—**Vagrant Verses.** Small crown 8vo, 5s.

NOEL, The Hon. Roden.—**A Little Child's Monument.** Third Edition. Small crown 8vo, 3s. 6d.

   The House of Ravensburg. New Edition. Small crown 8vo, 6s.

   The Red Flag, and other Poems. New Edition. Small crown 8vo, 6s.

NOEL, The Hon. Roden—continued.
    Songs of the Heights and Deeps. Crown 8vo, 6s.
    A Modern Faust, and other Poems. Small crown 8vo, 5s.

O'HAGAN, John.—**The Song of Roland.** Translated into English Verse. New and Cheaper Edition. Crown 8vo, 5s.

Publisher's Playground. Fcap. 8vo, 3s. 6d.

Rare Poems of the 16th and 17th Centuries. Edited by W. J. LINTON. Crown 8vo, 5s.

ROBINSON, A. Mary F.—**A Handful of Honeysuckle.** Fcap. 8vo, 3s. 6d.
    The Crowned Hippolytus. Translated from Euripides. With New Poems. Small crown 8vo, 5s.

SEAL, W. H.—**Visions of the Night.** Crown 8vo, 4s.

SMITH, J. W. Gilbart.—**The Loves of Vandyck.** A Tale of Genoa. Small crown 8vo, 2s. 6d.
    The Log o' the "Norseman." Small crown 8vo, 5s.
    Serbelloni. Small crown 8vo, 5s.

Sophocles: The Seven Plays in English Verse. Translated by LEWIS CAMPBELL. Crown 8vo, 7s. 6d.

SYMONDS, John Addington.—**Vagabunduli Libellus.** Crown 8vo, 6s.

TAYLOR, Sir H.—**Works.** Complete in Five Volumes. Crown 8vo, 30s.
    Philip Van Artevelde. Fcap. 8vo, 3s. 6d.
    The Virgin Widow, etc. Fcap. 8vo, 3s. 6d.

TODHUNTER, Dr. J.—**Laurella,** and other Poems. Crown 8vo, 6s. 6d.
    Forest Songs. Small crown 8vo, 3s. 6d.
    The True Tragedy of Rienzi: a Drama. 3s. 6d.
    Alcestis: a Dramatic Poem. Extra fcap. 8vo, 5s.
    Helena in Troas. Small crown 8vo, 2s. 6d.
    The Banshee, and other Poems. Small crown 8vo, 3s. 6d.

TYNAN, Katherine.—**Louise de la Valliere,** and other Poems. Small crown 8vo, 3s. 6d.
    Shamrocks. Small crown 8vo, 5s.

Twilight and Candleshades. By EXUL. With 15 Vignettes. Small crown 8vo, 5s.

Victorian Hymns: English Sacred Songs of Fifty Years. Dedicated to the Queen. Large post 8vo, 10s. 6d.

Wordsworth Birthday Book, The. Edited by ADELAIDE and VIOLET WORDSWORTH. 32mo, limp cloth, 1s. 6d.; cloth extra, 2s.

Wordsworth, Selections from. By WM. KNIGHT and other members of the Wordsworth Society. Large crown 8vo. Printed on hand-made paper. With Portrait. Parchment, 12s; vellum, 15s.

YEATS, W. B.—**The Wanderings of Oisin,** and other Poems. Small crown 8vo, 5s.

NOVELS AND TALES.

BAKER, Ella.—**Kingscote Stories.** Crown 8vo, 5s.
    Bertram de Drumont. Crown 8vo, 5s.

BANKS, Mrs. G. L.—**God's Providence House.** Crown 8vo, 6s.

CRAWFURD, Oswald.—**Sylvia Arden.** With Frontispiece. Crown 8vo, 1s.

GARDINER, Linda.—**His Heritage.** With Frontispiece. Crown 8vo, 6s.

GRAY, Maxwell.—**The Silence of Dean Maitland.** Fifteenth Thousand. With Frontispiece. Crown 8vo, 6s.

GREY, Rowland.—**In Sunny Switzerland.** A Tale of Six Weeks. Second Edition. Small crown 8vo, 5s.
    Lindenblumen and other Stories. Small crown 8vo, 5s.
    By Virtue of his Office. Crown 8vo, 6s.

HUNTER, Hay.—**The Crime of Christmas Day.** A Tale of the Latin Quarter. By the Author of "My Ducats and my Daughter." 1s.

HUNTER, Hay, and WHYTE, Walter.—**My Ducats and My Daughter.** With Frontispiece. Crown 8vo, 6s.

INGELOW, Jean.—**Off the Skelligs.** A Novel. With Frontispiece. Crown 8vo, 6s.

LANG, Andrew.—**In the Wrong Paradise,** and other Stories. Crown 8vo, 6s.

MACDONALD, G.—**Donal Grant.** A Novel. With Frontispiece. Crown 8vo, 6s.
    Home Again. With Frontispiece. Crown 8vo, 6s.
    Castle Warlock. A Novel. With Frontispiece. Crown 8vo, 6s.
    Malcolm. With Portrait of the Author engraved on Steel. Crown 8vo, 6s.

MACDONALD, G.—continued.
 The Marquis of Lossie. With Frontispiece. Crown 8vo, 6s.
 St. George and St. Michael. With Frontispiece. Crown 8vo, 6s.
 What's Mine's Mine. With Frontispiece. Crown 8vo, 6s.
 Annals of a Quiet Neighbourhood. With Frontispiece. Crown 8vo, 6s.
 The Seaboard Parish: a Sequel to "Annals of a Quiet Neighbourhood." With Frontispiece. Crown 8vo, 6s.
 Wilfred Cumbermede. An Autobiographical Story. With Frontispiece. Crown 8vo, 6s.
 Thomas Wingfold, Curate. With Frontispiece. Crown 8vo, 6s.
 Paul Faber, Surgeon. With Frontispiece. Crown 8vo, 6s.
 The Elect Lady. With Frontispiece. Crown 8vo, 6s.

MALET, Lucas.—Colonel Enderby's Wife. A Novel. With Frontispiece. Crown 8vo, 6s.
 A Counsel of Perfection. With Frontispiece. Crown 8vo, 6s.

MULHOLLAND, Rosa.—Marcella Grace. An Irish Novel. Crown 8vo, 6s.
 A Fair Emigrant. With Frontispiece. Crown 8vo, 6s.

OGLE, Anna C.—A Lost Love. Small crown 8vo, 2s. 6d.

PALGRAVE, W. Gifford.—Hermann Agha: an Eastern Narrative. Crown 8vo, 6s.

Romance of the Recusants. By the Author of "Life of a Prig." Crown 8vo, 5s.

SEVERNE, Florence.—The Pillar House. With Frontispiece. Crown 8vo, 6s.

SHAW, Flora L.—Castle Blair: a Story of Youthful Days. Crown 8vo, 3s. 6d.

STRETTON, Hesba.—Through a Needle's Eye. A Story. With Frontispiece. Crown 8vo, 6s.

TAYLOR, Col. Meadows, C.S.I., M.R.I.A.—Seeta. A Novel. With Frontispiece. Crown 8vo, 6s.
 Tippoo Sultaun: a Tale of the Mysore War. With Frontispiece. Crown 8vo, 6s.
 Ralph Darnell. With Frontispiece. Crown 8vo, 6s.
 A Noble Queen. With Frontispiece. Crown 8vo, 6s.
 The Confessions of a Thug. With Frontispiece. Crown 8vo, 6s.
 Tara: a Mahratta Tale. With Frontispiece. Crown 8vo, 6s.

Within Sound of the Sea. With Frontispiece. Crown 8vo, 6s.

BOOKS FOR THE YOUNG.

Brave Men's Footsteps. A Book of Example and Anecdote for Young People. By the Editor of "Men who have Risen." With 4 Illustrations by C. Doyle. Ninth Edition. Crown 8vo, 2s. 6d.

COXHEAD, Ethel.—**Birds and Babies.** With 33 Illustrations. Second Edition. Imp. 16mo, cloth, 1s.

DAVIES, G. Christopher.—**Rambles and Adventures of our School Field Club.** With 4 Illustrations. New and Cheaper Edition. Crown 8vo, 3s. 6d.

EDMONDS, Herbert.—**Well Spent Lives**: a Series of Modern Biographies. New and Cheaper Edition. Crown 8vo, 3s. 6d.

EVANS, Mark.—**The Story of our Father's Love,** told to Children. Sixth and Cheaper Edition of Theology for Children. With 4 Illustrations. Fcap. 8vo, 1s. 6d.

MAC KENNA, S. J.—**Plucky Fellows.** A Book for Boys. With 6 Illustrations. Fifth Edition. Crown 8vo, 3s. 6d.

MALET, Lucas.—**Little Peter.** A Christmas Morality for Children of any Age. With numerous Illustrations. Fourth Thousand. 5s.

REANEY, Mrs. G. S.—**Waking and Working**; or, From Girlhood to Womanhood. New and Cheaper Edition. With a Frontispiece. Crown 8vo, 3s. 6d.

Blessing and Blessed: a Sketch of Girl Life. New and Cheaper Edition. Crown 8vo, 3s. 6d.

Rose Gurney's Discovery. A Story for Girls. Dedicated to their Mothers. Crown 8vo, 3s. 6d.

English Girls: their Place and Power. With Preface by the Rev. R. W. Dale. Fifth Edition. Fcap. 8vo, 2s. 6d.

Just Anyone, and other Stories. Three Illustrations. Royal 16mo, 1s. 6d.

Sunbeam Willie, and other Stories. Three Illustrations. Royal 16mo, 1s. 6d.

Sunshine Jenny, and other Stories. Three Illustrations. Royal 16mo, 1s. 6d.

STORR, Francis, and TURNER, Hawes.—**Canterbury Chimes**; or, Chaucer Tales re-told to Children. With 6 Illustrations from the Ellesmere Manuscript. Third Edition. Fcap. 8vo, 3s. 6d.

STRETTON, Hesba.—**David Lloyd's Last Will.** With 4 Illustrations. New Edition. Royal 16mo, 2s. 6d.

WHITAKER, Florence.—**Christy's Inheritance.** A London Story. Illustrated. Royal 16mo, 1s. 6d.

PRINTED BY WILLIAM CLOWES AND SONS, LIMITED,
LONDON AND BECCLES.

MESSRS.

KEGAN PAUL, TRENCH & CO.'S

EDITIONS OF

SHAKSPERE'S WORKS.

THE PARCHMENT LIBRARY EDITION.

THE AVON EDITION.

The Text of these Editions is mainly that of Delius. Wherever a variant reading is adopted, some good and recognized Shaksperian Critic has been followed. In no case is a new rendering of the text proposed; nor has it been thought necessary to distract the reader's attention by notes or comments

1, PATERNOSTER SQUARE.

[P. T. O.

SHAKSPERE'S WORKS.

THE AVON EDITION.

Printed on thin opaque paper, and forming 12 handy volumes, cloth, 18*s*., or bound in 6 volumes, 15*s*.

The set of 12 volumes may also be had in a cloth box, price 21*s*., or bound in Roan, Persian, Crushed Persian Levant, Calf, or Morocco, and enclosed in an attractive leather box at prices from 31*s*. 6*d*. upwards.

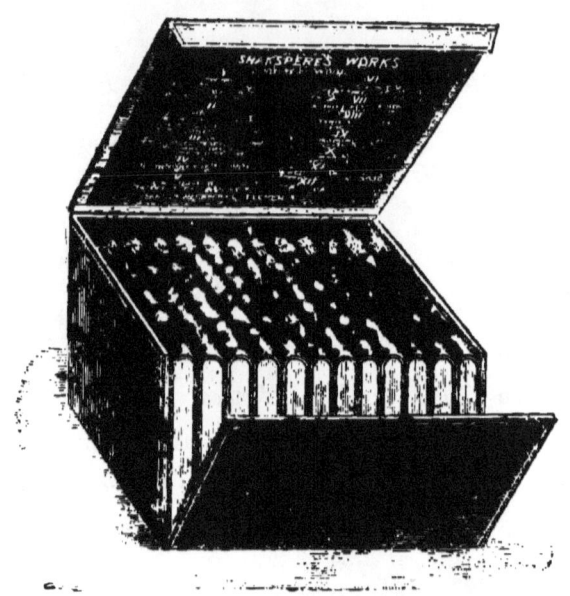

SOME PRESS NOTICES.

"This edition will be useful to those who want a good text, well and clearly printed, in convenient little volumes that will slip easily into an overcoat pocket or a travelling-bag."—*St. James's Gazette*.

"We know no prettier edition of Shakspere for the price."—*Academy*.

"It is refreshing to meet with an edition of Shakspere of convenient size and low price, without either notes or introductions of any sort to distract the attention of the reader."—*Saturday Review*.

"It is exquisite. Each volume is handy, is beautifully printed, and in every way lends itself to the taste of the cultivated student of Shakspere."—*Scotsman*.

LONDON: KEGAN PAUL, TRENCH & CO., 1, PATERNOSTER SQUARE.

SHAKSPERE'S WORKS.

THE PARCHMENT LIBRARY EDITION.

In 12 volumes Elzevir 8vo., choicely printed on hand-made paper, and bound in parchment or cloth, price £3 12s., or in vellum, price £4 10s.

The set of 12 volumes may also be had in a strong cloth box, price £3 17s., or with an oak hanging shelf, £3 18s.

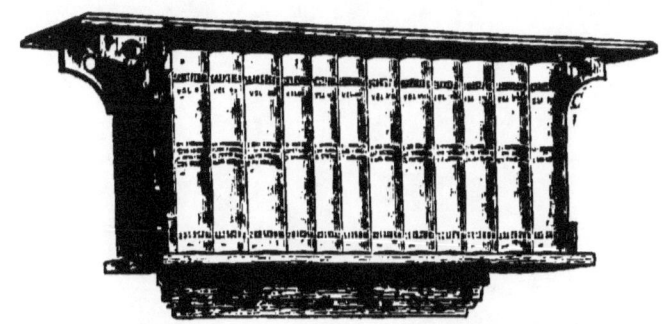

SOME PRESS NOTICES.

". . . There is, perhaps, no edition in which the works of Shakspere can be read in such luxury of type and quiet distinction of form as this, and we warmly recommend it."—*Pall Mall Gazette.*

"For elegance of form and beauty of typography, no edition of Shakspere hitherto published has excelled the 'Parchment Library Edition.' . . . They are in the strictest sense pocket volumes, yet the type is bold, and, being on fine white hand-made paper, can hardly tax the weakest of sight. The print is judiciously confined to the text, notes being more appropriate to library editions. The whole will be comprised in the cream-coloured parchment which gives the name to the series."—*Daily News.*

"The Parchment Library Edition of Shakspere needs no further praise."—*Saturday Review.*

Just published. Price 5s.

AN INDEX TO THE WORKS OF SHAKSPERE.

Applicable to all editions of Shakspere, and giving reference, by topics, to notable passages and significant expressions; brief histories of the plays; geographical names and historic incidents; mention of all characters and sketches of important ones; together with explanations of allusions and obscure and obsolete words and phrases.

By EVANGELINE M. O'CONNOR.

LONDON: KEGAN PAUL, TRENCH & CO., 1, PATERNOSTER SQUARE.

www.ingramcontent.com/pod-product-compliance
Lightning Source LLC
Chambersburg PA
CBHW032105230426
43672CB00009B/1641